OVERCOMING INDIFFERENCE

OVERCOMING INDIFFERENCE

Ten Key Challenges in Today's Changing World

A Survey of Ideas and Proposals
for Action on the Threshold
of the Twenty-First Century

Edited by
Klaus Schwab

New York University Press
New York and London

The opinions expressed in this book do not necessarily reflect the views of the
World Economic Forum, New York University, or New York University Press.
The papers in this volume were contributed by the authors in their personal
capacities, and they (the authors) are solely responsible for their views.

Library of Congress Cataloging-in-Publication Data

Overcoming indifference: ten key challenges in today's changing
world / edited by Klaus Schwab.
   p. cm.
  ISBN-0-8147-8008-3
  1. Economic policy. 2. Social policy. 3. Economic forecasting.
  4. Social prediction. I. Schwab, Klaus, 1938-
HD87.09 1995
338.9--dc20   94-24536
                                 CIP

New York University Press books are printed on acid-free paper,
and their binding materials are chosen for their strength and durability.

Manufactured in the United States of America

Indifference is the eighth deadly sin. When an understandable focus on one's own situation turns to neglect for the troubles of others, hostility toward those in different conditions and even conflict can be the result.

In contrast is the will to involvement. Early involvement can solve problems before they grow too great. Cooperative involvement can redound to the benefit of all. Sustained involvement can transform the world for the better.

The United Nations is a machine for involvement. Through its mechanisms peoples everywhere can engage their problems together. Individuals, nongovernmental organizations, regions, and states all have their place in the world organization. Through this unique universal means, the prospects for the future can become brighter than ever.

Boutros Boutros-Ghali
Secretary-General
United Nations

CONTENTS

CHAPTER 2
MAINTAINING GLOBAL SECURITY

CHAPTER 5
LIVING IN THE NEW INFORMATION SOCIETY

CHAPTER 6
KEEPING PACE WITH A GLOBALIZING ECONOMY

CHAPTER 9
ENSURING NATIONAL POLICY-MAKING IN A
GLOBAL WORLD

CHAPTER 10
REENGINEERING THE CORPORATION

FOREWORD

Klaus Schwab

This project, which took shape over the last year, was conceived in the context of two separate yet related activities. Initially, the inspiration for a review of changing basic assumptions flowed from the work of the United Nations High-Level Advisory Board to Secretary-General Boutros Boutros-Ghali.

As cochairman of the Advisory Board's panel on "Linkages Between Economic, Social, and Political Developments in a Changing World," I became convinced that my panel's mandate was potentially unmanageably broad. As a result, we began our work in late 1993 by consulting a series of experts regarding the challenges to the international community. Our goal was to secure a solid analytical foundation for the panel's recommendations to the Secretary-General. The high quality of the work done by these experts gave rise to the first thoughts of publishing a book.

The effort to survey experts in a variety of fields was also consistent with the intellectual program for the 1994 Annual Meeting of the World Economic Forum in Davos, Switzerland. The symposium's theme was "The Changing Basic Assumptions of the World Economy," but it quickly became evident that we also needed to reassess the fundamental assumptions of global society as a whole. This need to actively confront our future, however, met with indifference at all levels of society. We just seem to be overwhelmed with the complexity of the task. For this reason and in accordance with the title of this book, the 1995 Annual Meeting will have as its theme, "Overcoming Indifference: Building the Fundament for the Twenty-First Century."

Thus, this book and the two Annual Meetings reinforce each other in their global message. The title itself is based on the text by Professor Elie Wiesel, who develops this theme in his contribution to this book.

Consideration of the broad range of issues that needed to be addressed proved a challenge. Because structure and substance are imperatives when grappling with such amorphous concepts as "fundamental assumptions," the undertaking demanded both a coherent analytical framework and clearly delineated subject matter.

The analytical framework moves beyond a mere passive recognition of change and beyond commonplace lists of megatrends toward a constructive response to change. All of the contributors present their opinions in a format that stresses proposed actions. With a few exceptions, they identify the old and new assumptions, the consequences of change, and, critically, their proposed actions in response to the changed assumption.

Substance was the second issue governing preparation of this collection. An abstract collection of thoughts would serve little purpose, so the contributions were organized according to ten key "challenges" to the world today. Representing issues that present acute risks to humanity, the book's ten chapters survey revised assumptions of ideology, politics, society, and the economy. While neither all inclusive nor mutually exclusive, they together point out the immense parameters of change.

Much thought was given to the selection of contributors. Many political figures and academics, most of them constituents of the World Economic Forum, forwarded their views. In addition, business leaders provided constructive analyses grounded in the realities of the changing global economy, and the World Economic Forum's Global Leaders for Tomorrow, a group of young leaders born after 1950, contributed their naturally forward-thinking perspectives to the collection.

I must extend my thanks first to all the contributors. Because of their efforts, the text should at a minimum raise awareness of some of the critical challenges facing the contemporary world. Perhaps some of the proposed actions might even prove feasible, challenging the prevailing assumption that the world is short of new ideas. My deepest gratitude goes to George V. Vassiliou, former president of Cyprus. His expertise in political and business issues made him the ideal person to write the invaluable introduction to the text, as well as to the individual chapters. These introductions provide an overview to the vast intellectual material in the book. Next, I must thank Paul Boesen and Regula Waltenspuel. Paul managed the initial phase of this project. Regula maintained contact with a very diverse, high-level group of international contributors who also appreciated her skills and dedication. This undertaking would have been impossible without their collaboration. Finally, thanks to Maryse Zwick, whose daily support proved invaluable on this as on other projects.

INTRODUCTION

George V. Vassiliou

The Demise of the Old Assumptions

The first rays of the dawn of the twenty-first century are already visible, but there is no jubilation—only uncertainty and anxiety about the future. The contrast with the prevailing mood one hundred years ago is too great to miss. At the end of the nineteenth century, there was a feeling of boundless optimism, symbolized by the celebration of the Diamond Jubilee of Queen Victoria and encouraged by the substantial progress of science and discoveries, and a feeling of security in the relative peace prevailing throughout the world. Many believed that we had conquered the future. Yet the twentieth century turned out to be the most destructive in the long history of humanity. Two world wars on an as yet unprecedented scale, the beginning and end of the Russian Revolution, the death of millions of people in concentration camps, and now, as the century slowly approaches its final days, the tragedy of enthnonationalism and tribalism around the world, from Bosnia to Rwanda.

The Challenges We Face

However, at the same time, the twentieth century has been a period of unprecedented economic, scientific, and technological growth. Never before has so much progress been made in such a short span of time. The first people have walked on the moon; the conquering of outer space has begun. Atomic energy has been harnessed. The telecommunications revolution has turned the planet Earth into a global village. Science and technology are progressing in every field at an extremely fast pace, with no signs of slowing down. As one of the contributors points out, ninety percent of the engineers that ever lived in the world are living and working today. Whatever the achievements of science and technology until now, much more is to come, among other things, computing, biogenetics, process engineering, robotics, the information highways, and transportation.

Only a few years ago, the Cold War ended. The subsequent demolition of the Berlin Wall and the reunification of Germany signaled the beginning of a new world order in which peace, international justice, and a respect for human rights were expected to prevail. This process produced results, as illustrated by the celebrations that followed the first free elections in South Africa and the inauguration of President Mandela and by the beginnings of an Arab—Israeli peace after the signing of the agreement by Arafat and Rabin. Many thought that at long last humanity had conquered its future; some claimed that we had reached the "end of history." This optimism was extremely short lived. Subsequent developments—wars, ethnic strife, violations of human rights, and the economic recession—have shattered this spirit of optimism. Most of the contributors express feelings of malaise, fear, and angst concerning the future. In a remarkably short period, humanity has moved from the prospect of the "end of history" to the prospect of the "Clash of Civilizations."

What Reasons Are Behind This New Mood?

Change and development have been so rapid that we have lost our sense of direction. Almost all of the assumptions that the post-World War II generations believed in are no longer valid, but no new assumptions or beliefs have yet taken their place. A few examples of formerly accepted assumptions that are no longer valid will illustrate this point.

1. The world is divided into two conflicting blocks, with the United States and the Soviet Union maintaining the balance of power and peace in the world.

> Well, the world is no longer divided into two blocks. One block has completely disappeared; the other has lost the cohesion provided by fear of the adversary. One superpower is left, the United States, which is neither willing nor able to police the world on its own.

2. Nationalist ideals were a phenomenon that belonged to nineteenth-century Europe and to twentieth-century anticolonial struggles.

Unfortunately, the ugly face of ethnonationalism is very much a reality today. Every day we witness on our television screens the tragedy of warfare and killings.

3. People had convictions and believed in well-defined, but different, ideologies that laid down the path to the future. Many believed in a future socialist "arcadia"—an ideal world in which there would be no more poverty, and the creative powers of humanity would be liberated. Others fought the communist system and believed in the absolute goodness of free enterprise and democracy.

The socialist experiment in the Soviet Union has now collapsed, together with the Soviet Union itself. The concept of democracy and free markets has triumphed, but we still do not see the end of history, only a continuing uphill struggle in search of a better world.

4. People have mastered nature. Pessimistic Malthusian forecasts have proved unfounded. The creative abilities of people have no limits.

The Rio conference has shattered this assumption as well. We now know that we live in a world with a very fragile ecosystem, that the environment in which we live is in danger of being destroyed, and that the unchecked growth of the population throughout the world is bringing nearer the prospect of a Malthusian-type catastrophe. Production of grain is already falling behind population growth worldwide.

5. Growth creates employment and work for all. Mass unemployment belongs to the past.

Unfortunately, we now know only too well that growth can occur without the creation of employment. Mass or structural unemployment, as it is now called, is becoming endemic in Western Europe and many other parts of the world.

6. With growth, the gaps between rich and poor people within a country and between rich and poor countries will grow smaller and smaller.

For a time this was true, but recent statistics show that the gap between rich and poor is widening, and the divide between the developed and most of the developing countries is becoming a huge chasm.

7. The welfare state is the crowning achievement of social policy in the West. It is the answer to the communist threat, the basis on which democratic systems are built, and the means for providing peace and security and avoiding social conflicts.

Today the welfare state is attacked by all sides. Its institutions are in danger of collapse because of rising unemployment, the increased cost of health care, and the aging of the population.

8. The world is organized on the basis of a number of nation-states that have supreme control and responsibility for managing the economy, the environment, and conditions of life within their territories.

The globalization of the economy and the risks posed by environmental destruction, political uncertainties, and strife are now continuously undermining the nation-state, which has to surrender many of its powers to newly created multilateral and regional organizations. Multilateralism and regionalism are rapidly growing and attacking every single vestige of the nation-state.

9. "Big is beautiful" is the concept for the enterprise. Mass production is the answer to all problems.

Big is no longer beautiful; reengineering and flexible small-scale production is the order of the day.

10. Free trade can cure all problems and lead to increased prosperity throughout the world.

Now, with the completion of the latest Uruguay Round, there is already more talk about *fair* than *free* trade, and the free traders of yesterday are becoming the protectionists of today.

11. High quality goes with high wages and the Third World has low wages with low quality.

No longer are high-level quality and technology the monopoly of the rich. Developing countries can combine high quality, high technology, and high productivity with low wages.

We could go on enumerating old certainties that are no longer valid or introducing new assumptions based on social, economic, and political developments. There is no need, however; the point has been made. The old assumptions, or most of them, are dead. New ones have not yet been formulated. The usefulness of this collection is that it presents the ideas and suggestions of so many leading thinkers and personalities from the political, business, and academic worlds. The case is made convincingly that we cannot go on living and behaving as we did in the past. There is a warning, but not a feeling of hopelessness: by adopting the right policies, humanity can address the new challenges. The varied and interesting contributions have been successfully grouped together by Klaus Schwab into ten chapters, each dealing with a major challenge.

Final Comments

The chapter introductions highlight the main challenges, identify some of the new assumptions that are replacing the old ones, and help the reader focus on subjects of personal interest.

The challenges ahead of us, the tasks we need to perform as the twenty-first century approaches, are all too clear—protect the environment; achieve sustainable development; create the conditions that permit all humans to work, have a decent standard of living, and live in dignity in a society where moral values reign supreme; reconcile the nation-state with the needs of global governance; raise corporate management to the standards required by our globalized economy; integrate Asia and other developing parts of the world, particularly Africa, and reduce the gap between rich and poor countries; and keep the peace and eliminate conflicts within states.

This list could extend almost indefinitely. Some may wonder whether we can ever successfully meet these challenges. Humanity has always faced challenges and, in the end, no problem remains unsolved. What matters is whether the solution is the result of deliberate rational policies or the result of crisis and catastrophe. To succeeded in the difficult tasks ahead of us, to progress without experiencing the purgatory of a major catastrophe, we need first to care and then collectively try.

The usefulness of this collection lies in the fact that it brings to our attention the problems and challenges we face. Hopefully, after reading this volume, the reader will feel more interested, more committed. Because our worst enemy and the biggest challenge we face is indifference. Elie Wiesel expresses this eloquently in his closing words:

> The opposite of love is not hate but indifference. But this applies to other concepts as well. The opposite of education is not ignorance but indifference. The opposite of beauty is not ugliness but indifference. The opposite of life is not death but indifference to both life and death.
>
> Is this the new assumption we all seek now to accept? No, it is an old one. In fact, it is as old as human hope which has helped us triumph over fear.

CONTRIBUTORS

Esko Aho, Prime Minister of Finland.

Roger C. Altman, former Deputy Secretary, U.S. Department of the Treasury.

J.E. Andriessen, Minister of Economic Affairs, The Netherlands.

Robert U. Ayres, Sandoz Professor of Environment and Management, INSEAD, Fontainebleau, France.

Percy Barnevik, President and Chief Executive Officer, ABB Asea Brown Boveri, and Chairman of the Board, Sandvik AB and Skanska AB, Sweden.

Lincoln F. Bloomfield, Professor of Political Science emeritus and Senior Lecturer, Massachusetts Institute of Technology.

John Bohn, President and Chairman, Moody's Investors Service, USA.

Philip Bowring, Columnist, International Herald Tribune.

F. Romeo Braun, Executive Vice-President, Nestlé S.A.

Lester R. Brown, Founder, President, and Senior Researcher, Worldwatch Institute, and a MacArthur Fellow.

Colin Chapman, Managing Director and Editor-in-Chief, Financial Times Television.

Kenneth Clarke, Chancellor of the Exchequer, United Kingdom.

André de Clercq, Vice President, Corporate Research and Development, Barco NV.

Jacques-Yves Cousteau, Captain, French Navy, and President, The Cousteau Society/Equipe Cousteau.

Gustav Däniker, Major General (ret.), Federal Department of Defense, Switzerland, and Council Member, International Institute for Strategic Studies, London.

Howard Davies, Director General, Confederation of British Industry.

Guillermo de la Dehesa, Chief Executive Officer, Banco Pastor, and Chairman, High Council of Chambers of Commerce and Navigation.

Robert L. Dilenschneider, President and Chief Executive Officer, The Dilenschneider Group.

Roxanne Lynn Doty, Assistant Professor, Political Science, Arizona State University.

Jeffrey Edington, Board Member and Executive Director, Technology, British Steel.

Craig Fields, former Director, U.S. Department of Defense, Advanced Research Projects Agency, and former Chairman and Chief Executive Officer, Microelectronics and Computer Technology Corporation.

Hans-Peter Froehlich, Member, Board of Management, Institut der Deutschen Wirtschaft, Cologne, Germany.

Victor K. Fung, Chairman, Hong Kong Trade Development Council; Chairman, Prudential Asia Investments Ltd; and Chairman, Li & Fund Group.

Patrick Glynn, Resident Scholar, American Enterprise Institute for Public Policy Research.

Carl H. Hahn, Chairman of the Board (ret.), Volkswagen AG; Chairman, Board of Director, Saurer Gruppe Holding AG; and Director, The British Petroleum Company p.l.c., TRW, and PAC-CAR, Inc.

Gert Haller, State Secretary, Ministry of Finance, Bonn, Germany.

Michael Hammer, President, Hammer and Company.

Steve H. Hanke, Professor of Applied Economics, The Johns Hopkins University, and Vice President, FCMI Financial Corporation.

Philipp M. Hildebrand, Member, Executive Board, World Economic Forum.

Joseph P. Hoar, General (ret.), U.S. Marine Corps; former Commander in Chief, U.S. Central Command; and Co-Chairman of the Middle East Forum of the Council on Foreign Affairs.

Lutz Hoffmann, Professor of Economics, Free University of Berlin, and President, German Institute for Economic Research.

Samuel P. Huntington, Eaton Professor of the Science of Government and Director, John M. Olin Institute for Strategic Studies, Center for International Affairs, Harvard University.

Eiichi Itoh, Managing Director, Kokusai Denshin Denwa (KDD) Research Institute, Inc.

DeAnne Julius, Chief Economist, British Airways.

Sergei Kapitza, Professor of Physics, Moscow Institute for Physics and Technology; Senior Researcher, Institute for Physical Problems, Russian Academy of Sciences; Vice President, Academy of Natural Sciences of Russia; and President, Euro-Asian Physical Society.

Robert D. Kaplan, Contributing Editor, The Atlantic Monthly.

Alan Kay, Apple Fellow, Apple Computer.

Tommy T.B. Koh, Ambassador-at-Large, Republic of Singapore; Director, Institute of Policy Studies, Singapore; and Chairman, National Arts Council, Singapore.

Hans Küng, Professor of Ecumenical Theology and Director of the Institute for Ecumenical Research, University of Tübingen.

Robert Z. Lawrence, Albert L. Williams Professor of International Trade and Investment, John F. Kennedy School of Government, Harvard University; Nonresident Senior Fellow, Brookings Institution; and Research Associate, National Bureau of Economic Research.

Ho Khai Leong, Lecturer, Department of Political Science, National University of Singapore.

Jean-François Lepetit, President and Chief Executive Officer, Banque Indosuez.

James Lilley, former U.S. Ambassador to China; former U.S. Ambassador to the Republic of Korea; and former Director, American Institute, Taiwan.

Ernst-Moritz Lipp, Senior General Manager, Dresdner Bank.

Rajiv Mehrotra, Filmmaker and Trustee-Secretary of the Foundation for University Responsibility of H.H. The Dalai Lama.

Paul M. Minus, President, Council for Ethics in Economics.

Gary L. Moreau, President, Oneida Ltd.

Masayoshi Morita, Deputy Director, Japan Institute for Social and Economic Affairs.

Jacob Needleman, Professor, Department of Philosophy, San Francisco State University.

Sadako Ogata, United Nations High Commissioner for Refugees.

Robert B. Palmer, President and Chief Executive Officer, Digital Equipment Corporation.

Andrés Pastrana Arango, Lawyer; Journalist; and Leader, Columbian New Democratic Force Party.

Gunter Pauli, Chairman, PPA Holding and the Mozarteum Belgicum.

Niels Helveg Petersen, Minister for Foreign Affairs, Denmark.

Heinrich von Pierer, President and Chief Executive Officer, Siemens.

Sandra Postel, Director, Flobal Water Policy Project, Cambridge; Adjunct Professor, Tufts University; and Senior Fellow, Worldwatch Institute.

Neil Postman, Professor of Media Ecology and Chair, Department of Culture and Communication, New York University.

David de Pury, Co-Chairman, ABB Asea Brown Bovery.

U.V. Rao, Chief Executive Office and Managing Director, Larsen & Toubro, Ltd.

Wolfgang H. Reinicke, Research Associate, Brookings Institution.

Franck Riboud, Member of the Board, Danone Group.

Riordan Roett, Sarita and Don Johnson Professor and Director of the Latin American Studies Program, The Johns Hopkins Nitze School of Advanced International Studies.

Gabrielle Rolland, Vice President, European Institute of Leadership.

Daniel Roos, Professor of Civil Engineering; Director, Center for Technology, Policy, and Industrial Development; Director, Program for Technology, Management, and Policy; Director, International Motor Vehicle Program; Massachusetts Institute of Technology.

Joël de Rosnay, Managing Director, Development and International Relations, Cité des Sciences et de L'Industrie.

Luis Rubio, Director General of the Center of Research for Development, Mexico City.

Enrique Ruete, Chief Executive Officer, Roberts Group; Chairman, Argentine Business Council; and Director for Argentina, Latin American Business Council.

Mohammad Sadli, Professor Emeritus of Economics, University of Indonesia.

Carl Sagan, David Duncan Professor of Astronomy and Space Sciences and Director, Laboratory for Planetary Studies, Cornell University.

Ghassan Salamé, Director of Studies, Centre National de la Recherce Scientifique (CNRS), and Professor of International Relations, Institut D'Etudes Politiques.

Sven Sandstrom, Managing Director, World Bank.

Fritz Scharpf, Director, Max-Planck-Institut für Gesellschaftsforschung.

Jaime Serra Puche, Minister of Trade and Industry, Mexico.

George Shen, Chief Editor, Hong Kong Economic Journal.

Haruo Shimada, Professor of Economics, Keio University.

Horst Siebert, President, Kiel Institute of World Economics, and Member, German Council of Economic Advisors.

Fred L. Smith, President, Competitive Enterprise Institute, Washington, D.C.

Robert Solomon, Guest Scholar, Brookings Institution.

Tom Sommerlatte, Senior Vice President and Managing Director, Arthur D. Little, Inc.

Noordin Sopiee, Director General, Institute of Strategic and International Studies (ISIS), Malaysia.

Robert N. Stavins, Associate Professor of Public Policy, John F. Kennedy School of Government, Harvard University.

Makoto Taniguchi, Deputy Secretary-General, Organization for Economic Cooperation and Development (OECD).

Terence Taylor, Fellow, Center for International Security and Arms Control, Stanford University.

Frank Trümper, Managing Director, Bertelsmann Foundation.

Martin van Creveld, Professor, Department of History, Hebrew University.

Hugo Vandamme, President and Chief Executive Officer, Barco NV.

George V. Vassiliou, Chairman, MEMRB International, and President (1988-1993), Cyprus.

Michael Vlahos, Adviser, U.S. Navy and Republican Party.

Eberhard von Koerber, Executive Vice President, ABB Group, and President, Asea Brown Boveri Europe.

Hans-Dieter Vontobel, Chairman, Vontobel Holding AG.

Paul Walsh, Chief Executive Officer, The Pillsbury Company.

Elie Wiesel, Andrew W. Mellon Professor of the Humanities, Boston University. He is the recipient of the 1986 Nobel Peace Prize.

Rosanna Wong Yick-Ming, Chairman, Hong Kong Housing Authority, and Executive Director, Hong Kong Federation of Youth Groups.

Chapter 1
Coping with the Disintegration
of Value Systems

Introduction

George V. Vassiliou

The world, particularly the industrialized world, is beset by anger. Its traditional repositories of value—religion, ideology, community, family—are all falling under siege. Basic values are withering in face of rapidly accelerating change, and societies worldwide are threatened by the undermining of tradition. What awaits our societies when they lose respect for tradition, that underlying guarantor of societal values?

Jacob Needleman expresses the thoughts and anxieties of all contributors to this chapter when he writes: "There is no such thing as a purely material crisis," but the "the crisis in values . . . is at the root of all issues." Throughout history, people have confronted difficulties stemming from economic changes, environmental issues, wars, natural disasters, and personal health by relying on their value systems. Today, those value systems are endangered. In addition to the problems and crises that the contemporary world is facing, including crime, drugs, and the destruction of the environment, as Needleman points out, the intensification and diffusion of the market economy is endangering indigenous value systems, religious teachings, and social wisdom. Scientific, rationalistic technology and emerging market economies must be balanced with indigenous age-old wisdom. His advice is clear. Progress in technology and science must be accompanied by a deeper understanding of human nature, morality, and the natural world. He recommends that scientists and political leaders, who have a particular sensitivity to the purely spiritual, moral dimension of human life, make a special effort to study and learn from other cultures.

Michael Vlahos goes much further. He argues that "the Modern," defined as the materialistic way of looking at and explaining life, has ended. "What is happening to the ship of knowledge—our reality—is that the vessel is being rebuilt, not remodeled," and he looks forward to a spiritual and religious revival of the guiding certainty of belief.

Modern world patterns endanger family values, points out Rosanna Wong Yick-Ming from Hong Kong. The traditional, extended family, which was the basis of all Asiatic, as well as of many European societies, has been giving way—initially to the nuclear family and now to the one-parent family. Society and the state thus have an even greater obligation to participate in the care of children. All of these changes and transformations have affected traditional industrialized societies. As John Bohn indicates, the United States is struggling to combat a variety of problems, including individual excesses, the breakdown of law and order, and a corroded educational system. As a result, the United States, which can no longer serve as an example to the rest of the world, must initiate a national "realism and renewal" effort that will restore those values on which this great experiment in democracy was founded.

In contrast to the West, East Asia embodies values that offer an alternative—and more positive—approach to today's world. According to Tommy T.B. Koh, these include a less individualistic philosophy and greater emphasis on education, savings, cooperation between employers and employees, and respect for law and order.

Such principles, however, find few adherents in the new ghettos—the "gray areas," says Hans-Dieter Vontobel, where lawlessness reigns increasingly. New ghettos are being created—in the geographical sense—in metropolitan centers, and, in the metaphorical sense, for example, in the world of drug addicts. In these ghettos one's sense of justice degenerates. Instead of security, violence prevails, and a social Darwinist ethos reminiscent of early capitalism takes hold.

The functioning of the capitalist system is also endangered by the degeneration of ethics because capitalism is based on the assumption that the players in the market are basically honest. As Paul Minus points out, ethics were woven into the very fabric of Western society. It is therefore essential to cultivate the values of our society, to pay more attention to the ethical behavior of people, and to establish policies to overcome unethical practices. In this effort, the business community must play a major role, but behavior within companies must also change. Patrick Glynn urges a deemphasis on the rigid, pyramid-type modes of organization in favor of genuine cooperative models of management, based on individual empowerment, distribution of authority, and an ethic of service. In addition, Enrique Ruete argues for higher standards of conduct in government and business, while Rajiv Mehrotra proposes a greater effort by the media to promote human values.

The need for global ethics is obvious, and as Elie Wiesel illustrates by a quotation from Chesterton, "When people cease to believe in God, it is not that they believe in nothing, but they believe in anything."

Wiesel makes a passionate plea for greater understanding and tolerance toward one another: "Moral behavior, in the next century, must mean people's acceptance of the other who is not far from us, since he dwells in us. . . . We have known times when we were united in fear. Shall we be united in hope—tomorrow?" A similar argument is made by Hans Küng, who points to the fundamental role that religions play in world politics. In his opinion, they are not the overriding factor, but provide the cultural foundation for antagonisms and conflicts between nations. He believes conflicts between civilizations can be avoided and, towards this objective, argues for a dialogue between religions and a consensus on basic principles of global ethics that are common to all religions.

-1-
There Is No Such Thing as
a Purely Material Crisis

Jacob Needleman

Description of Change

The crisis in values is not merely one of many problems facing today's world; it is at the root of all issues. Although people have always faced difficulties resulting from changes in economics, health, geology, climate, war, and natural disaster, their value systems enabled them to adjust effectively. Perhaps in no previous era have people had to face such challenges without a guiding sense of *why*, of the ultimate purpose for living. The desire for mere physical survival, without an underlying sense of greater purpose, is not enough to enable people to preserve the social order. This is particularly true in a society coping with massive contemporary socioeconomic and geopolitical upheavals, many of which have been caused or accelerated by the spread of new technologies. To bring the element of meaning into human life can no longer be secondary to purely socioeconomic, political, or public health goals. The sources of moral behavior, sacrifice, and nonegoistic aspiration lie in the spiritual realms and must be restored or retained in the stream of human life.

Reasons for Change

Almost without exception, redefining humanity's basic assumptions begins and ends in the realm of values and human meaning. For humanity as a whole, as well as for nations and individual people, *there is no such thing as a purely material crisis!* The present world crises, including increasing crime, drugs, the widening gulf between rich and poor, the spread of sexually transmitted diseases, the destruction of the environment, the population explosion, the impotence of governments, are examples of the worldwide erosion of philosophical and moral guidance in the conduct and interpretation of life. Just as biological species are being destroyed by the effects of population growth, advancing technology, and the intensification and diffusion of the market economy, so too are countless indigenous value systems, religious teachings, moral systems, bodies of medical knowledge, and social wisdom that is encoded in customs, rituals, and symbols that are less and less appreciated and understood in their native contexts.

New technologies are replacing the traditional roles of philosophy and spiritual ideas. Scientists can manipulate the brain to produce sensations of happiness and mastery and rearrange the genetic code. Biological and economic techniques can be used to transform the meaning of personal identity, birth and death, work, and the family unit. These techniques have introduced an overwhelming dehumanizing influence into modern culture, which is now dangerously unbalanced. It is this imbalance between scientific, "rationalistic" technology and market economies on the one hand, and indigenous, age-old wisdom on the other that is manifested in the crises of ecology, public health, and societal instability, as well as in the growing sense of individual despair, meaninglessness, and moral impotence.

Probable Consequences

The pressure to learn and use new technologies is breeding confusion. People are taking sides for and against technology and find no way to consult their own inner feelings. The moral education of human beings, their ability to adjust in times of difficulty, is in danger of being entirely neglected. Without the cultivation of this capacity, which lies at the very heart of *moral power,* the present material and social crises of the world can only intensify, while new dangers, not yet foreseen, will appear. It is no exaggeration to say that the survival of humanity depends on the reanimation of the age-old search for inner truth.

Proposed Actions

The international community needs to support inquiries into the effects of technology on human life, inquiries that are not motivated by political or commercial considerations, or by the need to reach immediately applicable solutions. This crisis of meaning and value cannot be repaired overnight, and the discerning eye must discriminate between what in this situation is actually reparable and what is intrinsic to the human condition itself. We must drop the illusion that there will ever be a totally managed and explained world, or even a world without a preponderance of sorrow and pain. Nevertheless, crucial aspects of the current crisis have been created by perceptions and assumptions that are correctable. These must be identified and studied.

The same impartial approach should be applied to studying traditional and indigenous cultural forms, many of which contain a treasury of human wisdom. Discernment here is imperative; we must discriminate between forms and teachings that have preserved wisdom and those that have degenerated into superstition and dangerous half-truths. Simultaneously, respect must be shown for customs that have only the benign purpose of maintaining the identity of a group.

Such a program is limited without a deepened understanding of the vision of human nature, morality, and the natural world that lies at the heart of all spiritual teachings. We have to do more than merely tolerate the variety of religious and cultural forms in the world in the spirit of noninterventionism. We need to *understand* what these teachings are trying to pass on to people and, based on this understanding, have the courage to admit where we see the violation of human life—possibly even in revered traditional contexts. Not everything indigenous and ancient is good, true, or benign; just as not everything in the sweep of modern science, technology, and economics is harmful to the world or individuals. There is immense good in science, along with the bad that is implicit in its unbalanced applications; there may be immense danger in traditionalism, apart from the so far underappreciated greatness in its authentic spiritual, philosophical, and moral roots.

The first practical is to identify a handful of men and women who can come together to think about the actual meaning of spiritual and religious traditions, as well as art and culture, in the regions and among the peoples of the world. These individuals need not be academicians or appointed religious leaders. They may be scientists, businesspeople, statespeople, artists, writers, schoolteachers, and engineers. Their principal qualification will be a sensitivity to the purely spiritual/moral dimension of human life, together with a knowledge of traditional teachings within their own cultures and a willingness to exchange insights with representatives from other cultures, *without carrying any special political or social agenda into the exchange.*

Do such people exist? How can they be found?

-2-
The Death of the Modern
Michael Vlahos

Description of Change

To the American poet, Archibald MacLeish, as he wrote in "Hypocrite Auteur,"

A world ends when its metaphor has died. . . .

We all thought that the world ending was the world of communism; its place: the Soviet Empire; its metaphor: the Cold War.

We were wrong. A much bigger world, of much longer standing, is slowly dying. That world is what we have come to know as "the Modern...." The death of Soviet communism was just the death of the Modern's most wayward child. And when the first of us goes, we suddenly see the whole brood grown old.

Reasons for Change

What has caused the death of the Modern?

- Leadership has failed because the elite has failed. The sense that there are no leaders in the West has become a lament. But "Where are the leaders?" is not a call for good people, but rather a cry against the leadership class itself and the regime system it appears to own. The elite is not producing leaders because its ethos has become corrupt. Witness the endless Liberal Democratic Party scandals in Japan and American contempt for Washington, the federal bureaucracy, and Congress. People believe that the entrenched elites no longer know what it is to lead and serve the people, and having lost that trust, they are abrogating their authority to rule.
- Elites have been rejected by their own people. People who feel abused by a system that no longer seems to represent them become angry. And when they feel angry, they want to get even. Look at Canada, its ruling Conservative party simply destroyed; or Japan, its LDP overthrown in spite of its 38-year lock on political power; and Italy, its people turning to neofascists in preference to the cozy corruption of the "legitimate."

Look at what happened to the Socialists in France, and what is about to happen to the Tories in Britain. Look at the 20 percent of Americans who voted for Ross Perot. Perversely, demagogues and marginal movements have greater legitimacy precisely because they have not been corrupted by decades in power.

- The elite have unwittingly undercut their own legitimacy. The pattern is familiar. The sons and daughters of a current ruling cohort attack their parent's paradigm. Postmodernism, existentialism, and deconstruction are attacking other schools of thought within the Modern itself. They attack the Modern's impulse to sell its agenda to the people by appealing to the nostalgia embedded in popular values. The Modern understood that people, so unlike their elites, were still spiritually rooted in the world before the Modern; so modernism sold its policies by insisting they would uphold—even extend—the comforting old world of family and community. But beginning in the 1960s, the Modern's own young became revisionists. They began to say that tying our agenda to old values is unacceptable; it is a lie. Today, the young elite's brief is simple. All of modernism's nostalgic falsehoods must go, from family values to the melting pot. The trouble with this theory is that people do not believe in deconstruction, they believe in what these young elites would destroy.

- Elite policies have publicly failed, with governments getting deeper into debt. Nostalgic association, however, was irrelevant, because the policies that comprised modernism's core agenda were failing. They actually had often succeeded in making worse things that desperately needed to be made better. Poverty and unemployment have become more widespread and persistent because programs are state administered and subsidized. Medical care is costlier and less available because it is state run (with the United States on the way to this policy). The people are kept in their place because of the inferiority of state-run schools and their inability to avoid paying taxes, as they elite often can. The Modern promised that government run by enlightened public servants would do better, would not be venal, and would improve the quality of life for all people. Ask any person today whether or not it has delivered.

- People's way of life is eroding. Not only has the Modern failed to deliver on its vision, but what good already existed has been unexpectedly eroded. People like to reflect on the personal effects of progress. Is my life getting better? What kind of future can my children hope for? People in all three of the Modern's culture areas feel more uncertain and less hopeful about the future.

- In Europe, people are concerned about unemployment and falling wages, especially without the cushion of social democracy's welfare state. Their world is now beset by alien immigrants, competition from Asian economies that produce more for less, and arrogant Brussels Eurocrats who seek to control all aspects of their lives.
- In North America, people are afraid that the very glue of their lives is softening. They see a society defined by crime, anomie, and incivility, where the American dream exists only for the Yuppie few. The American elite has a lock on the rewards to come from economic revolution, and Americans know what it means not to share in those rewards.
- In Japan, the all-knowing system run by bureaucrat and daimyos has failed to keep Japan's world stable and secure. The Japanese people did what they were told, and in return, the system gave them security. Now, at many levels, all at once, this world is coming apart.
- There is a fearful wrenching of the context of people's lives. Economic revolution, even as it brings growth, also means restructuring. This is a cold term for the end of many people's job community. For many in the West, the last economic upheaval created an industrial world where one's job was one's family—one's mooring. Many of these communities are dying; many more will soon feel the noose. The loss of job communities among certain labor niches has already had a devastating cultural impact. For example, the withering of lower-skill industrial jobs in cities has been a material factor in the destruction of the black inner cities. Is it so different for French fishermen or Japanese rice farmers?

Probable Consequences

In the West, people assume that Big Change as social revolution cannot happen again, because the state (and its elites) will take care of the people, will respond to their needs in the face of change and uncertainty. (But, did not the Soviet state take care of its own?)

Cassandra's curse was to be both right and disbelieved. So there can be no probable consequences, only consequential possibilities. And we can describe them.

- In Europe, working people are fighting for their hard-won way of life. They will find leaders to protect their world and will turn to ideas that allow them to celebrate their identity. The preservation of social democracy may turn Europe into an uncompetitive backwater, but it will be a more democratic, if highly nativist, bastion. But it must keep its glacis cleared, that means managing, perhaps even repressing, its border areas to the east and south.

- In North America, the idea of the Modern will be remade as people wrestle with the fundamental questions of identity. What is the United States? What is Canada? Old party systems will be overthrown in the United States, as they have been in Canada. Religious revivalism and ornery nativism now rampage against a modernist elite, which marshals the majority of state power against a people who speak only with their votes. The outcome is still uncertain.

- In Japan, new meaning is forced by shocks from without the country—shocks can unleash national energy. The great Asian social conflicts of the early twenty-first century will challenge Japan. There will be no return to the American womb, so the Japanese must look to themselves for solutions. When they have done so before, interesting and sometimes terrible things have happened.

The death of the Modern does not make violent social revolution inevitable, or even likely. Nor does it make core culture areas weak and ineffectual as they remake their societies. Europe need not slide back to where it was ten centuries ago; the United States and Canada need not take the road to another war of civil visions; Japan need not find its identity in the theater of national insecurity. This is like flipping through old sketchbooks.

But something big always happens in a Big Change.

Proposed Actions

The best action is to see what is happening for what it is. This is also the hardest action, especially for us, the elite, the upholders of the Modern. It is hard to see the erosion because modernism has deliberately subdivided knowledge.

Think of our reality as a vessel holding all knowledge. Imagine the hull of this stately ship as a warren of compartments, each of which has as a permanent watch its own academic or professional knowledge guild of specialists. Each watch would know what was happening within its own compartment, but little of what was happening in others. A crew so specialized and subdivided would have a full understanding of its own ship space, but no sense of how the ship as a whole worked. There would be no captain, no watch on the bridge.

What is happening to the ship of knowledge—our reality—is that the vessel is being rebuilt, not remodeled. Thomas Kuhn wrote about the struggle of a new paradigm to be born. He looked at change in the paradigm of science, a single community of knowledge. What we are witnessing is a birth struggle not simply in one knowledge world, but among several simultaneously. We see it in the physical sciences, as scientists rethink what they once believed could be quantified—time and space itself. We see in the social sciences, as its practitioners change their calculus of human behavior, explaining why some societies work while others fall apart. We see it in economics, where models of rational control are yielding to those, such as human culture, that are beyond the field's sway. We see it in psychology, where new drugs can treat mental illnesses that analysis still cannot assuage. We see it in philosophy, which must acknowledge that reason alone cannot give meaning and which now desperately seeks a sense of the sacred that will willingly inhabit the mental universe of the Modern. We see it even in schools of management, where the robotic doctrines of Frederick Taylor—so beloved by Lenin—now give way to management philosophies that seek efficiency and productivity gains from the liberation of the individual from those very robotic structures of personal control.

The shocks to our macroparadigm—if we were to name the Modern according to Kuhn—have come from its own failed experiments. They have built up an accretion of contrary evidence that can no longer be accommodated in yet another revision of theory. This has happened to the Einsteinian universe, the Freudian mind, and, of course, the Marxian economy. It is happening at last in the realm of political philosophy.

These shocks to the Modern's macroparadigm mean that those who rule the Modern no longer have a pantheon to believe in. The gods of the Western elites lie shattered in the great acropolis of the state, while those with temporal authority try to pick their way through the rubble as though nothing has changed. Is not the acropolis still standing; its walls still not breached?

But without the guiding certainty of belief, without the comfort and the strength that only these ideas can offer, elites bring to their electorates an almost visible hollowness of spirit. This is why there is no leadership in Europe, American, and Japan. The elites no longer believe in themselves.

The surest sign of the death of the Modern is this loss of confidence among its elites. And, in the terrifying absence of belief, they are all the more afraid of new ideas or popular insurgencies. Witness the fear among the U.S. elite of the so-called "religious right"; among European elites of "ultranationalism"; or in Japan, simply of the word "reformation." Their fear drives them to master those who threaten, rather than to puzzle through why their motivating political urge is to control instead of lead.

The Modern will not long survive. It has ceased to work, people no longer believe in it, and it just does not fit the new ways things will be done. The new world being made by economic revolution needs a new idea to give it voice. It needs a new elite that can lead the way.

And who will do this, if not we? There are others, to be sure. But what is also sure is that the new metaphor, the one that succeeds the Modern, is awaiting only its name.

But will that word be spoken by us?

-3-
The Breakdown of
the Family
Rosanna Wong Yick-Ming

Description of Change

The structure of the family has always depended on, among other factors, a society's religious system and economic base. Although still the basic unit of social organization, the family unit is weakening in the modern world.

In Hong Kong and China, for example, the interdependence of family members has an economic and religious basis. Since young people still tend to live with their parents until marriage, they make substantial contributions to the family's income. This pattern is no longer true in a more individual Western culture, where young adults are eager to pursue independent lifestyles. At present, 64 percent of Hong King's residents live in nuclear families, and this percentage has grown in the last ten years.

In addition, parents are increasingly pressured to earn higher incomes, so that their families will enjoy an improved standard of living. As a result, young children often do not receive the day-to-day care and attention that they need to develop into responsible citizens. With both parents at work, grandparents unable to assist, and the breakup of community units, children may suffer from inadequate supervision. When parents do return home, they are often too tired and preoccupied to communicate effectively with their children.

Reasons for Change

As a result of rapid urbanization, the world population explosion, and the spread of international capitalism, local traditions and family loyalties are giving way to the demands of the market. These changes mean that smaller units of production, where people felt secure in their value systems and of their place in society, have rapidly eroded. Within countries, the breakdown of local economies and higher urban wages lure people from villages to cities. Rural depopulation and the consequent breakup of stable communities is a cause of major social change in many countries, including Japan and France. Internationally, the differential in standard of living and GNP between rich and poor countries encourages many workers to migrate to foreign countries to find work, sending remittances back home. Sometimes, the entire nuclear family migrates, in which case links with the extended family are weakened. Other times, just the man of the family (for example, Turkish workers in Western Europe) or the woman (for example, the 125,000 Filipina domestic helpers in Hong Kong) migrates, leaving behind a family, often with young children.

Probable Consequences

Without daily contact with parents, children grow up in a spiritual vacuum, where the highest value is placed on money and the acquisition of material commodities. The worldwide marketplace now offers a tempting range of consumer goods, the very acquisition of which alters—in fact, often minimizes—social interaction within and between families. Television, for example, has replaced conversation and homemade family entertainment. Similarly, the possession of washing machines mean that women no longer interact at the communal washing place. Through advertising, young people are constantly aware of new technologies and life-styles. The clear message is that immediate acquisition of these products is essential for peer acceptance. Credit cards and bank loans have taken "the waiting out of wanting," so that the attribute of saving for a much-prized purchase will soon be consigned to the dustbin. The built-in obsolescence of these sought-after goods guarantees that this cycle never ends.

People who cannot afford these goods increasingly resort to illegal activities to acquire them, as is evidenced by the growth in crime worldwide. After years without basic commodities and a lack of freedom of expression, Russia is in the wake of an inflation that accompanied the drive to develop a market economy. One result has been a breakdown in law and order, as people become rootless in the pursuit of materialism. As people in poorer countries rush to catch up with people in richer countries, they are less likely to remain committed to family, community, and nation. Without the firm support of a stable family, dissatisfied young people may be increasingly vulnerable to drug pushers and a promiscuous life-style.

Proposed Actions

Current politicians and policymakers must be aware of the dangers of a world in which people have no moral direction, no spiritual life, and no sense of community responsibility. The breakdown of communism in the

Eastern bloc and the subsequent ending of the Cold War is a hopeful direction for humanity. Attention can now focus on developing policies of cooperation and mutual assistance.

Leaders, governments and their agencies, as well as the various arms of the United Nations, must support programs of family-life education and intergenerational communication. Educational and social programs for young people should emphasize community service and compassion for those less privileged, while encouraging the young to use their skills and training for the benefit of society. There are some admirable examples of unselfish use of professional expertise, such as Orbis, *Médecine sans Frontières,* and Operation Smile. International youth exchange programs help young people view themselves as part of an entity larger than just their own family or peer group. It is hoped that such exchanges will foster a sense of unity and brotherhood in tomorrow's leaders, values that they will pass on to their own children. Youth exchanges are already being successfully operated in Hong Kong between local young people and those of China, Canada, and Germany. Finally, owners of the mass media must become more responsible as they have a powerful influence on many people who rely on the media for information and entertainment.

The Decline of the United States as an Inspiration to Emerging Nations

John Bohn

Description of Change

Since 1945, the U.S. system of democracy, which accommodated differences, individual liberty, and responsibility within a market-driven economy, served as a model for developing countries. Clearly, a stable legal order, a fair court system, and equal opportunity based on individual effort contributed to U.S. economic success. As such, the United States had enormous influence in shaping institutions and policies around the globe and in providing hope to the world's populations.

Recently, however, other economic systems have produced dramatic growth. This at a time when the United States is combating individual excesses, a breakdown of law and order, a corroded educational system, and growing national fragmentation based on race, history, culture, and perceived inequality of benefits. The result is national and international skepticism as to the ability of the United States to set and sustain a national agenda, let alone a global one. As a result, the United States is losing its place as the role model in the international arena.

Reasons for Change

America's sense of nationhood has been pressured by globalization and advances in technology. Although instant communication has brought world problems to its compassionate and solution-hungry electorate, it has also made the nation's own failures globally visible. Without the Soviet threat to unite the country, interest groups have begun to overpower the nation's traditional value system. At the same time, the energy inherent in change is creating destabilizing challenges abroad.

Probable Consequences

The decline of the United States as an accepted reference point during these particularly turbulent times is accelerating instability. Developing societies will turn away from the American example toward Darwinian self-interest. Any influence the United States might have exerted through its financial aid policies is diminishing as funds allotted to world development decline. For developing societies in search of economic growth and a sense of meaning, the fragmentation of the United States will send interest groups searching for immediate short-term advantage, provoke military confrontations as well as cultural and religious clashes, and encourage ethnic turmoil.

Proposed Actions

The United States must initiate a national program of "realism and renewal" that will restore basic values, put the nation's economic house in order, and replace individual self-indulgence with a sense of national worth. Once rediscovered, these values must be elaborated through international organizations, such as the United Nations. Without such national renewal, other claimants to moral leadership, whether political or religious, will struggle fiercely during the twenty-first century, with consequent instability and bloodshed.

-5-
The Positive Values
of East Asia

Tommy T.B. Koh

Description of Change

For the past hundred years, the values of the West have dominated the world. This assumption that West stood for the Best and that the Best must be Western is changing as East Asians are gaining respect for their traditional values.

Reason for Change

This more positive self-image is largely the result of the spectacular rise of East Asia in the world economy. Led by Japan, and followed by Korea, Taiwan, Hong Kong, ASEAN, China, and Vietnam, the economies of East Asia have the world's highest growth rates. Because of their increasing interdependence, created through trade and investment, they have maintained their buoyancy despite recession and comparatively sluggish growth in the OECD economies. Economic success has given East Asians the self-confidence to deal with the West as equals.

East Asians are also benefiting from the rising tide of social problems in the West—the breakdown of the family; rising crime rates; and the decline of civil society. In East Asia, by contrast, the family remains strong; social welfare exists but does not erode the work ethic or the sense of personal responsibility; and cities are safe for law-abiding citizens. East Asians therefore believe that their point of view, whether on economics, moral values, social governance, or the concept of good government, is legitimate and worth sharing with others.

On the whole, East Asians prefer consensus over contention. Thus, they believe that the rights of the individual must be balanced by the rights of the family and society; that the family is the building block of society; that education is important; and that frugality is virtuous. They have faith in the work ethic, in national teamwork, and in communitarianism.

Probable Consequences

What are the consequences of the rise of East Asia? There are at least three possible scenarios—Samuel P. Huntington's scenario of "civilizational conflict"; a world order based on universal values; and a community of nations based on partial convergence of universal values. The first two are least likely. The world does not appear to be heading toward conflict based on clashes of civilizations, but a complete convergence of values throughout the world would be an unrealistic expectation. Since there is, however, a growing core of universal values, the third scenario is the most logical. Outside this core, we must respect each other's point of view. Better still, we should learn from them.

Proposed Actions

The avoidance of future conflict requires mutual understanding. Success should not make the East smug and arrogant; it should continue to learn from the West. At the same time, the West should drop its stance of moral superiority, acknowledge that some of its moral, economic, and social prescriptions have proven to be flawed, and admit that it can learn some valuable lessons from East Asia.

-6-
Pirates in Modern Society
Hans-Dieter Vontobel

Description of Change

In the urban centers of the industrialized world, gray areas are emerging. These areas are characterized by self-interest and a limited respect for state authority and law. They have become true ethnic-cultural ghettos, in which the social and constitutional bases of society and state are being eroded. In gray areas, such as the drug scene, organized crime eventually finds fertile ground for its activities. In society's ineffective approach to these problems, the values that underlie our public order are continuously questioned, challenged, and brought into discredit—if only through well-intended appeasement by the authorities. This process leads people to question the constitutional state and the fundamental principles of liberty.

Reasons for Change

These gray areas have evolved as basic values have been replaced by comparative lawlessness, increased adherence to social Darwinism, and social disintegration. In modern society, "demand instead of serve" has become the motto. Respect for the law has suffered from the relative loss of basic ethical rules and justice, as well as from excessive violence in the media. As social Darwinism spreads into economic policy, some people are regressing to early capitalist practices. Clearly, affluence has prompted waywardness, material values have proved insufficient substitutes for conventional norms, and the welfare state invites abuse.

The obvious inability of modern economies to come to terms with unemployment has intensified these problems, because it results in the social exclusion of millions of people. Many of the industrialized countries are experiencing a potentially disturbing phenomenon, in which second-generation immigrants are often deliberately rejecting social and cultural integration. This attitude has repeatedly resulted in clashes between the practices of the Western secular state (for instance, in its schools) and the religious beliefs and traditions of immigrants.

We are experiencing, on a more philosophical level, the end of the Age of Enlightenment, the end of the Jacobin tradition of public order and structure, and a loss of faith in the scientific and material progress. The French author Alain Minc has brilliantly described this new *Zeitgeist* in his recent book *Le Nouveau Moyen-Age* (The New Middle Ages [Paris: Gallimard, 1993]).

Probable Consequences

What sort of a new age have we inaugurated, and toward what sort of future do we look? Those who most need to be integrated into society are converting to the ways of the pirates. As a result of the ineffectiveness of social welfare programs, they often turn to nonaltruistic groups, such as organized crime, for economic and social support. This gives organized crime a vital foothold in these communities. As crime increases, traditional values concerning the state and the rule of law are discredited. People who continue to respect these values become increasingly xenophobic and extreme in their political views.

Proposed Actions

Western societies must take positive action to preserve their basic values. Social welfare policies alone will not be sufficient, for the silent acceptance of the growing disintegration of social values is undermining the very basis of the constitutional role of the state. There are no easy solutions. The state must abandon the anesthetizing (and at the same time fatalistic) political discourse that plays down problems and adopt policies that deal more effectively with the issues of multiculturalism. Such policies include schooling programs for immigrants and their children and reformation of the social welfare system. Ignoring the reality by suggesting instead that we live in the best of all worlds (an approach many politicians prefer), only helps the pirates enlarge their gray areas.

Toward an Ethic for the Twenty-First Century

Paul M. Minus

Description of Change

The post-Cold War era has witnessed the acceleration of a fateful change: the weakening of the generally accepted ethical standards that were nurtured in the West over centuries and gave many people both a vision of the common good and an incentive to seek its realization.

Never as compelling or effective as its proponents wished, this ethic nonetheless came to be woven into the fabric of Western society, providing a high degree of social cohesion and individual purposiveness. Moreover, it gained worldwide recognition through the spread of Western ideas and institutions during the nineteenth and twentieth centuries.

The effects of this ethical decline have been evident recently in such diverse phenomena as the upsurge of family violence and drug abuse, the increased divisiveness of social and political life, and the conspicuous scandals uncovered in the upper levels of business organizations. The same decline has also been a key factor in the failure to cope aggressively with such ominous global developments as the spread of the effects of poverty and malnutrition among children and the degradation of the natural environment.

However, recent years have also witnessed an accelerated, albeit uncertain, quest for a new ethic—an ethic that will restore such basic values as freedom, responsibility, and justice, will restate these values in ways that embrace key values of non-Western cultural traditions, and will demonstrate their relevance to difficult political, social, and economic problems.

Reasons for Change

The decline of the traditional ethic can be traced to the diminished influence of such long-standing teachers of values as religion, the schools, and the family; the heightened depersonalization, fragmentation, and insecurity of modern life; and the failure of mainstream institutions to recognize how much the welfare of individuals, organizations, and the planet is tied to values and ethics.

Similarly, the search for a new ethic has been propelled by a complex combination of factors, including a nostalgia for what is seen as best in older ways, a fear of the possible results of failure to change course, and a perhaps instinctive recognition that the challenges of a new millennium require a new ethical compass.

Probable Consequences

A continued erosion of the traditional ethic—offset by no advance of the new ethic—may well propel the world further down the path of social disarray and disintegration. "Where there is no vision the people perish" is an insight as relevant today as it was in biblical times.

Particularly important is the fact that recent technological advances have given people unprecedented power by which to affect both the natural environment and the human community. Guided by narrow interests, this power can lead to considerable decay and misery; but guided by a larger vision, it can create an expanding realm of peace and well-being.

Proposed Actions

Every possible effort must now be made to strengthen the efforts already launched to develop and apply a new ethic. Steps to be taken in this direction include:

- fostering greater public awareness of how critical this issue has become for the future of humanity.
- increasing investment of resources by the business sector.
- supporting efforts now under way among the major world religions to identify fundamental ethical teachings common to them all.
- accelerating international collaboration among the business, government, academic, and religious sectors so as to engage the issues of ethics and values constructively.

The proposed major role of the business sector in this effort merits further comment. As is demonstrated by ethics incentives undertaken recently by such business organizations as *Keidanren* in Japan, *Confindustria* in Italy, and the Conference Board in the United States, the business community has begun to treat these matters with unusual seriousness.

This fresh interest is due partly to recognition that the capitalist system and efficient business transactions presuppose the presence of an "ethical infrastructure" that leads people to deal with each other honestly and fairly. It is in the direct interest of corporations to repair this ethical precondition of business enterprise where it has declined, to nurture it where it has not yet fully emerged, and to extend it worldwide as an indispensable basis for an efficient global economy.

Other recent developments are also pushing business to pay fresh attention to the issues of ethics and values noted below.

- In a time of mounting public pressure for business to assume greater responsibility for preserving the natural environment and for renewing communities, how far should business organizations go in this direction?

- In a time of far-reaching reconsideration by business of its purposes and processes, to what degree should it embrace such newly recovered values as community, cooperation, participation, and empowerment?

- In a time of growing global involvement by corporations among peoples and cultures with which they have had little previous association, should business distinguish between conduct that is ethically appropriate for it in "home" settings and conduct that is ethically appropriate for it in "host" settings?

- In a time of the ascendance of market economies over a discredited communism, what should business do to foster a humane capitalism, especially in lands that have experienced long years of communist domination and are now passing through a difficult period of transition?

- In a time of emerging interest among corporate executives around the world in the ethical dimensions of business policy and operations, how can this interest be effectively integrated and implemented in the organizations they lead?

It may well be—as some business leaders now believe—that greater attention to these questions by corporations will not only contribute to a better world, but will also win them new customers and clients. Those who "do good" will also "do well."

Business leaders can address this issue most constructively in dialogue with their counterparts in the education and religious communities. Academic specialists, especially those who have developed the new discipline of business ethics, have helpful technical expertise to contribute to this venture, and religious ethicists from the Buddhist, Hindu, Islamic, Jewish, and Christian traditions, especially from their more progressive wings, have considerable experience to offer in relating high ethical standards to the daily struggles and difficult dilemmas of life.

Some international business-driven collaborative organizations, such as the International Chamber of Commerce and the World Economic

Forum, have now placed ethics issues on their agendas. And some, such as the Council for Ethics in Economics, have also developed business/education/religion partnerships as their normal mode of seeking global consensus on an ethic for the twenty-first century and for the new global economy.

It is clear that people around the world are eager for bold new steps on behalf of a humane future for the human family. The time is ripe for leaders who are ready to engage in this quest.

-8-
Religion and Modern Value Systems

Rajiv Mehrotra

Description of Change

With the growing erosion in interpersonal values, we need to reemphasize the importance and influence of religion. Historically, the teaching of values was inextricably linked with religion, and political power often derived from "divine" or religious authority. However, both Western liberal democracies and later communist dictatorships sought to distance themselves, at least formally, from religion.

Reasons for Change

The impact of technology has made human interaction increasingly impersonal. We communicate through electronic pulses, fight wars by remote control, and fulfill many of our needs without direct human interaction. As a result, we have an illusion of autonomy, a feeling of decreasing independence from the family or the community.

The cultivation of values has accompanied the development of a structured religious faith. As organized religion failed to keep pace with larger societal imperatives and the perceived promise of science to provide solutions to human dilemmas, the influence of religion declined or, in many cases, was perverted. This was particularly true in the technologically advanced world, where the modern state pursued a synthetic secularism that was based on an intellectual commitment to an empirical, rational world view and an effort to ensure that the state was not seen to be endorsing one religion over another.

Religion has, however, survived as an influential factor in interpersonal and international relationships. Although religion appears more dominant in Islamic states, it is an emerging force in the postcommunist world of Eastern Europe and still wields enormous influence in countries that purport to be deeply committed to secularism. In the United States, for example, where the President-elect takes the oath of office with one hand on a Bible and invites a member of the clergy to deliver a prayer, an estimated 65 percent of the people are active members of a church or synagogue, and religion remains a major factor in regional conflicts.

Recently, indices of development have been based solely on economic growth, higher productivity, ever-improving material standards of living, and, where convenient, political freedoms. These are inadequate standards by which to measure human aspiration and progress.

Probable Consequences

Our growing sense of the differences among people has diminished our humanity and led to an insensitivity to the real predicaments of others. On a more tangible level, violence is increasing even in affluent cultures, such as the United States. The wealthy and the successful are frequently insulated from the plight of those less fortunate. Throughout the world, gross inequities exist in the consumption of natural resources and the inability of more than half of the world's population to access what the other half considers only a bare minimum for survival. In the long run, indifference threatens us all. What happens in one part of the world—or even to a single human being—has an impact on everyone. More than ever, we are confronting vast and complex challenges, whose implications are not always immediate and tangible.

Proposed Actions

As members of the global community we need to cultivate a sense of universal responsibility, based on an understanding of the interdependence of people with each other, with their environments, and with their "spiritual" sides. It will change the way we treat ourselves, each other, and our physical environment.

The media and the educational system are two major instruments of change. With the media increasingly driven by financial imperatives, it is likely to prove more difficult to influence. The educational system, however, which remains largely under state direction, can emphasize the importance of interdependence and impart a philosophy that combines altruism and compassion without treading on secularistic toes.

We also need to create global structures and institutions that promote a sense of universal responsibility—an awareness of interdependence— and work with religious traditions toward creating a better, more harmonious world. An international organization should be created under the aegis of the United Nations that will promote human values, without endorsing any one faith. It will encourage dialogue and interaction among the different religious traditions, as well as serve as a resource for conflict resolution in religious disagreements around the world. It will have a central governing body, a security council, whose membership will include the heads of different faiths, well-known scholars, and activists from the voluntary sector.

-9-
A Global Ethic as the Alternative to the Clash of Civilizations

Hans Küng

In 1918 the twentieth century had its first opportunity to replace the fashionable nationalism of the day, which had collapsed with the end of World War I, with a new and more peaceful global world order. This was prevented, however, by the popular ideologies of fascism, communism, national socialism, and Japanese militarism. Subsequently, these ideologies proved to be catastrophic mistakes even for their adherents, and the world was set back by decades. Instead of a new world order, there was world chaos. In 1945, thanks to obstruction by Stalin's Soviet Union, the second opportunity for a new world order was missed. Instead of world order, the result was world division.

In 1989 these reactionary ideologies, including that of a self-righteous anticommunism, ended; the time for monolithic ideologies and their wars seemed to be over. Once again, the idea of a new world order was propagated, admittedly without doing anything to achieve it. But the new wars, particularly the Persian Gulf War and the war in the Balkans, have sobered us all. Has the third opportunity already been lost? Are we now heading not for a new world order, but for a new world disorder? Instead of peace among nations, are we destined to an inevitable "clash of civilizations" as the American political scientist Samuel P. Huntington recently predicted.

Clash of Civilizations?

This prediction is correct in one respect: In most current conflicts, from Karabakh via the Gulf War and Bosnia through to Kashmir, fighting is basically not about civilization and religion, but about territories, raw materials, and trade and money. What is at stake are economic, political, and military interests. But ethnic/religious rivalries form the permanent framework within which the political, economic, and military conflicts can be justified, inspired, and exacerbated at any time for the purposes of territorial conflict, political interests, and economic competition. These factors can no longer be omitted when analyzing the political realities of our time. The major civilizations are not the overriding factor in world political conflicts, but rather offer a continuing cultural foundation to all antagonisms and conflicts between nations. The great religions of the world also belong to this cultural background

Anyone who is not totally blind to history realizes that current frontiers in Eastern Europe (and to some extent in Africa, too) are somewhat irrelevant in comparison with ancient frontiers, which were based on race, religion, and religious denomination. Such frontiers include those between Armenia and Azerbaijan, between Georgia and Russia, between Ukraine and Russia, and also between religious groups in the former Yugoslavia. The complexity of the problems in Yugoslavia can only be understood if you bear in mind that for more than 1000 years, basically since the division of the Roman Empire into East and West, Yugoslavia had not two different civilizations, but two different paradigms of Christianity. To this has been added the Moslems, the only autochthonous Moslems in Europe. The results are that:

- contrary to the views of all the superficial politicians and political scientists who fail to see the underlying causes of world conflicts, religions do play a fundamental role in world politics—and this was claimed by Toynbee long before Huntington.
- religions are growing, but not in Toynbee's sense of growing into a single uniform religion consisting of Christian, Moslem, Hindu, and Buddhist elements in the service of a uniform human society. To be realistic, you have to take into account their potential for conflict as rivals.

The Alternative: Peace Between the Religions

In view of possible conflicts between civilizations and between religions, does not the future look rather gloomy for humanity? If future conflicts are primarily between civilizations, then these are, so to speak, unavoidably in the nature of things. So will the future of human beings be one of continuous, endless wars?

No, conflict between civilizations can be avoided. How? In the short term, we must strive for increasing the unity of the West, increasingly cooperating with Latin American and Europe, increasingly cooperating with Russia and Japan, and restricting the military strength of Islamic and Confucianist states. In the longer term, this collision of civilizations can only be avoided by a deeper understanding of the fundamental religious and philosophical foundations of civilization. Huntington was the one who recognized this and emphasized that it would be no easy task to identify those elements that are shared in common by Western and other civilizations.

So the programmatic antithesis to the "clash of civilizations" reads like this: "Without peace between the religions, war between the civilizations. No peace between the religions without dialogue between the religions. No dialogue between the religions without fundamental research into the religions." The first result of this fundamental research already exists in the form of the Global Ethic Declaration made by the Parliament of World Religions on September 4, 1993, in Chicago.[1]

This declaration, which I worked on for the parliament, starts with the fundamental difference between law and ethics. Legal agreements, such as treaties and laws, are to be found in abundance in our world, both nationally and internationally. But what use are laws without ethics—without the individual being willing to adhere to these laws? What is the point of arms limitation agreements if there is no desire for peace? Religions can play a vital role in this respect. The Global Ethic Declaration aims therefore to accept the United Nations Declaration of Human Rights (1948) and to confirm on the basis of ethics what was therein ceremonially proclaimed on a legal level.

This declaration, which was signed by people of all the major religions, witnesses the experience that:

- laws, rulings, and conventions on their own cannot create or enforce a better world order.
- the realization that the peace, justice, and maintenance of the world depends on the readiness of people to accept legislation.
- the commitment to law and freedom assumes a consciousness of responsibilities and duties, and that therefore people's minds and hearts must be addressed.
- law without reality cannot be upheld indefinitely, and that therefore a new world order requires a global ethic.

A global ethic in this sense does not mean a new world ideology or a universal world religion beyond all existing religions. It definitely does not mean the dominance of one religion over all others. A global ethic means a basic consensus with regard to existing binding values, unalterable standards, and personal principles. Without a minimum basic consensus on ethics, any community will sooner or later become vulnerable to chaos, dictatorship, and individual despair. Indeed, without a global ethic, humanity does indeed risk "the clash of civilizations."

---

[1]The Chicago text is available in H. Küng (ed), *Erklärung zum Welthethos. Die Deklaration des Parlamentes der Weltreligionen,* Munich 1993 (Piper 1958); it is available in English translation, *A Global Ethic. The Declaration of the Parliament of the World's Religions* (London/New York, 1993). It is currently being translated into other languages.

The Global Ethic Declaration starts with the continuing difference between religions. It specifically states:

> our various religious and ethical traditions are often founded in fundamentally different ways on the basic concepts of what aids or damages man, what is just or unjust, and what is good or evil. It is not our intention to hide or ignore the fundamental differences between the individual religions. At the same time however, the Declaration states clearly that, for the sake of the peace of mankind, the religions need to emphasize more clearly what they already have in common. Included in this is the principle found in all religions that every person must be treated humanely. So every individual, whatever his age, sex, race, skin colour, physical or mental ability, language, religion, political view, national or social origin, has a dignity which is inalienable and inviolable. In order to protect this the Declaration reiterates a principle, the golden rule which has proven its worth for thousand of years in many religions and ethical traditions of mankind: "Do unto others as you would be done by." Or, to put it more positively, "However you would like to be treated, treat others that way." This principle "should be the inalienable and absolute standard for all aspects of life, for family and communities, for races, nations and religions."

This principle includes concrete standards. From it can be derived four comprehensive and ancient guidelines—eternal verities—which are to be found in most religions of the world: an obligation to a culture of nonviolence and of respect for life; an obligation to a culture of solidarity and a just form of world commerce; an obligation to a culture of tolerance and honesty in life; and an obligation to a culture of equal opportunities and the partnership of man and woman.

Finally, the Global Ethic Declaration ends on a hopeful note: "The world cannot be changed for the better without a change in the consciousness of the individual. We argue for a change in collective consciousness at both an individual and a collective level, for a wakening of spiritual strength through reflection, meditation, prayer, and positive thinking, for a return to the heart. Together we can move mountains. Without taking some risks and being prepared to make a sacrifice, there can be no fundamental change in our situation. Therefore, we commit ourselves to a joint global ethic, to better mutual understanding, and to a way of life that is socially acceptable, promotes peace, and is at one with nature."

-10-
From Hierarchy to Cooperation
Patrick Glynn

Description of Change

Increasingly, cooperative forms of behavior are gaining favor over hierarchical organization and competition. Many businesses are moving away from rigid structures toward cooperative models of management based on individual empowerment, redistribution of authority, and an ethic of service. These companies, such as Levi-Strauss, many new small firms, and some smaller, experimental units in more traditional organizations, are prospering far ahead of the old dinosaurs. Similarly, in politics, those states following a violent or competitive path are suffering economically and spiritually (Serbia is one extreme example), whereas those seeking greater openness and cooperation with other nations are enjoying expanded prosperity. In daily life, the best-adjusted and most prosperous individuals are those who primarily give service to others, rather than advance their careers at the expense of others.

We have long thought in terms of individualistic competition and the "survival of the fittest." Now, we are seeing evidence that cooperative behavior, which integrates considerations of ethics and experience, values, and efficiency, has an evolutionary advantage over more predatory approaches. For example, for many years it was assumed that communist governments, by virtue of their ruthlessness, had a strategic advantage over more loosely organized, consent-based democracies. In the 1960s, many Western observers even believed command economies to be superior to market economies. Events in recent years, however, have demonstrated the evolutionary superiority of democratic/market systems, extending even into the military realm.

The collapse of communism was quickly followed by a parallel "paradigm shift" in business thinking and practices; this shift was reinforced by tumultuous shakeouts in many industries. The enthusiasm among many business executives for "empowerment/team" approaches reflects a growing recognition that treating customers or employees indifferently or exploitatively has real long-run costs. Business itself has undergone in *Fortune's* words, "the Western equivalent of the collapse of communism," with vast, rigid, hierarchical, command-oriented (and once seemingly impervious) corporate structures falling the hardest. A wealth of experiential evidence and study data now supports the economic advantages of more participatory, less hierarchical management structures, as well as what might be called "altruism in the workplace." For example, companies actively fostering volunteerism and community service enjoy increased profitability and attract better personnel. Marketing data, meanwhile, show consumers giving greater weight to a company's record on social responsibility and environmental records in their purchase decisions. A new kind of company is emerging—one that employs radically unorthodox, humanistic approaches to management, with impressive bottom-line results. At the same time, a growing body of psychology literature is stressing the importance of sound values, charitable behavior, and conscious spirituality to the overall contentment and health of individuals.

Reasons for Change

Humanity is in the midst of a major spiritual and psychological realignment. The long era of selfish struggle among individuals, organizations, and nations is gradually passing. Its demise is signaled not only by the dramatically peaceful collapse of the Berlin Wall, but also by higher levels of cooperation on both local and global scales. The essence of the new global alignment is a coming together of separate individuals, organizations, and nations into a complex, highly differentiated, but ultimately unified, global organism. Information—communication—will be the lifeblood of this new global organism. It is, after all, the information revolution that peacefully undermined the Soviet Union and which continues to challenge hierarchy and repression in all its forms, including authoritarianism and paternalism in the workplace. At the human level, television, which is gradually becoming globally available, enables people to identify to an unprecedented degree with individuals of different races, cultures, and geographic circumstances. Operationally, knowledge itself is becoming collectivized, no longer apprehensible by the single mind working in isolation, but rather through cooperative efforts among various people with diverse talents, intuitions, and perspectives. One sign of this is the proliferation of new joint ventures between long-time business rivals for purposes of research and development; even competitors must now pool talent and expertise to keep pace with the rapid advance of knowledge.

Probable Consequences

Those individuals, organizations, and polities that persist in playing by the old rules of hierarchy, competition, and attack will encounter increasing resistance, while those that work with the new forces of cooperation and peace will attract greater resources to their efforts. In this transitional era, the global scene will be characterized by sharp contrasts between a large, expanding zone of prosperity and peace on the one hand, and pockets of colossal failure, violence, and destruction on the other. Those who genuinely reorient themselves toward an ethic of service will have little to fear, although news reports, which focus disproportionately on negative events, may at times paint a misleadingly foreboding picture of rapid global developments.

Proposed Actions

At present, states, organizations, and individuals should institute reforms that emphasize cooperation with and service to others. In addition, pockets of negativity cannot be allowed to affect the whole. Thus, on the international level, outlaw states need to be contained through diplomatic and economic means, as well as by the select and restrained use of military instruments. Domestically, governments must be prepared to alleviate problems arising from dislocations caused by collapsing structures, such as workers laid off by ailing, mismanaged companies or refugees fleeing from collapsing states. In general, the level of dislocation can be lessened by major efforts to communicate the new formula for prosperity to those business and political centers that continue to resist change. By now, the evidence is manifold. Whether in political and economic experience, management theory, or psychological research, genuinely cooperative behavior produces far better results than egoistic, aggressive, or Machiavellian approaches. The sooner this insight becomes an explicit and central part of our global information culture, the smoother and less violent will be the transition to the new global reality.

-11-
The Need for Standards
of Conduct in
Government and Business
Enrique Ruete

Description of Change

Open and responsible conduct by government, public officials, and business leaders are key factors in a country's success. The fight against corruption has become a significant challenge for each country's society and leaders, as new moral values impose penalties on those whose conduct and attitudes favor a few at the expense of the many.

Reasons for Change

Over the years, public officials in authoritarian states with monopolistic powers exercised considerable discretion in applying price and exchange controls, subsidizing particular activities, deferring taxes, providing credit, restricting commerce, and other similar measures. Even though these acts are technically legal, they often favor a small and defined number of people. In many such countries, citizens and international business leaders have lost faith in the credibility of the system and its officials.

In most countries where corruption is a crucial problem, public officials assume little or no responsibility for their actions. In addition, the roles of the media and public opinion are limited; freedom of expression is not fully recognized and the use of these tools to influence public opinion and thereby control government activities is not fully understood. Although corruption is most visible in the misconduct of public officials, the business community can also be guilty of seeking or obtaining advantages by engaging in unfair competition and dishonest dealing.

Probable Consequences

If governments and societies do not seriously address this problem, these countries will continue to isolate themselves from the international business community. They will also undermine the essential principles that should govern people's lives, substituting speculation and profiteering for the ethics of work, saving, and production.

Both government and private business will be more successful if they follow ethical standards of behavior. In general, political parties, legislatures, courts, and public officials need social acceptance and respect to effectively fulfill their responsibilities; they cannot live long under the shadow of suspicion. Similarly, corporations and other economic agents can only validate their activities through fair dealing, honest reporting, and legitimate profits.

Proposed Actions

A nation's leaders must behave in an exemplary manner as they conduct the fight against corruption. If they do not have well-defined concepts of honesty, people will lose faith in them and their subordinates. By denouncing immoral activities and demanding openness and efficiency from leaders, public opinion can substantially reduce corruption and improve individual conduct.

The state should protect its own system with realistic and efficient legislation that will, among other effects, establish effective judicial procedures, require justification of unusual personal financial gain by government officials and business leaders, and mandate that political parties and candidates publicly disclose information about fundraising and sources of campaign financing.

Finally, the educational system should teach students the importance of moral values and convey the message that progress can be achieved through a set of values that emphasize self-improvement, thrift, and respect for other people's rights.

-12-
The Need to Overcome Indifference

Elie Wiesel

May I begin with a parable and conclude with an aphorism? A solitary wanderer was lost in the forest. He yelled "help, help" but no one answered. After days and nights of anguished walking, he met an old man. "It is God who sent you," exclaimed the wanderer, "help me find the way out." And the old man, with a smile, his finger pointing behind him, said: "I myself am lost. All I can tell you is—do not go that way. I just came from there."

Is this the message the twentieth century—the most violent in recorded history according to Hannah Arendt—will bequeath to the next? Plato thanked the gods every day for being born a Greek, a male, and free—and in the time of Socrates. But who among us would affirm his or her happiness for being born in the century of Auschwitz, the Gulag, and Hiroshima? Can we prevent the coming era from falling into the abyss which, in more ways than one, is still open?

Our century will be judged—and judged severely—in metaphysical and ethical terms. Its failures and deceptions throw a dark light on the human condition. Is it wise, is it useful to confront it now?

It is my humble opinion that Lot's wife was unjustly punished. It is important to look backwards. We cannot but listen to the advice given by Kierkegaard and Walter Benjamin: In order to comprehend the future, one must contemplate the past. Our traumatized generation's past represents a disquieting and exulting mixture. In it, the mystery of evil is matched by that of good. The nuclear component is at once a possibility of life and a potential cause of annihilation.

On the international scene, certain signs are encouraging—the end of apartheid in South Africa, the premises of a necessary and inevitable peace in the Middle East, the triumph of democracy—or rather the end of dictatorships—in Eastern Europe. Are we then justified in greeting a new dawn and its blessings? If we do so, what about the conflicts that tear territories and souls apart? How can they be appeased or, at least, explained? Will we ever understand the hatred of some and the compassion of others? The human spirit has never accomplished, not destroyed, as much in such a short period of time. Yet, fifty-five million casualties—victims of warfare, systematic violence, and daily massacres—have occurred in how many decades? And the scandal still continues. It continues in the former Yugoslavia, in Ireland, and in certain parts of India. People kill for God, so to speak, not realizing that when one kills for God, one kills against God. In how many lands do we see how many men and women inflict suffering, shame, and death on one another?

Still, at the same time, physicians prolong life, scientists discover cures for so-called incurable diseases, defenders of ecology protect nature, and world leaders elaborate economic systems to assure the happiness of the individual. We discuss global issues; we recognize the fact that the planet is shrinking. We live in more than one place; we participate in more than one adventure. Never have we lived so close to one another; we know here what is happening far away. Distances no longer count. We watch the same news reports, read the same novels, and listen to the same live concert broadcasts. There is no longer what one would call local culture. As philosophers would say, not without humor, everything is in everything. On our level, there have never been as many conferences and gatherings of political scientists. It is as if we were all afraid of coming unprepared to the threshold of the century and the millennium. What will remain of our turbulent and tormented era—the conquest of space and the human body or its monuments of ashes?

That the twentieth century remains marked and fashioned by political fanaticism, just as the Middle Ages were by religious prejudice, is beyond dispute. The two totalitarian ideologies that shaped its vision of itself—and I do not compare them—have both, in varying degrees, adopted a quasireligious vocabulary. While trying to change people and alter their destiny, they would to transform their followers in jailers and executioners, and their victims in slaves and objects. Was not communism a form of messianism, but without God, and Nazism a kind of paganism worshipping man's evil power? How is one to understand a society that has enabled them to exist and flourish? The reevaluation of its goals and methods is in order. How could medical doctors serve death in Nazi Germany without diminishing themselves? How could creative thinkers, poets, novelists, and musicians sing Stalin's praise without betraying their humanity? Both Nazism and communism—again, I do not compare one to the other—possessed a mystical fascination over those who believed in them. Both were universal in scope. As for democracy. . . . Look at the way it functions in the former Soviet Union. And yet, and yet, I believe there is no substitute for democracy. So, what are we to do now?

All those betrayed ideals, all those broken promises. The age of hypocrisy has followed that of absurdity. My generation needed much faith and courage to build and rebuild on the ruins of our illusions a new temple to illuminate man's heart. For a while, after the war, philosophers echoed Nietzsche's desperate outcry that "God was dead." What replaced God? Chesterton has said: "When people cease to believe in God, it is not that they believe in nothing, but they believe in anything." In other words, after 1945, spiritual chaos reigned in the world. And now? Are we witnessing a rebirth of religion or religiosity, as in Russia or in the Muslim world? If so, it is our duty to respect religion as much as politics, but they must remain separate. When religion becomes political, or when politics turns into a religion, we are all in trouble.

The battle is far from being won. Intellectuals are being assassinated in Algeria, dissidents persecuted in Iran. Religious intolerance keeps growing. Jewish extremists and Catholic fundamentalists do not resort to violence, but they too are carriers of hatred. Do not they realize that religious hatred is a contradiction in terms?

As for secular hatred, it has not vanished either. Xenophobia, racism, anti-Semitism, neo-Nazism—how are we stop them from entering the new century? Would I transgress some rule here were I to suggest the theme for your next forum. Namely, "the perils of hatred?" I propose it in my capacity as teacher, writer, and witness. Whatever triumphs might be obtained by our contemporaries in any field of intellectual endeavor, they could easily be jeopardized if we allow fanaticism to progress and seduce all those who need bread, joy, peace, and compassion.

Intolerance is never an option. This is what this century has taught us. Thus, in many places under the sun, men and women of goodwill and resolve have established a new kind of spirituality and even of secular religiosity. I refer to their valiant fight for human rights.

Their faith—and mine—is that victims have certain rights over us. We owe them something. And it is up to them to define that "something." Seneca understood that the Roman Empire was declining when he saw that the morals of the vanquished were superior to those of the victors.

The prisoner in his cell, the hungry child frozen in fear or burning under blazing skies, the old man besieged by sorrow, and the desperate mother dominated by shame—they tell me what my ethical conduct ought to be. Whatever happens to them affects my conscience and my very being. Not to respond to their plight is to refuse them—and myself—a place in civilized society. What is more important than to live in freedom? It is to help others gain freedom.

Moral behavior, in the next century, must mean people's acceptance of the other who is not far from us, since he dwells in us. Is that a reason to despair? Despair is never an answer; despair is only a question. We have known times when we were united in fear. Shall we be united in hope—tomorrow?

In conclusion, as promised, a brief aphorism that I have repeated for years. The opposite of love is not hate but indifference. But this applies to other concepts as well. The opposite of education is not ignorance but indifference. The opposite of beauty is not ugliness but indifference. The opposite of life is not death but indifference to both life and death.

Is this the new assumption we all seek now to accept? No. It is an old one. In fact, it is as old as human hope which has helped us triumph over fear.

Chapter 2
Maintaining Global Security

Introduction
George V. Vassiliou

During the Cold War, global security was maintained by the two super-powers and the fear of a nuclear holocaust. Although the fear of nuclear war receded as the Cold War ended, the problem of global security remains even more acute. Today, security is not threatened by war between states, but by conflicts within states. States now recognize the futility of fighting neighbors to gain territory, but entities within states, particularly those not recognized as sovereign by the international community, have grown increasingly violent. To respond to this problem, the global infrastructure needs to be restructured and reoriented. World War I was capped by the Treaty of Versailles and the League of Nations and World War II by the Bretton Woods Institutions and the United Nations, but no such new post-Cold War framework steadies the international system. Low-intensity war, virulent nationalism, and a resurgent protectionism threatens to shatter the "new world order." Ethnic conflicts, criminal activities, and terrorism are all around us.

Under these new conditions, writes General Joseph Hoar of the U.S. Marine Corps, "formal alliances, such as NATO and the former Warsaw Pact, built around an ideological core and against a known opposition, have proven unable to adapt to these threats." The UN has also been unsuccessful in coping with the "emerging paradigm." He recommends strengthening the UN, particularly the Security Council and the Secretariat, to deal more effectively with problems of world security.

We must also intensify global awareness of weapons proliferation, particularly weapons of mass destruction. Because the UN has limited resources, regional organizations and ad hoc coalitions should be developed that would operate with the support of the Security Council.

According to Ghassan Salamé, international security is also threatened by a slowly emerging division between countries benefiting from the new world order and those that feel increasingly isolated. In these circumstances, the UN risks becoming a "residual organization" that can take effective action only when the major powers permit it. Salamé proposes to strengthen the UN by increasing the representation of developing countries in the Security Council, coopting Germany and Japan, and revising the Charter to give the General Assembly a more decisive role in shaping policy.

The greatest danger to international security, however, is ethnic conflicts and ethnonationalism, problems we are not ready to combat. Although progress has been made in conflict management and in peacekeeping, Riordan Roett argues that we still have not learned how to make peace. Hence his emphasis on effective diplomacy, transparency, and greater control in armament sales, and the need for regional cooperation. In these conditions, according to Terence Taylor and Gustav Däniker, countries must establish guidelines—parameters and standards of collective behavior, and security coalitions will have to rely on interlocking political, military, security, and economic elements that are equitable and responsive to the interests of all parties.

The explosion of crime is dealt with by many contributors, among them Martin van Creveld, Robert Kaplan, and Lincoln Bloomfield. They attribute this problem to the growing gap between rich and poor, as well as the increasing suffering of the unemployed and the urban ghetto underclass. As businesses and individuals rely more and more on private security agencies for protection, the concept of the state's monopoly over the armed forces is undermined.

As a result of these problems, people are emigrating in search of better lives. As Sadako Ogata points out, these new migrational waves are themselves a major threat to world stability. Combined with growing unemployment within countries, the presence of new immigrants has led to the reappearance of racist tendencies in many countries.

In addition, the drug trade, which devastates the very fabric of society in many countries, is another threat to world security, as demonstrated by Andrés Pastrana Arango. To deny criminal elements the profits from drug trafficking, serious consideration is being given to legalizing the use of drugs.

But, in the end, the spread of democracy is itself the best way to combat conflict and instability. It is well documented that the danger of conflict decreases with the strengthening of democracy. We should all rejoice that in spite of so many negative developments in recent years, democracy is spreading to more countries than ever before. The time has come, however, as Samuel P. Huntington points out, for a tactical halt. The emphasis should not be so much on spreading democracy to even more countries, but rather on consolidating and deepening democratic institutions in the countries that have recently acquired them.

-1-
The Changing Environment of World Security

Joseph P. Hoar

Description of Change

The new century brings the promise of a secure, stable environment in which all nations may flourish. Everywhere, emergent globalism is challenging us to rethink old assumptions. In particular, the technological revolution, with its information "superhighway," has connected nations, businesses, and people as never before.

With the end of bipolar politics, dominated by the conflict between the United States and the former Soviet Union, the United Nations may finally emerge as the force its founders intended—a force capable of influencing, if not managing, the planet's future. The stakes have never been higher, nor the potential rewards greater. With the shift toward globalism, the future security arrangements of the UN and individual nations must provide the stability essential to an increasingly complex and interdependent world.

Witness in Somalia, Bosnia, the former Soviet Union, and Saddam's Iraq early indicators of future challenges to world security. Clearly, our first priority is to prevent damage by rogue states that use force or the threat of force to achieve their objectives.

Formal alliances, such as NATO and the former Warsaw Pact, built around an ideological core and against a known opposition, have proven unable to adapt to these threats. Similarly, the UN has experienced difficulty in trying to cope with the challenges of the emerging paradigm.

Reasons for Change

This century has seen events and trends that redefine the nature of conflict and security. Nations have expanded, contracted, and experienced the demise of their colonial systems. In their wake, countries drawn on the map by imperial fiat have foundered. Since 1949, an East-West confrontation based on ideological differences resulted in alliances formed around the United States and the Soviet Union. This confrontation carried with it the threat of global war. The collapse of the United States-Soviet bipolar system in the 1980s and the dissolution of the Soviet Union in the early 1990s opened the door to deeply rooted sources of conflict that had earlier been kept in check by the United States-Soviet balance. Future security requirements will be determined by the globalism that resulted in part from the relaxation of the restraints imposed by the old bipolar system.

The continued development of weapons of mass destruction, as evidenced by advances in weapons-related technology and the availability of increasingly lethal weapons, is the most influential factor affecting international security. The easy acquisition of high-tech, long-range weapons systems is a lure for states seeking to guarantee their security and expand their influence. The result, however, is a false sense of security; in reality, these weapons only increase the potential for conflict. Present and future global security require deterring and restraining the proliferation of these weapons.

Perhaps the most influential aspect of the new technology is the unrestricted flow of information across borders. Increasingly, nations can monitor events as they happen and rapidly detect any provocation or offensive military posturing. At the same time, modern communications can mobilize world opinion by bringing home the brutal images of war and suffering, thereby changing dramatically national and international responses. In addition, because information is pervasive, global interest groups can coalesce without regard to national boundaries. The trend toward globalization of information and growing interdependence in commerce, for example, will change current concepts of national sovereignty. Multinational businesses and economic organizations demonstrate this process when they try to influence a state to modify its behavior.

Another trend is the creation of global institutions that, through broad consensus, take a world view of such issues as the environment and propagate ideals for human behavior. The International Red Cross, the World Bank, the International Monetary Fund, *Médecine sans Frontières*, the World Health Organization, and a number of UN-sponsored organizations, such as the Commission on Human Rights, not only help to clarify these ideals, they also advocate global consciousness.

Probable Consequences

As the changes occur, defensive blocs and formal alliances that were concerned with containing an ideological enemy must adapt to survive. The new test of cooperative security arrangements will be their ability to address a broader range of interests. Although the opportunities ring with hope, translating common interests into unified action is always a challenge. Regional political and economic arrangements, for example, will be faced with maintaining a more complex charter as both constraints and opportunities multiply.

There will be increased pressure for the ascendancy of the rights of the global community over individuals and states—particularly as global resources become more scarce, the environment deteriorates, and ideals crystallize on issues such as human rights. The UN may choose to create legal frameworks, as illustrated by the Law of the Sea Convention, within which to protect these resources. Global interest in the planet's resources will also affect functions normally associated with sovereign nations. The undiminished national interests of major powers, however, will figure prominently in determining what actions are taken. Consequently, the international community will be in constant pursuit of a balance between its world agenda and what its most powerful constituent members will define, at times separately, as their national interests. Arguably, the new globalism supposes greater convergence of interests, but as a natural occurrence, especially considering the needs of major powers, there will be limits to the compatibility of interests.

The world may ultimately come to see the UN as a potentially effective organization for achieving world security. The UN would be expected to prevent conflict through financial assistance, developmental aid, and preventive diplomacy. To achieve these goals, the structure of the UN, particularly the Security Council, and the influence of individual members would have to change. The world community already views the veto power of individual Security Council members as a Cold War remnant that undermines the Council's ability to act. In addition, emerging regional powers will demand a greater role in decision-making.

A major threat to world security will be challenges from states that threaten force in a desperate attempt to retain power and dominate their neighbors. Because penalties such as market mechanisms are insufficient to prevent such aggression, nations will eventually join in regional groups to coerce rogue states into compliance. In this environment, effective deterrence may depend on the demonstrated ability of nations whose interests are most at stake to quickly forge ad hoc coalitions.

Proposed Actions

The international community should first assess the capability of the UN to meet its expectations. This assessment should recognize that increased global orientation will raise the premium placed on security. If the UN is to be the primary instrument of world order, its many roles must be carefully analyzed and its strengths and weaknesses weighed. For example, as a political forum of formidable moral influence, to what role should the UN aspire militarily? Analysis should appraise what activities the UN does best as well as recommend improvements.

Such a sweeping reassessment would offer a timely check on UN preparedness to handle the future. The time is right for redefining the instruments of international policy. Any redefinition of the UN should include a pragmatic plan that will empower it to meet future needs. The key is the Security Council. Although globalism continues to spread, the constant nexus for decisive action will remain shared national interests. For the foreseeable future, the UN will find the legitimacy of its more significant actions in the Security Council. The Secretariat, the organizational apparatus of the UN, is constrained by having a less well-established constituency. Therefore, a twofold approach to functionally aligning the UN is required.

1. Continue to develop the Security Council as the primary UN avenue for decisive security actions; and

2. Sharpen the administrative capability of the secretariat and associated staff, including enhancement of the military operations cell.

Concurrently, the international community must develop a program to increase global awareness of weapons proliferation, particularly weapons of mass destruction. The first step is to establish the baseline of existing weapons and weapons programs. Next, world opinion should be mobilized in support of freezing programs at the baseline, with controls to monitor and punish violators. This problem calls for a full-scale effort that would exploit the opportune circumstances of global trends. Not only the UN, but international and regional coalitions will be required to stop the spread of these weapons and their technology.

Next, despite the new global orientation, the UN will not necessarily handle all security threats throughout the world. While the UN perfects the means to prevent war, it should also encourage alternatives to UN leadership tailored to certain situations. For example, the growth and development of political and regional organizations would be especially useful in less-developed regions, where ties with the global system are most tenuous. The result would be many organizations operating within and sharing the responsibilities of the community. Ad hoc coalitions would further reinforce this result by adding an appropriate measure of flexibility. Such coalitions would operate best with the UN's, that is, the Security Council's, political backing.

Lastly, a fundamental assumption of the new world view merits continuing thought. The global village, metaphorically at least, envisions a change in the behavior of nations, which will relate to each other in much the same fashion as people do within a nation. Because this may oversimplify the complex imperatives of national interests and may also expect too much too soon, we must approach the changing world with a renewed vigilance at least equal to the newfound optimism.

-2-
Inclusion/Exclusion: The New Dynamic in the World System

Ghassan Salamé

Description of Change

The end of the Cold War was followed by a fundamental change in the world power structure that brought about a host of conflicting trends. For example, some military/ideological alliances, such as the Warsaw Pact, disappeared; others, such as NATO, expanded. Some conflicts were more easily settled, as in the Middle East and South Africa; others, as in Afghanistan, were exacerbated and/or transformed into civil wars. In addition, new conflicts erupted because of the diminished capabilities of the Great Powers to regulate events. Ad hoc military coalitions were easily assembled in some cases (Kuwait) and much less so on other fronts (Bosnia). Many countries in Europe and Asia were liberated from their satellite status and became fully emancipated while, elsewhere, countries, such as Iraq, still have stringent limitations on their sovereignty. A number of state apparati (e.g., in Somalia and Ethiopia) collapsed with the end of support from their distant, suddenly uninterested, patrons. Although most countries are enjoying a renewed sense of freedom, many feel isolated in the new world system and are competing intensely for attention and relevance on the world scene. This is evident in the rivalry among developing and newly emancipated countries for aid and foreign investment and the delocalization of business.

Reasons for Change

The causes of these conflicting developments include the disappearance of aid based on strategic needs, the weakness of many regional alliances, the increasing number of aid and investment seekers, the erosion of solidarity based on common ideological values, and the persistent low prices of oil and raw materials. Some groups of countries have strengthened their institutional bonds, as is illustrated by the European Community (EC) or the signing of the North Atlantic Free Trade Agreement (NAFTA). Humanitarian aid, very fashionable from 1990 to 1992, is now more limited and selective. Some countries, such as Rwanda and

Tajikistan, have aroused international interest; others, only slightly less tragic, have not.

Probable Consequences

These changes have both domestic and international effects. Domestically, the feeling of irrelevance in the world induces calls for "authenticity," stronger attachment to traditional values, the triumph of nationalist/populist trends, "retraditionalization" of societies, and, in some cases, the resurgence of religious fanaticism coupled with xenophobia. Hospitality to foreign ideas, institutions, and people themselves, such as tourists or NGO members, is diminished. Internationally, many countries feel more vulnerable, less relevant, and isolated. A deep rift is slowly emerging, not so much between civilizations, but between countries that think they can be included in a "winning" grouping and those that feel excluded from the new arrangements. Symptomatic of this division is that many East European countries want to join the European Union (EU) or NATO as soon as possible. Russia itself wants to be a full member of the G-7 group. Both Germany and Japan are now ready and willing to be permanent members of the United Nations Security Council. Some Latin American countries envy Mexico's inclusion in NAFTA and the EU. The feeling of exclusion is transformed domestically into a condemnation of those leaders and parties unsuccessfully seeking the country's integration into some "winning" grouping.

Those excluded from these strong groupings feel estranged from the world; this could lead to their refusal to accept universal norms and organizations. This is evidenced by the fact that the UN currently intervenes only in those areas where the interests of a permanent member of the Security Council are not directly at stake. There is serious risk that the UN will become a residual organization, intervening only in those areas where the great powers are willing to let it intervene.

Regionalization could become the euphemistic cover for the formation of new zones of influence, in which newly emancipated countries are either integrated on an unequal basis or left to themselves. A very strong causal relationship already exists between a loss of position in the world and the emergence of extremist forms of nationalism, such as religious militantism. The idea of a "clash" between the major civilizations is therefore understood as an ex post facto rationalization of this exclusion.

Proposed Actions

To integrate all nations into the new world order, the following measures are recommended:

- Developing countries should be better represented in the Security Council. The likely inclusion of Germany and Japan could strengthen the image of the P-5 (later P-7) group as an exclusive club for the economically stronger members of the world community. The door would have been opened for new members, only to make large parts of the world feel even less represented. A more subtle form of wider representation with rules of rotation in the membership of the P-5 group will become necessary to erase the image of the government of all by the few.
- The UN Charter should be revised so that the General Assembly, where all states are represented, would have a more decisive role in shaping UN policy.
- Regional organizations should have a stronger role in conflict prevention and resolution through a more determined effort on the part of the Great Powers to take these organizations even more seriously than some of their members do.
- Regional goupings, joint ventures, and peace-keeping forces should be encouraged by a reformulation of aid. States should be invited to participate in these regional groupings, to abide by regional contractual rules, and to be rewarded somehow for doing so.

-3-
The Need for a Strategy of Stabilization

Gustav Däniker

Description of Change

From the 1950s until 1989, the outbreak of World War III was pre-vented by a strategic system of deterrence based on the principle of "mutual assured destruction" with nuclear weapons. This principle was ethically dubious, but calculable, and imposed stability by preventing the nuclear powers from challenging each other.

With the collapse of the Warsaw Pact and the Soviet Union, the bipolar system of world politics, dominated by the conflict between the two superpowers, ended. All at once, a significant number of domesti-cally unstable states arose in Central and Eastern Europe. Numerous border disputes and minority issues remain unsolved; some have already led to open conflicts, as in Georgia and the former Yugoslavia. The potential danger from new conflicts, including wars both international and civil, is considerable.

Reasons for Change

With time, people in the former Soviet Union became disillusioned. Their standard of living was not improving, Western democracies were prospering, and the CSCE-process brought demands for human rights and freedom of information. By the mid-1980s Soviet leaders, particu-larly Gorbachev, instituted changes designed to strengthen the Soviet economy, including domestic reforms and a foreign policy based on cooperation instead of confrontation. But the dynamics of these measures made evolutionary development impossible. Although the collapse of Soviet communism occurred without bloodshed, it had serious con-sequences for the military strategy, economics, and social fabric of the region. Although Western "victors" tried to avoid humiliating the East-ern Europeans, many conservatives and nationalists, who felt exposed to the West, formed alliances in many countries and the armed forces are trying to increase their strength.

In the meantime, the balance of power outside Europe has also shifted. An arc of crisis stretches from North Korea, Southeast Asia, and

India to the Middle East and the Maghreb. Against the few positive developments, such as in Cambodia and South Africa, stand many setbacks, such as in Latin America. The national state is oscillating between new strength and crisis. Its replacement by the "clash of civilizations" and regional or ethnic entities is conceivable, but will not occur without the use of force.

Probable Consequences

Wars, particularly civil wars, have returned to the northern hemisphere. These conflicts confirm that existing global and regional organizations, including the United Nations, CSCE, NATO, and WEU, which are built on the system of nation-states, do not represent a sufficient principle of order. Neither their statutes nor international law deal with all aspects of these new developments. The same is true of the instruments available to them to implement security policies and principles of order. They are largely powerless in the modern world of religious fanaticism, organized crime, revolutions by minority groups, poverty-stricken masses, and unscrupulous and brutal warlords. Economic crises, the AIDS epidemic, and the drug problem make it even more difficult to find solutions to world problems. Each nation appears preoccupied by its own problems and addresses primarily its own interests. As a result, the world is threatened by greater and greater chaos.

Proposed Actions

Western countries, in collaboration with the UN, must develop a sustainable strategy of stabilization aimed at conflict prevention and successful crisis management. This strategy, which needs the support of governments and private forces, would include suitable diplomatic, economic, charitable, and military policies. It is not only a question of being prepared for the "worst case" anymore, it is rather a question of advancing the "best case" with all suitable means. The long-term goal is a geographically expanding area of sustainably stabilized, domestically peaceful, socially balanced, and mutually friendly nations that do not have ambitions for territorial expansion. The instruments of such "sustainable strategy" are as numerous as the policies described above. Diplomacy and good services are among them, as are economic cooperation and assistance in developing democratic, legal, market-economic, and social structures. The capability for military intervention is an important, but not the decisive, component.

Fundamentally, all of these activities may be summarized under the notion of "stability projection." It marks the necessary dynamics, but at the same time underlines the contrast to the former "power projection" of many nations. But traditional security mechanisms, based on a policy of deterrence, are still strongly entrenched in national defense strategies. They need to be replaced by a dynamic, evolutionary process that will both prevent relapses into policies that exclusively serve the power ambitions of individuals and, if possible, diminish the possible success of the atavistic use of force. The framework of this new strategy must include the containment of crisis areas, the ability to pacify troubled regions, and the capability to eliminate obstinate troublemakers.

"Stability projection" will be successful only if supported by the people involved. Their hopes, cultures, energies, and specific qualities are the indispensable framework for effective and sustainable stabilizing efforts from outside. Therefore, caution and psychological skills are very important.

Unfortunately, the existing collective security systems are only conditionally suited to promote stabilization. More is needed than the often-implored "mutually reinforcing support." Westerners must change their consciousness to reflect that new global dangers cannot be addressed by building walls, fencing oneself in, or preparing for a bloody defense, but rather by a fundamental new policy, based on priorities and probability of success, that gradually advances stabilizing elements into regions and states whose troubles and potential for violence could sooner or later spread. It is not a question of humanitarian aid alone, but of the choice between sustainable common security or chaos. Above all, Western nations must learn to redefine long-term national interest in terms of the benefits from international cooperation in building democratic, legal, free-market, and social structures throughout the world. Tackling this herculean task is justified by looking at the unpleasant alternatives. At least in the area of the CSCE, the goal appears attainable. Perhaps then it will gradually spread to other regions.

A new approach is also required for determining the nature and use of military forces in peace-keeping and peace-enforcement tasks. Modern forces, designed for defeating a classic adversary, are helpless when faced by bold warlords supported by a handful of fanatic combatants. The rapid development of effective nontraditional fighting tactics and nonlethal weapons is indispensable. Stabilizing interventions also need to be legitimized by a combination of international law, the close coordination of military and civilian efforts, and utmost circumspection at any demonstration of power.

Elements of this sustainable strategy of stabilization are already developing or in place. It is paramount that it becomes an integral part of every nation's policy and is implemented step by step.

-4-
Are Nation-States
Becoming Obsolete?
Mohammad Sadli

Description of Change

Nation-states have been the building blocks of the world community since the nineteenth century. Nationalism is a concomitant paradigm.

After World War II, the existence of newly independent states, as a result of decolonization, was based on the same premise. But many new states, particularly those in Africa, remain fragile, because nation building did not begin until after independence was achieved. States whose nation-building efforts began before independence—as part of the national movement— have been more successful, although they often face serious problems.

Reasons for Change

These new states learned that with independence and development came new forces for internal tension. Ethnic, religious, and regional sentiments have produced separatist movements—even civil wars—in some newly independent states. For example, not all regions shared equally in the fruits of economic development; some provinces felt left out. Peripheral areas did not enjoy living under the heavy shadow of the center. Finally, nation building often applies the idea of the melting pot by suppressing ethnic identities. Questions arise over whether the profits from local resources should go to the entire nation or to the province and people in their area of discovery?

Young nation-states tend to often have centralist and authoritarian regimes on which they depend for economic development. If, however, the profits do not compensate for perceived discrimination from the center, then fledgling states become exposed to centrifugal forces. The fragility of new nation-states was dramatized by the break-up of Yugoslavia, which for a long time after World War II was regarded as a successfully developing country.

Then, there is the break-up of the Soviet Union, which was based on an old European imperium. Some experts attribute the difficulties of African countries to the irrational geographical boundaries of the postcolonial nation-states, which were drawn up haphazardly by Western colonial regimes without regard for natural boundaries, cultural groupings, and related factors.

Probable Consequences

The breakup of the former Soviet Union and Yugoslavia is a reenactment of "Balkanization"; only time will tell if it will have good or bad connotations. In contrast, the breakup of existing nation-states in African and elsewhere is viewed negatively. As a continent, Africa already has the largest number of ministates. The ruling elites cling to the status quo, while others promote regional, or even continental, integration. Is regionalism a possible resolution to the problem of nation-states? European experimentation with integration is closely watched, but what is feasible in Europe may not be adaptable elsewhere. It is also true that political processes take a long time to mature.

The newly independent states prefer to contain ethnic, tribal, or regional forces by giving them greater autonomy. Although recognizing that many nation-states were established on artificial and haphazard bases, there is also a conviction that redrawing borders, creating additional nation-states, and balkanizing a region further will not solve the problem. The Western community is compounding these internal and regional difficulties by insisting on the right of self-determination for all people, including the right to become independent. Ethiopia is experimenting with this option, but hopes that ethnic minorities will not exercise the right to become independent if they are granted greater practical autonomy. The question is, however, how will the nation-state fare if the center is weakened too much?

Proposed Actions

The role of the international community is unclear in this changing world. For decades, a dominant West, or some of its constituent powers, tried to impose its value system on the East (that is, Asia) and the South. Now, however, China, which opted for a different course of reform, is seen by peoples of the East and the South as a better model. If China continues to prosper, it will become more democratic in its social and political life. At the same time, it becomes very problematic whether the trauma and the social and economic hardships of the breakup of the Soviet Union into democratic entities will be worth the effort. If Russia continues its chaotic transition and economic deprivation, it may produce another authoritarian regime.

If the international community is restructured in a form where the Western superpowers are not the only parties making rules, where the voices of the East (Asia) and the South (developing countries) are better heard and observed, then it can mediate efforts to find a solution for troubled nation-states. But it must be an open-ended experiment, without a preconceived final model. General principles of democracy, human rights, rule of law, and so on, should be upheld; the transformation should be peaceful and gradual, taking into account local idiosyncrasies.

-5-
The Transformation of War

Martin van Creveld

Description of Change

Between 1648 and 1945, the most important wars were fought between political entities known as states. In the future, wars will be fought by and against entities of a different kind, namely entities that do not own large, continuous, distinct pieces of territory and are not recognized as "sovereign" by the international community.

From 1945 to 1993, the majority of all wars—perhaps 80 percent of them—have been of this new kind. The number of casualties was much greater and the political significance immense. Since 1948, no state has succeeded in using war to move an international border by so much as a single inch. During the same period, however, war as waged by political organizations other than states—guerrillas, terrorists, and so on—has brought down the most powerful empires in history and caused the globe to change its color.

Reasons for Change

The most important reason for the change has been the spread of nuclear weapons, which has neutralized the ability of more and more states to effectively fight their neighbors. As a result, all wars since 1945 have been fought either between or against third- and fourth-rate military powers.

The second reason is that following both world wars, the prevailing ideas concerning the role of force in international relations has changed. In 1946 the United Nations Charter, which is the most subscribed-to document of all time, explicitly prohibited attempts to alter national borders by force. Consequently, concepts that as recently as the 1930s and 1940s were the stock in trade of international law, that is, the "right of conquest" and "subjugation," have disappeared without a trace.

Third, as any number of wars all over the world have shown, modern conventional military technology—the tanks, the APCs, the artillery pieces, the fighter bombers—is largely irrelevant in waging war against organizations rather than states. Thus, states have realized that even if they should succeed in expanding by force, the only outcome is likely to be a protracted guerrilla war with little prospect of success.

Probable Consequences

These developments have eroded the state's monopoly over the use of armed force. This process, which began in the Third World, is now spreading elsewhere. Examples are events in the former Yugoslavia, Georgia, and Tajikistan, and the mortar attacks on Heathrow Airport in early March 1994.

Unless this development can be arrested, modern civilization, including all the accomplishments of democracy, liberalism, science, and technology, is doomed. The developing world is not catching up with the developed world. Rather, much of the developed world is likely to sink back to a less-advanced level. The future will be a cross between Latin America, where the state has never really succeeded in imposing its monopoly on violence, and the former Yugoslavia, which has recently witnessed the disintegration of that monopoly.

Proposed Actions

If the above analysis is correct, then the dangers stemming from the spread of nuclear weapons to new states have probably been exaggerated. However, to prevent these weapons from falling into the hands of guerrillas and terrorists, an international organization, possibly under UN auspices, should be established.

States should realize that future threats to their security are likely to come less from the outside than from the inside. Accordingly, a coherent international program should be established to deal with this threat. Such programs can succeed. For example, since about 1985, the problem of skyjacking has all but disappeared because of improved security and the unwillingness of governments to provide terrorists with asylum.

Finally, states must develop an effective policy for dealing with the drug problem. Not only is the combination of desperate need and astronomic profits impossible to arrest, but it is drug money that stands behind much of international terrorism. As conducted today, the war on drugs probably does more harm than good. To eliminate this most important economic mainstay of international terrorism, consideration should be given to legalizing all or most drugs.

-6-
The Explosion of Crime and the Criminalization of War

Robert D. Kaplan

Description of Change

Until recently, unprovoked crime was manageable, and war was characterized by a neat division of states, peoples, and armies. Now, however, crime is exploding both in the West and the developing world. And, as state power breaks down, the distinctions between armies and populations, between war and crime, and between soldiers and criminals, erode. Guerrilla armies in Liberia and Sierra Leone, as well as crime networks in the Caucasus, are but some examples of the intermingling of crime and war. Nor is this phenomenon limited to the developing and postcommunist worlds. Many American inner cities are becoming uninhabitable lands, where conventional state authority is ineffective.

Reasons for Change

Many nations have become dysfunctional. Sinking GNPs, surging populations, and diminishing resources are making a greater number of places ungovernable. Ninety-five percent of the world's population growth is among its poorest citizens; 90 percent of that group lives in overcrowded urban or urbanizing areas. As a West African official said, almost all of the world's new children are being born to "people who are completely unequipped to bring up kids in a modern society." The soaring rise in the number of children born out of wedlock, especially in American inner cities and in certain polygamous societies in the Third World, results in unsocialized youths prone to criminal violence. The breakup of the nuclear family and income disparities among people are also factors in this undeniable phenomenon.

Behavior is crucial. The key factor is not what decisions are made nor what opinions are expressed, but rather how decisions are made and how opinions are expressed. For example, it is less significant that people in a South African homeland choose to participate in a national election than the fact that they rioted as a means to express this opinion.

Places where riots are frequent means of protest are an example of social breakdown and chaos.

Probable Consequences

"National security" will increasingly be viewed as a local concept. Major state armies will grow smaller, as private security firms grow and fill the gap. States will die if they cannot offer minimal physical protection to their citizens; their role will be filled by tribal ministates and urban mafias that can offer "protection." The areas of daily life controlled by mafias in the former communist world may become more significant than those controlled by existing states. To the average person, politics will mean less and personal security more. The most interesting aspect of the fighting in the Balkans and Caucasus is its criminal nature, in which drug cartels in Albania and Serbia, for instance, are extremely relevant to the trajectory of events. The UN will have less credibility among Western taxpayers, as more of its member nations in Africa and elsewhere collapse.

We are on the verge of a second Cold War, which will be fought against the forces of global disorder. Human civilization is entering a phase akin to puberty. The "deep" future may be very bright, but the coming decades could be difficult, as population growth stabilizes and new forms of government emerge. Crime, in the meantime, is a "background noise"—more or less a symptom of this disorder.

Proposed Actions

The idea of using draconian means to reduce birthrates in poor areas of the world and among uncivil elements of society, as extreme as it sounds, is actually being voiced by some ideologically moderate columnists. Just as nature will increasingly drive politics in the twenty-first century, so will science. And science is unstoppable. It will come up with better birth control means and behavioral drugs to modify criminal behavior. As crime increases, people will demand any and all means of protection. States cannot be saved; Liberia, Somalia, and Georgia are merely the first over the edge. Many states are creatures of the modern world, which was born at Westphalia, more or less, in the seventeenth century and is now more or less dying. The UN cannot save states that are dead on arrival. It will have to try to improve societies from within.

In the meantime, the Western governments, which previously doled out aid on the basis of a third world country's anticommunism, should now give out aid based on how serious a country is about reducing its population growth and preserving its natural resources. Encouraging both literacy among rural women and neighborhood self-help organizations is important; these are crucial to filling the societal vacuum created by weakening central governments.

-7-
The Dilemma of
"Law and Order" in
the World at Large

Lincoln F. Bloomfield

Description of Change

At all levels of society, the idea of "law and order" means creating and enforcing rules of conduct within a civil society. Unfortunately, in the international community, the phrase has never had a comparable meaning. Indeed, some people scoff at the very notion of an international community, citing egregious national misbehavior and weaknesses in the international system that together dominate daily news reports.

As with so many sweeping assertions, that view reflects a half truth. International law has existed for centuries in limited, but important, sectors, such as diplomatic immunity and laws of the sea. An undramatic but genuine revolution took place during the postwar years, as international bodies began to monitor and regulate in fields that governments could not handle alone—from global frequency allocation to international mail, trade, epidemic control, air safety, global weather forecasting, nuclear plant inspection, missile technology transfers, refugee programs, and regulations for the seabed and outer space.

With that said, it is on the crucial "peace and security" front that the organized international system stands or falls in the eyes of the public. In 1945, a new start was made with the United Nations Charter, which criminalized open military aggression across recognized borders and stigmatized violations of fundamental human rights. It took almost half a century for the UN, finally freed from Cold War hang-ups, to begin to confront violations of these basic norms. But even during the Cold War, with its system gridlocked, an extraordinary political intervention—UN peace-keeping—was devised. More than a dozen UN peace-keeping or observation missions were fielded to preserve fragile truces in the Middle East, Cyprus, and elsewhere.

Reasons for Change

With the unprecedented backing of the West, Russia, and China, the UN Security Council in the early 1990s finally began to confront new aggressions and humanitarian outrages. Iraqi aggression in the Gulf was reversed, and a new surge of UN peace-keeping and election-monitoring missions in 18 hotspots deployed 80,000 personnel from 57 countries. For the inward turning industrial/democratic powers, "assertive multi-lateralism," as some called it, seemed an ideal substitute for unilateral power projection at a time when worldwide economic interests demanded a stable political environment.

But the new security agenda featured misbehavior within state boundaries—a category traditionally excluded from UN jurisdiction. Clashes between states had not ended. But removing the heavy hand of communist rule in much of Eurasia unleashed nationalist and ethnic passions kept under wraps since the breakup of the Ottoman and Austro-Hungarian empires. The end of strategic influence seeking by the superpowers left weak states to sink or swim.

Some of the new cases represented the wreckage of states such as Yugoslavia, which broke up into its component pieces. Some represented so-called "failed states," where government evaporated into anarchy and local warlords contended bloodily for control, such as Liberia, Somalia, Angola, Rwanda, and Haiti. These and other countries, including the Sudan, Myanmar (formerly Burma), Iran, and parts of the trans-Caucasus and southwest Asia, confronted the world community with morally intolerable behavior, ranging from suppression of democracy and deliberate refugee creation to famine and slow-motion genocide, all inside state borders. The very meanings of peace-keeping, peace-making, and "humanitarian enforcement" were being transformed, with a powerful assist from worldwide television coverage.

Inevitably, intervention into civil strife severely tested the UN. In Bosnia, the Western democracies forgot history when they tolerated nearby genocide until it was too late. In Somalia, a handful of casualties (fewer than New York experiences in a slow week) created an American back-lash against intervention, reinforced when a handful of hoodlums on a Port au Prince dock humiliated the United States and the UN. The difficulties experienced in the "three cases from Hell" threaten to reverse a hopeful step in developing even minimal international law and order.

Probable Consequences

The result of these setbacks could be a step back to a time when political crimes within a state, even if they outraged the world's conscience, were ignored. It is not even certain that such a clear-cut case of aggression as that of Iraq against Kuwait would soon again be as vigorously opposed. There will be additional cases of state breakup or breakdown, arousing passions of nationalism, tribalism, and religious fundamentalism that sharpen rather than harmonize differences. The irony is that simultaneously, state authority continues to erode in the face of borders—ignoring mutual economic and technological interdependencies. The latter add up to a tight and sensitive worldwide economic and financial web that cannot function effectively or profitably in a lawless environment.

The only rational conclusion is that a better system must be developed for effective conflict management. The errors and weaknesses on the part of both the major countries and the UN itself should not be allowed to define the future.

Proposed Actions

Success in achieving minimal global "law and order" means learning to live with inconsistency in tackling international "criminality," both because a still-primitive "community" can fail from overload and because the acquiescence of Russia, China, and major "southern" countries is also a condition of a global, rather than an alliance or regional, system. Still, several reforms could improve the system's capacity for improved conflict limitation and management.

An efficient international secretariat drawn from many cultures and constituencies is an oxymoron. However, financially strapped members can demand more efficiency from the UN Secretariat and force other reforms to the extent that mismanagement is a genuine obstacle. Standby peace-keeping forces can be useful once decisions are made by the political authorities. Of course, the real reason for UN inaction is always lack of agreement among the big powers.

Finances are a genuinely neuralgic impediment to effectiveness, starting with the price of peace-keeping missions demanded by the states themselves. Something is dreadfully wrong with a system where, decade after decade, the richest country in the world undergoes annual crises about whether to pay it overdue bills, leaving the UN regularly bankrupt. Two major changes are needed to eliminate the "tin-cup" approach to running a multibillion dollar enterprise.

One immediate step is to reduce the United States' unrealistic 25 percent assessment to a more realistic 20 percent, thereby depriving the U.S. Congress of a perennial—and legitimate—grievance. More drastic, but equally urgent, is an agreement on a surcharge on all international electronic communications. Tiny in size, this could pay for all peace-keeping activities and end the annual agony and embarrassment of the system. As at present, not one cent would or could be spent for security operations that the permanent members did not favor, but the serious business of conflict management could be carried on with something approaching dignity.

Inevitably, the Security Council will expand. One recommendation is to add four permanent, but nonvetoing seats, for Germany, Japan, India, and South Africa. A more radical proposal is to eliminate the great power veto on all but Chapter VII enforcement actions. If the modern economically linked world of states and, increasingly, potent nongovernments can ill afford a turbulent and unpredictable international landscape; if the UN is not really very good at peace enforcement; and if the United States does not want to police the world, the obvious logical alternative is to become far more serious about conflict prevention and preventive diplomacy.[1] Three readily available strategies, so far rarely applied, are:

1. Maximum publicity. This runs against the grain of traditional low-key diplomacy, but thanks to global media coverage by such nongovernment watchdogs as CNN, the BBC, and Amnesty International, the "spotlight function" can play an increasingly important role.

2. Deterrence. The strategy bearing that name helped keep the peace during the Cold War and is relevant to such avoidable disasters as Bosnia, where timely and believable UN and/or European Union or NATO low-level action could have changed history.

3. Peaceful change. This means procedures to change the map peacefully and by diplomacy rather than war. Another "might-have-been" in the Bosnian tragedy was a 1992 proposal, reportedly agreed to by the parties but quashed by Washington,[2] to partition that fractured piece of real estate before rather than after the spilling of oceans of blood.

But, at the end of the day, conflict prevention and limitation depend first of all on committed and courageous political leaders. Even with that gift, those pondering how to maintain an acceptable level of international security would do well to remember Winston Churchill's caution that "the UN was not set up to get us to Heaven, but to save us from Hell."

---

[1]See Lincoln F. Bloomfield, "The Premature Demise of Global Law and Order: Looking Beyond the Three Cases from Hell." *The Washington Quarterly*, Summer 1994.

[2]According to David Binder, "U.S. Policymakers on Bosnia Admit Errors in Opposing Partition in 1992. *New York Times,* August 29, 1993.

Security Policy in a
World of Complexity

Terence Taylor

Description of Change

In the past five years, security policy has shifted from an East-West divide, based on ideological and economic competition, to a less well-defined and complex North-South divide, based, principally, on economic and technological power.

In response, the security policy of the more developed countries has undergone dramatic change. Former adversaries of Cold War days have joined in far-reaching cooperative security arrangements, including a heretofore unparalleled degree of transparency in military matters. NATO countries and those of the former Warsaw Pact have embarked on a partnership in sharing common security and economic interests. The leading developed countries seek to maintain their position and protect their technological advantage both for economic protection and to counter any perceived threats to their security.

In contrast, in the developing world, including the southern fringes of Central Europe, interstate disputes, civil wars, and ethnic and religious conflict appear rampant, leading to a continuing demand for both conventional weapons and those of mass destruction.

A further layer of complexity has been superimposed by the emergence of new and fragile democracies, whose difficulties are multiplied as the freedom of travel for individuals has increased the migration of talent from key sectors of their academic institutions, industries, and medical services.

Reasons for Change

The change flows from the collapse of the Warsaw Pact and the breakup of the Soviet Union. With the fading of global superpower competition, regional powers must provide for their own security and economic interests. They are impelled to seek ways of advancing their economic and, in some cases, military ambitions, so they do not fall even further behind the pace of technological change in the developed world.

The end of the superpower confrontation is also responsible for increased ethnic conflict and related territorial disputes. For nearly four decades, these disputes were subsumed by the East-West confrontation. With the lessening of global military tension, however, regional disputes are resurgent.

In addition, supplier states have not been completely successful in efforts to restrict the transfer of advanced technology with military applications to developing countries, many of which distort their economies through expenditures aimed at acquiring the military means they believe necessary to guarantee their security and national survival.

The pace of change has been accelerated by advances in information and communications technology. Because this makes it more difficult for authoritarian regimes to survive, their ultimate goal is to acquire advanced technologies and equipment that will permit the local production of weapons. Thus, there is a shift in emphasis from the transfer of complete weapons systems to the acquisition of components and technology. Within such countries, the best scientists and engineers are enticed from peaceful projects to weapons programs by a combination of personal economic rewards and coercion.

Where democratic change has occurred or is in progress, many states in the developing world, Eastern Europe, and the former Soviet Union are struggling economically. Their goal is internal stability, with maximum independence from neighbors with tendencies toward hegemony.

Probable Consequences

The security gains following the end of the East-West confrontation could be seriously eroded if regional conflicts continue to increase. These conflicts wreak human suffering in terms of loss of life, injuries, suppression of civil rights and liberties, destruction of property, and damage to the environment. Supplier states must be careful about strengthening restrictions on technology transfer in an effort to stem weapons proliferation and pursuing protectionist economic policies. These actions may so severely restrict economic growth in the developing world that further instability results. In the longer term, these policies will also have a deleterious effect on economic stability in the developed world. Unless action is taken promptly, this downward spiral could be further accelerated by the migration of talented scientists and engineers to the major industrial powers.

Proposed Actions

During the next decade, security policy must concentrate on resolving conflicts in regions of instability by political action that is based on a strategy of cooperative security. At the global level, there needs to be a substantive overarching dialogue encompassing countries of North and South, which builds on the UN General Assembly's areas of general agreement on security matters. The leading powers should make greater investments in such activities as the process put in hand under the General Assembly's resolution on Transparency in Armaments.[1] This resolution established the UN Conventional Arms Register, which resulted in negotiations between supplier and importing states on transfers, holdings, and national production of major conventional weapons. Further, the Conference on Disarmament is debating the subject of transparency in relation to weapons of mass destruction and transfers of technology. Greater effort needs to be applied to these negotiations, with the objective of developing meaningful measures that enhance confidence and security. In particular, the dialogue on technology transfer should enable technology transfers for peaceful purposes and lessen the need for one-sided regimes based solely on denial. An example of a cooperative regime, including security assistance and economic and technical cooperation, is the Chemical Weapons Convention,[2] which has elements of a paradigm for future security regimes as well as for improving existing regimes. President Clinton, in his address to the General Assembly in September 1993, suggested the possibility of developing the Missile Technology Control Regime into a cooperative arrangement encompassing both suppliers and importers. The time for action on such proposals is overdue.

At the regional level, organizations can play a leading role in developing a security dialogue that is all encompassing. It would include not just military matters and political disputes, but also economic, scientific, and technical cooperation. The progress achieved to date in the Middle East peace process is an example of what can be accomplished within a region where there are seemingly insolvable disputes. The UN could help by reinforcing and redeploying its regional centers on a more flexible basis. For example, there could be one now supporting the process in the Middle East. North Asia might be an appropriate area for another. This need not inhibit the major powers from playing a facilitating role to broker agreements and provide security assurances.

These regional efforts could be enhanced by encouraging the development of regional science and technology centers on similar lines to those being set up by the European Union, Japan, Russia, and the United

---

[1] UN General Assembly resolution 46/36L of December 9, 1991.

[2] Due to enter into force on January 13, 1995, or 180 days after the deposit of the 65th ratification, whichever is the later.

States. They would not only employ scientists and engineers formerly working on the weapons programs, but could also enhance higher levels of academic training within the regions. This could help stem the "brain drain" in the direction of the developed world, which would contribute to improving economic development and hence stability in the developing world. The economically advanced countries in G-7 would benefit by making, what would be for them, a modest investment in setting up such centers in places where there would be the most benefit.

Security regimes will be effective and durable only if they rest on interlocking political, military security, and economic elements that respond to the interest of all parties.

International Peace-Keeping after the End of the Cold War

Riordan Roett

Description of Change

Clearly, the current international system is ill prepared for the tasks of peace-keeping. The confusion over Somalia, the dismal efforts in the former Yugoslavia, and the controversy surrounding the role of the United Nations indicate the need for a reconceptualization of the use of force to restore and/or prevent the breakdown of order in diverse areas of the globe.

Reasons for Change

In hindsight, the precarious, but diabolically stable, bipolar world of post-1945 worked. There were confrontations, but no Armageddons. The nuclear balance weighed in at moments of high tension, such as the Cuban Missile Crisis of 1962. Regional surrogates were permitted—as with the Cubans in Africa—but those forces were clearly subordinated to the strategic goals of the Great Powers.

The next two decades will witness a continued fraying of the traditional nation-state system. The breakup of Czechoslovakia was peaceful, as was that of Ethiopia; that of Yugoslavia was not. Algeria and Somalia are only two of a growing number of nation-states on the brink of dissolution, civil war, or fundamental breakdown. Clearly, sorting out of the successor states of the former Soviet Union has only begun and boundaries will shift and be redrawn for some years to come.

Probable Consequences

Unless the key industrial and developing states can create a new consensus about the need for new guidelines over international peace-keeping, there is a real danger that international conflicts will increase because of multiplying border disputes, the risk of fundamentalism, and the revival of long-frozen rivalries. One school of thought, based on a belief in a natural logic to geographic shifts of state boundaries, argues that the time for international police officers has passed. Things will, somehow, work themselves out over time.

Nothing can be farther from the truth. The logical outcome of that benign posture will be an escalation of local and regional conflict. It will engender dramatic increases in immigration, further exacerbating nationalist tensions in the receiver countries. It offers opportunists and marginal political and religious elements the chance to challenge the new, evolving international order.

Proposed Actions

The United States will inevitably need to lead the effort to reconceptualize how to meet the challenge of maintaining order and furthering the cause of peace after the end of the Cold War. This cannot be done piecemeal; it will require wide and proactive consultation. The process must include the key players in Asia, Europe, and the Middle East. It will need to coldly analyze current and potential areas of destabilization and to emphasize the need for sufficient military muscle to convince challengers to accept the common goals of the international community.

This approach is broadly reminiscent of Europe following the Napoleonic Wars. Although a Concert of Europe does not have to be the formal model, the informal process of consultation, the role of the balancing power, and the commitment to the negotiated settlement of outstanding disputes are essential. Some will argue that the revival of collective peace-keeping will result in an effort to impose a "Pax Americana" or "Pax Transatlantica" on the world. It is essential to eschew that argument. Just as the United States has had to turn to China in dealing with the nuclear threat in North Korea, Japan and China will be fundamental pillars of the new efforts at international peace-keeping. The European Union will have to decide if it can foster a common foreign and security policy; if not, Germany must be included in the new inner circle of decision-making.

The argument smacks of realpolitik, and so it should. But it is a reliance on realpolitik in an international order entering a period of potentially chaotic transition. The time-honored concept of the nation-state may dissolve in some areas of the world. New boundaries will emerge through a process of conflict and confrontation. In this situation, the powers need to establish guidelines, parameters, and standards of collective behavior. Whether the UN is the appropriate forum within which to do so remains to be seen. What is clear is that without such an initiative, the international order is doomed to new Somalias, Yugoslavias, and Kurdish revolts. It is foolish to argue that the end of the Cold War has resulted in any sort of a "pax." It has, dramatically, done the opposite, thereby forcing us to accept the realities of conflict that will require management, direction, and at times the use of force to protect and enhance a generalized conception of the yet-to-be-defined new international order.

-10-
Race and International Relations

Roxanne Lynn Doty

Description of Change

Racism is not a new phenomenon, but the racism occurring today is linked with the emigration of Third World people to the wealthy, industrialized Western countries. Thus race and racism can no longer be considered purely domestic issues; they have implications of a global nature.

In the past several years, the world has witnessed a disturbing increase in the number of incidents with racial overtones. In 1988, for example, Italy experienced increased violence against its rapidly growing Third World immigrant population. In June 1991, Parisian mayor Jacques Chirac suggested that French workers included too many "polygamous North African welfare bums." In September 1992, former French President Valéry Giscard d'Estaing suggested that the country was facing an invasion of dark-skinned immigrants and prescribed the institution into citizenship of a "right of blood." Figures reported to Britain's Home Office conservatively suggest that there were 7,780 racially motivated attacks last year. Meanwhile, social committees of the European Parliament have twice looked at the increase in racist and xenophobic activity throughout Europe and concluded that it is growing worse. Nor is the United States immune from the nativism and racism linked with anti-immigrant sentiments.

Reasons for Change

During the age of European explorations, expansion, and colonialism, race relations were global relations. Concern with the issue of race coincided with curiosity about human beings in different geographic locales. After World War II and during the accompanying period of decolonization (roughly, 1945 to 1970), displaced persons and colonial subjects emigrated to the urban centers of the West, where they provided the cheap source of labor needed to recover from the devastation of war. Recent contractions of the world economy and economic difficulties experienced by individual countries have now led to increasing resentment toward new immigrants.

Thus, the movement of peoples across national borders is increasingly a global concern. As with earlier waves of emigrants, the motives include greater economic opportunity and freedom from political turmoil and violence. This is illustrated by the recent movements of refugees from Rwanda and Haiti. With such mass migrations, however, racism becomes relevant on several levels. Although the United States has been accused of racism for turning back Haitians seeking asylum, race also becomes an issue when immigrants and refugees are permitted to stay. In those instances, nativists and the growing number of long-term unemployed often oppose the new immigrants. In *Preparing for the Twenty-First Century,* Paul Kennedy argues that great waves of migration will continue and that enhanced efforts by states to control their borders are unlikely to succeed in the face of global demographic imbalances.

Probable Consequences

According to Eric Hosbawm, in *Nations and Nationalism since 1780,* xenophobia has become the most widespread mass ideology in the world today. It is now linked, inextricably, with racism. The result can assume various forms, from immigration control to the overt violence against foreigners in Germany, France, and Britain in the past few years. Even the United States has experienced xenophobic reactions to immigration as well as economic competition from Asian countries.

As a result, many Western nations, including France and Germany, are imposing increasingly restrictive immigration laws. The European Community will have to address this issue, because as boundaries between countries within the EC are becoming more flexible and fluid, individuals from nonmember countries may find it more difficult to cross them. A call for similarly restrictive legislation is being heard in the United States from citizens and politicians across the political spectrum. Such legislation often increases illegal movement across national borders, which has been difficult to control even with enhanced resources. One has only to look at the United States/Mexican border as confirmation of this problem.

Proposed Actions

Eliminating racism is an elusive ideal. On the international level, the formal ending of colonialism did not eliminate the division of the world into the racially "superior" and "inferior." The record in domestic policy is also mixed. The abolition of slavery and legal discrimination in the United States, for example, certainly did not end racial discrimination.

Some proposed solutions really just avoid the issue. For example, improved conditions in developing countries may simply alleviate the necessity for people to emigrate in search of work and political stability. The issue of racism, itself, is not addressed. On the global level, increased anti-immigrant violence should be treated as a violation of basic human rights. People must become more sensitive to ways in which tradition and cultural practices may support ideas of racial superiority.

How to promote such sensitivity is not an easy question to answer. Perhaps the most fruitful place to begin, but the slowest, is with the world's children. Where and how do they learn to hate? Where and how do they learn to define themselves as inherently different from others? Where do they learn that rights and obligations stop at national borders? Education on all levels should promote the notion that national boundaries are quite arbitrary, increasingly meaningless economically and politically, and often destructive of goals concerning the well-being of all people. How to promote this kind of education? Think globally, act locally, in elementary and secondary education by working with such organizations as TransAfrica and Amnesty International.

-11-
The Threat of Population Movements

Sadako Ogata

Description of Change

More people are being forced to flee their homes than ever before. The world refugee population has risen dramatically, now exceeding 20 million people, as has the numbers of those displaced inside their own countries. We are confronted with major humanitarian emergencies, notably in the former Yugoslavia, former Soviet Union, and Africa. Undefined numbers are also fleeing intolerable poverty. Some estimates of illegal migrants vary between 20 and 40 million. These figures mean that about one in every hundred world citizens has been forced to leave home. Large numbers seeking to enter Europe, as well as the proximity of emergencies in the Balkans and the former Soviet Union, have given added urgency to the problem for Western countries.

Reasons for Change

One immediate cause of flight is internal conflict, kindled by resurgent nationalism and ethnic and religious tensions. The massive proliferation of arms has increased prospects for continuing violence. Political causes are linked with socioeconomic ones, as environmental degradation, population growth, and poverty increase migratory pressures and exacerbate ethnic and communal tensions. Structural adjustments are taking their human toll in developing countries. Moves toward market economies in former communist countries, along with rapid economic growth in east Asia and Latin America, are widening the gap between rich and poor and increasing the risk for social discontent and violence.

Probable Consequences

Economic and social disparities will grow; ethnic conflicts will escalate, forcing more people to flee. It will be difficult to maintain the classical distinction between refugees, internally displaced people, and migrants. The international commitment to asylum will further weaken, and pressure will grow for local/national solutions inside the country of origin of displacement, as through the creation of a safety zone in northern Iraq. As strategic interests are redrawn and major countries are preoccupied with domestic concerns, the political will to deal with displacement in distant countries will diminish. Humanitarian assistance will increasingly be used as a substitute for political action. Anarchy and violence will deepen, leading to the disintegration of governmental authority, and eventually to chronic displacement and regional instability.

Proposed Actions

Isolated, piecemeal gestures should be replaced by a comprehensive strategy that recognizes the links between humanitarian crises, peace and security, and economic well-being. This strategy should also:

- give priority to prevention and resolution of refugee-producing conflicts. Preventive action presupposes greater involvement in domestic uncertainties and conflicts, and requires the UN and regional organizations to devise rapid political response mechanisms for conflict resolution, not only between states but within states.

- establish human rights monitoring mechanisms in conflict situations, as for example, through an international presence, and mechanisms for respect of minority rights. The establishment of the UN High Commissioner for Human Rights by the General Assembly is an important step, but will have little effect unless the issue of national sovereignty is addressed.

- formulate a development strategy of aid and trade in such a way as to promote better governance, respect for human rights, and rehabilitation of war-torn societies. Failure in development must be seen as a dangerous threat to democracy and freedom.

- develop fair, efficient, and expeditious procedures to differentiate between those fleeing war and violence and those fleeing poverty. International protection and assistance should be granted to the refugees and internally displaced until they can return home. Economic migrants should be dealt with in the context of immigration policies that recognize the demographic patterns and labor needs of the industrialized world as well as the aspirations of poorer countries in the East and South.

-12-
Drug Trafficking

Andrés Pastrana Arango

Description of Change

In the past two decades, drug production, trafficking, and consumption, as well as the criminal activity surrounding this industry, have become the most detrimental and destructive force affecting the fabric of societies worldwide. It is difficult to determine whether the consumption of drugs in developed countries has spurred the production of illegal narcotics in developing nations, or vice versa. In either event, international drug trafficking has become the largest illegal business in history.

Reasons for Change

Some of the fertile conditions in developing countries that encourage increased production of narcotics include rural poverty, faulty law enforcement in rural areas, the huge profit potential, and eroding moral values. Consumption seems to grow from a general social dissatisfaction and the deterioration of ethical principles.

Probable Consequences

The byproducts of the phenomenon of supply and demand are the powerful international crime organizations that have the wealth to corrupt public and private authorities, build worldwide distribution networks, and wage war against individual governments.

The negative effects of the drug industry on the nations of the world are difficult to summarize. Probably the most damaging is the effect on consumers. Addiction causes instability, reduced productivity, and a degeneration of moral values. It also causes sickness and may lead to death. Addicts become obsessed with maintaining or increasing their drug supply and usually resort to street crime or even drug dealing to fulfill their needs.

Violence also occurs from the distribution side, for example, as a result of territorial disputes among drug dealers. The crime of money laundering also increases as the drug trade grows. This corruption within international financial institutions creates instability in the system and generates a lack of confidence in depositors.

Another detrimental effect is damage to the ecosystems of drug-producing nations. Land used for coca or poppy production is illegally deforested; the plants themselves render the land infertile for regular crops.

Producing nations also face grave social, political, and economic problems. In Columbia, for example, drug money has been used by traffickers for social reform programs that create powerful political alliances. The government bureaucracy is under constant threat and is fearful of imposing laws against traffickers. The devaluation rate is kept artificially low because of the abundance of "narcodollars." Worst of all, assassinations and terrorism have taken the lives of important political figures, as well as hundreds of innocent bystanders.

Proposed Actions

The international community must immediately form a threefold action plan to fight drug trafficking that includes efforts to combat production, distribution (international and local), and consumption. If we fail to implement any one aspect of the plan, it will automatically nullify the efforts of the others.

The Fight Against Production

Most drug-producing nations do not have the resources or the infrastructure to effectively combat rural area drug farms. International commitments by both producing and consuming nations will be required for the search and destruction of production areas. Consuming nations should provide equipment (helicopters, chemicals, and so on), intelligence (satellite pictures and information), and money for personnel working in the area. To lessen any internal political frictions, these people should be citizens of the country where the specific operation is occurring.

The producing nations must reinforce their judicial systems to effectively convict growers and local distributors. Because of the power of the defendants, these cases should be tried in military courts with anonymous ("faceless") judges with special investigative powers.

To guarantee that the destroyed farms are not simply replanted with drug plants, a crop substitution program must be established, either as a separate government institution or as part of an existing agricultural department. Here again, international support is crucial, especially technology, equipment, access to markets in terms of lowering duties and other barriers to entry, and infrastructure (roads, communications, irrigation networks, electricity, and so on).

The Fight Against Distribution

This aspect of the plan requires the greatest degree of international cooperation, because it involves international patrolling and searching of brigades to stop international drug movements. Producing and consuming nations should each patrol their own boundaries. Everything in between should be patrolled by one international military force created especially for the purpose. This force should have a legal code of strict laws enforceable by its own judicial system. Both producing and consuming nations should appoint "drug judges" ("faceless" and military) to try those criminals either caught between boundaries or those facing charges in more than one country. These judges should cooperate in the exchange of information and proof to convict tried traffickers on all international counts to the full extent of the law.

The Fight Against Consumption

This part of the plan is probably the most expensive and slowest, but nonetheless crucial in our efforts. It is divided into three major areas and applies to all nations where consumption occurs, including drug-producing nations where drug use is increasing exponentially.

We should establish antidrug campaigns involving multinational companies, political figures, and celebrities, to spread the message to people in all countries. Schools should establish drug workshops that inform children about the damaging effects of drug use. Hospitals could conduct seminars to train parents on how to keep children away from drugs and what to do if a drug problem already exists.

Rehabilitation centers, free of cost to the users, should be set up in the main consumption cities of the world. We must also strictly enforce user and dealer laws in all communities. Convicted users must spend time in rehabilitation centers as part of their sentences.

To set these projects in motion, I suggest an international drug summit to be attended by the main producing and consuming nations, either in Bogotá, New York, London, or Geneva.

The time to act is now. Every day we wait allows the largest illegal business in the world to further destroy our societies, economies, and worldwide political stability. The effort must be international, requiring the cooperation of producer, distributor, and consumer nations.

-13-
Democracy's Challenge[1]
Samuel P. Huntington

Description of Change

The expansion of democracy is, without doubt, the single most important political phenomenon of the late twentieth century. After starting in southern Europe in Spain, Portugal, and Greece, this wave of democratization swept through Latin American and brought change to every undemocratic country in the Western hemisphere, except Cuba. It moved on to Asia, with the Philippines, South Korea, Taiwan, Pakistan, and Bangladesh all replacing authoritarian regimes with elected governments. In 1989, of course, it erupted in Eastern Europe, and then two years later, in the former Soviet Union. The democratization wave has also manifested itself in the increasing role of elections in Middle Eastern countries, such as Yemen and Jordan. In Africa, dictators have been voted out of office in a few countries, national conferences have occurred in several others, and most importantly, South Africa is now on the way toward democracy. Democracy has manifested itself in some of the most improbable countries. Albania, Mongolia, Nepal, Benin: A few years ago who would have thought that these countries would have elective governments by the early 1990s? Throughout the world, military juntas, dictators, and one-party systems have all been replaced by democratic regimes. The organization Freedom House each year publishes a comprehensive analysis of the state of freedom in the world. In 1972, it rated 42 countries as free; last year, it rated 75 in this class.

Reasons for Change

This dramatic expansion of democracy has two important consequences. First, although democracy does not necessarily solve the problems of in-

---

[1]This contribution is an abridged version of the 1993 Francisco Fernández Ordonez Annual Lecture and appeared in similar form in the March/April 1994 edition of *WorldLink*.

equality, corruption, inefficiency, injustice, or ineffective decision-making, it does provide the institutional setting to guarantee the freedom of the individual from gross violations of human rights and dignity. Democracy is a cure for tyranny.

Second, the expansion of democracy reduces the likelihood of war between nation-states. One of the most central facts of recent history is that since the advent of modern democracy in the United States in the early nineteenth century, democracies have, with only trivial exceptions, not fought wars with other democracies.

The expansion of democracy after 1974 has given rise to the view that we are in the midst of an all-encompassing global democratic revolution. Democracy is on the march, people have argued, and soon it should emerge victorious in virtually every country of the world. This view was, of course, particularly prevalent after the collapse of communism in Eastern Europe. "Democracy's won," one observer proclaimed. Others termed democracy "the wave of the future" and celebrated "the globalization of democracy." Francis Fukuyama heralded the end of history and, in his words, "the universalization of western liberal democracy as the final form of human government." It was just a matter of time until the last holdouts, be they Cuba, Burma, North Korea, or elsewhere, fell before the engulfing universalism of the democratic tide.

Probable Consequences

Yet I am doubtful that the spread of democracy in the world will continue during this decade at the same pace that it has during the past two—although it is true that I usually incline toward pessimism. Nonetheless, I believe that the wave of democratization which began in the mid-1970s and which spread to almost 40 countries, is now moving from the phase of expansion to the phase of consolidation.

There are several reasons for this belief. First, certain economic and cultural conditions favor democratization. These include a relatively high level of economic development and values, including Western Christianity, that are supportive of individual rights and democracy. At present, virtually all of the non-oil producing high-income or upper middle-income countries (as classified by the World Bank) are, with the exception of Singapore, democratic. Similarly, Western and Western-influenced nations, with the exception of Cuba and perhaps a few others, have become democratic. The countries that have not yet democratized are those where the conditions favoring democratization are weak. They generally tend to be either poor countries or countries with non-Western cultures. The 75 countries identified as free by Freedom House, for instance, include only five countries in Asia (Japan, South Korea, Mongolia, Nepal, Bangladesh), only two Islamic countries (Bangladesh and the Turkish Republic of Cyprus), and only three Orthodox countries (Greece, Bulgaria, and the Greek Republic on Cyprus). Apart from the Baltic republics, none of the countries of the former Soviet Union is classified as free.

At present, democracy prevails in western and central Europe, in North and South America, and on the fringes of east Asia. It is missing from much of the former Soviet Union, China, much of southern Asia, the Arab states and Iran, and much of Africa. Will democracy expand in these areas? The prospects for the expansion of democracy depend on the interplay of economics and culture.

Among the former Soviet republics, for instance, one can be reasonably optimistic about the future of democracy in the economically better-off and Protestant or Catholic Baltic republics. In the poor trans-Caucasian and Muslim central Asian republics, democracy's future is bleak. In the Orthodox republics, which occupy a middle ground economically, uncertainty prevails. In Russia, Boris Yeltsin has expanded presidential power, disestablished political parties, limited press freedoms, and prohibited criticism of his constitution and of himself. Yeltsin is making many needed reforms in Russia, but his principal model is Peter the Great—hardly a democrat. Yeltsin's Russia may or may not become a democratic Russia. What happens there will have an immense impact on political developments in other former Soviet republics, Mongolia, and Eastern Europe. Hence, the single most important foreign policy goal for the United States, and the West in general, is the consolidation of democracy in Russia.

During the past decade China has experienced extraordinarily rapid economic growth. In south China, in particular, a vigorous private sector has emerged and with it the beginnings of a substantial bourgeoisie and middle class. In due course these groups will provide the impetus for a political opening and movement toward pluralism and perhaps even democracy. That movement is unlikely, however, to occur either quickly or easily; peasants still form the bulk of the population and Confucian values and practices remain strong. In addition, the political leadership is outspokenly contemptuous of Western democracy and human rights and is committed to maintaining an authoritarian political system. In the longer run, however, if it continues, economic growth is likely to overcome cultural and political obstacles.

Thus, the prospects for democracy in Russia are uncertain in both the short run and the long run. The prospects for democracy in China are bleak in the short term but rather bright in the long term.

I do not argue that democracy can exist only in Western countries. That obviously is not the case, but its development in non-Western societies has, with only a few exceptions such as Turkey, been largely the result of Western influence, colonialism, or military occupation. Modern democracy was initially a product of Western Protestant culture. It came more slowly to Catholic countries, and the initial democratic transitions in the 1970s and 1980s were overwhelmingly in Catholic countries. In considerable measure, these transitions were the result of changes in the position of the Catholic church and of economic development that occurred in the 1950s and 1960s.

Economic development, consequently, can alter a country's culture and make it more supportive of democracy. If it occurs, economic development will presumably have this effect on Islamic, Buddhist, Orthodox, and Confucian societies. However, economic development surges in East Asia, even though cultural change is likely to be a lengthy process. Recent transitions to democracy have served the important function of extending democracy throughout almost all of the wealthier countries in the world and almost all countries that have largely Western cultures. Efforts to extend democracy further face much more significant obstacles than the democratization of the past two decades.

Another reason to be skeptical about much further democratization is the dialectical nature of history. Any substantial movement in one direction tends eventually to lose its momentum and generate counter-vailing forces. This has been true with respect to democratization. The current wave of transitions since 1974 is the third such wave in the modern world. The first originated in the United States in the early nineteenth century and culminated after World War I, at which time there were roughly 32 democratic countries in the world. A second wave of democratic transitions occurred after World War II and lasted until 1960. Then a second reverse got under way and by 1973, there were several fewer (30) democratic countries in the world than there had been ten years earlier (36). It is thus possible that a third reverse wave could materialize in the coming years. In some measure it already has. Sudan, Nigeria, Haiti, and Peru all made transitions to democracy, but now have dictatorial regimes. For the first time in more than a decade, Freedom House last year reported no net increase in the number of free countries in the world. Its latest report carries the headline, *Freedom in retreat.*

In this respect the democratic expansion since 1974 can be thought of as a military campaign, with country after country being liberated by the surging democratic forces. Even in the most dramatic of advances, however, it becomes necessary to pause, regroup, and consolidate one's gains. It would appear that the third wave of democratization may have reached that point.

Apart from southern Europe, the future of democracy in the new democracies is uncertain. A recent comprehensive survey by Larry

Diamond of the situation in Latin America concluded that "the region as a whole has reached the point of stagnation in progress toward democracy, with setbacks offsetting or even exceeding gains." In its 1992 report, Freedom House classified only ten Latin American republics as free, Cuba and Haiti as not free, and the remainder as partly free. In addition to Peru and Haiti, Venezuela and Guatemala have experienced coup attempts. In countries ranging from Brazil and Chile to Guatemala and El Salvador, the military remains a powerful behind-the- scenes force. The situation in Eastern Europe and the former Soviet Union is similarly precarious.

Proposed Actions

The international community faces major obstacles in extending democracy to non-Western and poorer countries. In addition, major problems, if not crises, exist in many of the countries where democracy has recently been introduced. As a result, the immediate priority is to strengthen these new democracies rather than to extend democracy to other countries. Consolidation, not expansion, is the order of the day.

Consolidation of the new democracies requires a variety of actions: promoting tolerance and the rule of the law, curbing the power of the military and former communist bureaucracies, and determining how to deal with those officials in authoritarian regimes who have grossly violated human rights. There are, however, two major areas in which experience provides some guidelines for making new democracies more robust.

Political institutions must be strengthened. The new democracies need to develop political institutions that will reduce fragmentation and stalemate, promote effective and responsible decision-making, and yet also prevent the overconcentration of power in any particular branch of government. These requirements at times conflict and the appropriate balance will differ from society to society. There are no institutional solutions which should be universally adopted; there are, however, institutional mistakes which should be universally avoided.

First, extreme forms of proportional representation should be avoided. They tend to create excessive fragmentation, as in Poland with 29 parties being represented in the legislature and no party controlling more than 13 percent of the seats. When the Poles reformed this system and introduced a 5 percent threshold for representation in parliament, the number of parties in the legislature dropped to six.

Second, the combination of a directly elected president with a legislature elected through proportional representation produces institutional deadlock and policy paralysis. If the chief executive and the legislators have different constituencies, there is little incentive to develop strong political parties, and stalemate and institutional conflict result. This can lead to the removal of the chief executives, as in Brazil and Venezuela, to successful or unsuccessful efforts at executive coups, as in Peru and Guatemala, or to the president largely ignoring the legislature and ruling by decree, as in Argentina. We can see this unfortunate combination at work now in Russia, where half the parliament was elected by proportional representation. To remedy these problems, Juan Linz and others have argued that Latin American countries should shift to a parliamentary system. This would not only reduce the discordance between legislature and executive but would also encourage the development of a two-party system.

Third, in general, a system with two strong parties is likely to provide a better combination of effective decision-making and responsible government than alternative types of party systems. A dominant party system, in which one party or coalition continuously controls the government, can generate massive corruption, as has happened in Italy, Japan, and India. A multiparty system with a parliamentary government also often makes political change difficult as the parties appeal to separate constituencies, elections tend to produce little variation in the distribution of votes among parties, and successive governments involve simply the reshuffling of coalitions of party insiders. A system with two strong parties, on the other hand, means that one party can govern and the other can provide both a responsible opposition and an alternative government in waiting. The dynamics of electoral competition will also tend to draw the two parties toward the middle of the political spectrum.

Finally, simple forms of majority rule do not work in societies severely divided along racial, ethnic, religious, or regional lines. No communal group will accept being in a permanent minority, permanently excluded from government. Depending on the size and nature of the communal groups in the society, some power sharing is necessary, such as is now envisioned for South Africa. Alternatively, voting arrangements can be structured so as to encourage parties and candidates to make multicommunal appeals, as with alternative vote system in Sri Lanka.

This is a time for constitutional innovation and institutional experimentation. There is much that the new democracies can learn from each other and from the experiences of older democracies, some of which, such as Italy, Israel, and Japan, are also altering their institutional structures.

A second major need in the new democracies is to promote economic reform, reducing the role of the state and encouraging more dependence on the market. Economic reform is a more complex and onerous task than political democratization. It is more difficult to organize markets than to organize elections. Economic reform also often imposes severe hardship on portions of the population. Most importantly, there have been virtually no historical precedents for economic liberalization since the dismantling of mercantilism in the early nineteenth century. New and old democracies have had to learn how to do it by doing it. Nonetheless some lessons do emerge from recent experience.

Governments best undertake economic reform promptly after they have won a clear electoral victory. They do not necessarily have to have committed themselves to reform; indeed, in several cases—Jamaica, Venezuela, Argentina—reform was undertaken by leaders who had appeared to favor populist expansionist policies. Forceful executive leadership is almost always necessary for reform, and this is one reason why a presidential or semipresidential system may be desirable in a new democracy. In the past few years there has been much debate over whether reforms should be introduced all at once, the shock therapy, or whether they should be done sequentially. Some sequencing is obviously necessary and conventional wisdom states that economic stabilization should come first, followed by marketization, the freeing of price and exchange rates, and then privatization. Overall, however, success seems more likely to come to governments which attempt these measures as quickly and as simultaneously as possible. Inevitably, groups hurt by the reforms try to moderate or reverse them, and if a government starts out with a major push for sweeping reforms, it has greater leeway to compromise without gutting the essence of the reform.

Outside agencies can provide needed discipline by making their assistance conditional on governments' imposing fiscal austerity, freeing prices, and curbing inflation. Undoubtedly, however, the greatest help which established democracies can give to the new democracies is to carry out economic reform themselves and reduce their import barriers.

The United States and the European Union actively hoped to promote the expansion of democracy in the 1970s and 1980s. Can they now help with the consolidation of democracy? They surely are better positioned to do that in the coming years than to push for the further extension of democracy to countries where it is now absent. Apart from Africa, these are generally areas where Western influence is limited and may often be deeply resented and resisted as a manifestation of Western arrogance and "human rights imperialism." The United States and the EU are, however, able to promote the consolidation of democracy in those regions where they helped to inaugurate it: Latin America, Eastern Europe, and peripheral east Asia. Supporting the consolidation of democracy in these regions should be a top foreign policy priority and, in the United States, it has become just that.

More than 150 years ago, Alexis de Tocqueville wrote that "a great democratic revolution is going on around us. . . . it is the most uniform, the most ancient, and the most permanent tendency to be found in history. . . . It is universal, it is lasting, it constantly eludes all human interference, and all events as well as all men contribute to its progress." Tocqueville was far too optimistic for his times. So also are those contemporary observers who have been hailing the global victory of the democratic revolution. At this point in history, democracy will be furthered not by efforts to extend it to societies where social and economic conditions are still unfavorable, but rather by the deepening of democracy in societies where it has been recently introduced. Democracy, as one analyst has said, has been fully consolidated in only three or four of the almost forty newly democratic countries: Spain, Portugal, Greece, and perhaps Uruguay. In all the others its future is in doubt if not in danger. If by early in the next century those dangers can be countered, those doubts eliminated, and democracy stabilized and consolidated in most of these forty countries, this generation of democratizers will have done its work well. Successful rounding out and completion of the third wave of democratization will lay the foundation from which a fourth wave can then be launched with far better chances to extend democracy to those non-Western and those less wealthy parts of the world where it is now absent.

Chapter 3
Facing the New Inequalities

Introduction
George V. Vassiliou

Equality has been the dream and the guiding light for philosophers, revolutionaries, and ideologists for centuries. The entire theory of socialism was built on the assumption that capitalism cannot lead to equality. On the contrary, Marx predicted, the growth of capitalism would lead to an ever-increasing gap between rich and poor. This did not prove true in the post-World War II world. In developed countries, the economic boom and the welfare state caused an unprecedented increase in living standards that substantially narrowed the gap between rich and poor. Simultaneously, Soviet-style socialism created equality for the huge majority at the lowest possible denominator and wealth and benefits only for the very few party members at the top. Thus, it became accepted that Marx's forecasts were wrong; a market economy was able to improve standards of living of the poor.

In the 1980s, however, this trend has been disturbingly reversed. Not only did the gap between rich and poor begin to increase again, as discussed by Howard Davies, but the gap between developed and developing countries also increased. According to Makoto Taniguchi, the only difference is that the developed group includes some of the "tigers" of the Far East and a few countries in Latin America. At the same time, the number of countries classified among the LLDCs has jumped from 24 in 1970 to 41 in 1990. We should not underestimate the potential for conflict if the developed countries do not take into account the needs of the developing countries. We should realize, points out the OECD Deputy Secretary General, that "all human beings are in the same, small, fragile boat called 'Earth.' The problems we must face and solve together transcend the difference between developed and developing country."

This growing inequality has other negative consequences. Franck Riboud points out the increasing exclusion of young people who, particularly in France, are finding it difficult to find suitable employment.

Esko Aho, the Prime Minister of Finland, points to the social tensions created by the rapidly changing demographic profile of many countries. As the proportion of the older population continuously increases, the dependency ratio rapidly deteriorates. This could lead to social tensions that would endanger the welfare state. In those countries where demographic trends cannot easily be reversed, the economic and social systems will have to adapt their policies to accommodate the realities of an aging society with low growth rates.

Gabrielle Rolland looks at the inequality between sexes. Although women may represent the majority of employees in many sectors in the industrialized countries, very few of them are in positions of power. In the developing countries, the position of women has worsened significantly in the last decade. To successfully address the challenges of the third millennium, women have to be given the opportunity to participate equally. This requires a concerted effort by all.

Inequality is not expressed only in incomes, however. The new technology and telecommunications revolution has created a new type of inequality—one based on the availability of and access to information. As Ernst-Moritz Lipp writes, the world is now divided between those who know and have access to information and the majority that does not. Within this framework, it is particularly important that the new communications elite is created more by the contact between persons in the global network than by contact with fellow workers or citizens. The elite make decisions without knowing that their information is incomplete and without the necessary understanding of social conditions, values, and needs of the societies involved. We cannot stop the growth of global network, but we can formulate policies to reduce the risk of isolation of the telecommunications elite.

The contributors have some suggestions, but do not offer detailed plans for reversing these growing inequalities. Their service, however, is in highlighting the facts and emphasizing the need for policy makers to begin a comprehensive effort to formulate programs that will reverse these trends.

-1-
The New North-South Conflict

Makoto Taniguchi

Description of Change

The end of the Cold War has changed the nature of North-South relations; the old paradigm, characterized by political and ideological confrontation, has mostly disappeared. Instead, the new landscape reflects
the emergence and rapid economic development of certain countries, particularly the dynamic Asian economies and some successful reforming
countries in Latin America. For example, Mexico is expected to join the
OECD by June 1994 and Korea in the near future. The term "North-
South" really does not fit today's situation; it is now more appropriate to
distinguish between "developed" and "developing" countries, "rich" and
"poor" countries, or more precisely, "high-income" and "low-income"
countries.

In the past three decades, the most striking phenomenon in the evolution of relations between developed and developing countries has been
the growing divergence among developing countries themselves. Not
only has the income gap widened between developed and developing
countries, it has widened considerably within developing countries. Consider the dynamic Asian economies and what the United Nations refers
to as the least developed countries—the LDCs. The economic development of the dynamic Asian economies (and other emerging countries
such as China) has been outstanding in recent years. In 1990, in terms of
per capita income, Singapore and Hong Kong were just behind New
Zealand, but already ahead of Ireland and Spain. Korea and Taiwan were
on a level with Greece. Based on present trends of relatively higher
growth in the dynamic Asian economies than in OECD countries, the
former could well be in the median OECD income range by the year
2000. Similarly, in Latin America, several reforming countries have
made economic strides.

However, although these few developing countries launched themselves on a successful path to development, the number of countries now
classified among the LDCs jumped from 24 in 1970 to 41 in 1990. Most
of these are in Africa. When we look at the present deplorable situations
in Mozambique, Somalia, Rwanda, and other conflict-stricken countries
in Africa, we cannot but suspect a direct causal link between grinding

mass poverty and the outbreak of military conflicts. For example, in 1990 Mozambique had the lowest per capita income in the world—US $80, which was 1/400th of that of Switzerland.

Reasons for Change

In the process of globalization of the world economy, potentially serious problems are beginning to surface—problems that can lead to serious friction, even open conflict, between mature developed countries and some of the more dynamic developing countries. This is doubtless natural and inevitable in what is rapidly becoming a borderless world market system. When the capacity of developed countries to adjust themselves structurally cannot keep pace with the increasing competitiveness of dynamic developing economies, friction is unavoidable.

Ideally, developed countries should make every effort to upgrade their productive apparatus based on high technology. But, as the corollary of this seems to be a "hollowing out" of the heavy and labor-intensive manufacturing sector, this has already brought about, to some extent, economic and social problems in the developed countries. For example, unemployment, especially in Europe, is already one of the most serious problems faced by OECD economies. It is predicted that total unemployment in the OECD area will reach 35 million by the end of 1994. In the process of rapid structural adjustment, skilled labor is very much in need, but unskilled labor will be increasingly poorly paid or join the rolls of the unemployed. As a result, unemployment and a widening income gap between different categories of workers in the OECD countries could lead to serious social problems during this decade.

Probable Consequences

If the gap between the rich and poor countries becomes too extreme, political tension will be created among regions and nations, with the attendant risk of insecurity and military conflicts, as we are seeing in some poorer regions in Africa.

As the 1989 report of the chairman of the OECD Development Assistance Committee pointed out, most of the poorer countries, particularly the LDCs, are suffering from the "vicious circle" of poverty, population explosion, and environmental degradation. If these countries cannot break this circle, it will be difficult, if not impossible, for them to achieve sound political, economic, and social development. At the same time, if their problems cannot be overcome, there may be adverse consequences for all the nations in the form of cross-boundary environmental damage, uncontrolled migration, refugees, and the spread of drugs and AIDS.

The potential for conflict should not be underestimated. Both developed and developing countries need to arrive at common understanding and value judgments on such global issues as population and environment. All human beings are in the same, small, fragile boat called "Earth." The problems we must face and solve together transcend the difference between developed and developing country. For this reason, the UN should be strengthened.

However, neither should we underestimate the importance of "South-South" cooperation (cooperation between more advanced developing countries and those which have been less successful), which is very often more effective than traditional "North-South" cooperation.

Proposed Actions

The potential for friction and conflict between mature developed countries and emerging developing countries may give rise to serious problems. Social strains will increase in mature developed countries, based on the growing phenomenon of long-term unemployment and the seeming lack of near-to-medium-term prospects to reduce unemployment. Even in the most developed countries, poverty has remained a persistent feature, made worse in some countries by falling real wages—in particular, for low-skilled workers—that create a "poverty trap." Widening income disparities can only place further strains on the social fabric. Additional friction may come from the burgeoning expenditure required for the increasing senior population. Health and pension costs could place a heavy burden on OECD economies and generate intergenerational tensions.

In the long run, developed countries have no choice but to proceed with the necessary structural adjustments required to cope with the rapidly changing world economic situation. The real challenge will be to avoid friction and conflict situations during this period of adjustment. Such friction generally damages all parties concerned, with a net negative effect for the world economy.

The dynamic developing economies still need inflows of capital and technology to assure future growth, while the mature developed economies need expanding markets for their exports. To set up more cooperative, interdependent, and mutually beneficial relations in a globalized world economy, there will be an even greater need for global rules of the game. International organizations, such as the OECD and the WTO, should take the initiative, together with other related organizations, in tackling such emerging trade issues as trade and the environment, new competition policy, strategic industry, and labor standards.

The Rich Get Richer, the Poor Get Poorer
Howard Davies

Description of Change

In deciding to reach a comprehensive GATT deal at the end of 1993, the developed world turned its back on protectionism, at least for now. It also threw open its doors to new and more intense competition from newly industrializing economies, competition that will have a dramatic impact on the structure of Western society. In some countries, notably France and the United States, the GATT deal was politically controversial (for different reasons in each case). Basically, certain sector interests felt their positions to be threatened. In Germany and the United Kingdom, on the other hand, there was very little popular concern and little public debate. The impact of growing competition from low-cost industrialized countries on the nature of Western societies was rarely the subject of informed argument.

Yet, the consequences of growing competition, especially from the Pacific Rim countries, will be dramatic for the welfare states of the West and, particularly, for the income distribution patterns of those countries. For a further discussion of this issue, see Fritz Scharpf's comments in Chapter 9.

Reasons for Change

For several decades up to the end of the 1970s, the gap between high- and low-income earners narrowed in most developed countries. There remained sizable differences in the spread of incomes from one country to another, with the United States the least equal and Finland the most equal among OECD countries. But the general direction of change was similar in each case. The tax and benefit systems were part of the story, reducing pretax differentials, but pretax differentials themselves also narrowed.

Since the late 1970s, the trend has begun to reverse. It changed first in the United States, then in the United Kingdom, and in the mid-to-late 1980s, in most, though not quite all, of Western Europe. The spread of incomes became wider; the incomes of the rich grew more rapidly than the average and those of the poor less rapidly. In fact the incomes of the poor declined in absolute terms. In the United Kingdom, for example, average income for the population as a whole rose by 36 percent between 1979 and 1991. But during that same period, the real incomes of the top tenth rose by 62 percent, while those in the bottom tenth fell by 14 percent. Similar trends, though not always as dramatic, have been seen in other European countries.

The causes of these changes are not entirely understood. Part of the reason can be found in changing social structures. For those at the bottom of the income distribution ladder, the single most important cause of poverty seems to be unemployment. And, as Scharpf argues, much of the unemployment among unskilled or semiskilled workers has come in the manufacturing industry, which is facing competitive pressures from low-cost producers. They are disproportionately affected by new competitors, whose advantage is low-labor costs. Another factor is the increase in family break-ups, which results in more single parents, especially young women, with child-care responsibilities. This makes it difficult, or even impossible, for them to work or be trained for work.

In principle, these impacts could be offset by changes in the tax and benefit systems in developed economies. A more steeply progressive income tax, combined with more generous benefits—particularly income supplements—paid to low income workers could change this picture. But the trend has coincided with an increasing opposition to high taxes, so that while pretax income differentials have been widening, top marginal tax rates and social benefits have been held down.

Probable Consequences

If these trends continue, the developed economies will have to cope with a growing "under class" that is increasingly separated from the mainstream economy and the imposition of heavier and heavier burdens on social services.

Proposed Actions

An effective response to this problem requires a combination of measures. That response should not, however, include protectionist measures. Not only does protection reduce the incentive for companies to become more competitive, it causes a dangerous build-up of resentment among newly industrialized economies. This resentment would eventually lead to ever-higher defense expenditures by wealthier nations. So the response must be to enhance competitiveness, while seeking to mitigate some of the most damaging social consequences of growing inequality.

A four-faceted solution is required:

1. Tight control of labor costs in developed economies. If average wages are allowed to rise too quickly, then unemployment, which is the single most important cause of relative poverty and family breakdown, will also rise.

2. Western economies must invest significantly more in education and training, particularly of those disadvantaged groups of unskilled workers who are being ejected from the industrial economy. That means devising programs that attract and hold the long-term unemployed. It also means providing retraining opportunities throughout a person's working life to allow individuals to recycle themselves back into the labor force at different points. A comprehensive retraining strategy will be expensive, but the alternative is worse.

3. Social benefit systems will need to become more entangled with particular disadvantaged groups and more sensitively related to the tax system.

4. Responding to the single-parent family problem, we must find ways of subsidizing child care to allow young women to remain in, or close to, the labor force during their childbearing years, even when there is no father at home.

This strategy will not be easy to follow. There will be many political objections. but the alternative is acquiescence in a growing level of inequality, which could have extremely damaging social consequences across the developed world.

Intergenerational Conflict

Esko Aho

Description of Change

Recent events at global, regional, and nation-state levels are best described as a process of fundamental change. Global integration involves difficult adjustments and potential conflicts characterized by unpredictability and a high degree of uncertainty.

In such a process of change, we need to rethink our basic assumptions about the main lines of development and consider alternative directions for an uncertain future. Identification of such options would shake up our "cognitive maps" and intellectual structures, thereby allowing us to make better decisions. We must prepare for the future now.

Reasons for Change

In the developed countries, we have become accustomed to thinking that "each day is better than the previous one." This expectation is based on what has been in historical terms an unusually long period of growth, high employment, and rapidly increasing standards of education.

The lack of economic growth in recent years has made expectations uncertain, especially among young people. With good reason, the young wonder about their position in the chain of generations. Has the future already been determined? Do the young have expectations that cannot be fulfilled in a changing world? What commitments have been made for the future? Will it be fair to us and our children?

The facts below long constituted a valid description of virtually all of the industrialized countries:

- Economic growth was fast; in Finland, real per capita GDP doubled in fewer than thirty years.
- Unemployment remained below 5 percent.
- By historical standards, the age structure of both the population as a whole and the work force was extremely favorable: the elderly accounted for a small proportion of the population and young age groups were very large.

- The seriousness of environmental problems was in fact recognized, although they were generally regarded as local, or at most local/regional issues.

The significant changes in these basic factors, as outlined below, lie behind the concerned questions asked by young people:

- For years, economic growth has remained below earlier levels and has sometimes even been negative; outlooks in the United States, Europe, and Japan are uncertain.
- Unemployment grew very rapidly, especially in Europe; the average rate for the European OECD countries is now approximately 11 percent; any expectations of rapid decline are probably illusory. The fact that in many countries unemployment among young people is substantially more general (approximately 20 to 35 percent) is the greatest source of concern.
- The age structure in the developed countries is changing rapidly. The segment of the population over the age of 60 is rising sharply in comparison with that of children and those of working age. Although at present the elderly account for less than 20 percent of the population, by the year 2020 they will represent nearly one-third. At the same time, population increases in these countries will rest entirely on immigration from the developing world, which will continue to struggle with its own explosive population growth.

  Due to change and probably continued high unemployment, the dependency ratio (the ratio of the nonemployed, such as the aged, children, and jobless, to the employed portion of the population) will rise to a historically high level. The size and structure of the work force will have an adverse effect on economic growth. Young people will have reason to fear that the quantitative superiority of the older generation, for example, within the electorate, may have an impact on the nature and direction of society as a whole.

- The young in particular understand that environmental issues are no longer exclusively local issues of protection. Rather, they constitute the "ultimate frontier" of the global economy and existing levels of consumption. The young understand that global environment problems can be solved only through broad, international cooperation, massive investment in environmentally sound technology, and profound changes in life-styles.

  Nor is it insignificant that rising national debts and corporate borrowing in developed countries are generating unprecedented pressure to reduce expenditure on social welfare, pensions, health, and education.

Probable Consequences

We are still not sufficiently prepared for this change. In 1993, I established a special task force on "generational welfare and responsibilities" to examine the nature of this change and its long-term impact.

The legacy left to posterity is a broad issue. Are the means for well-being being handed down from one generation to another? Will our legacy be larger or smaller than the one we received? What kind of an economy, what kind of human capital (for example, education), what kinds of natural resources and environments, what kinds of collective commodities, and what kinds of institutions will we leave? What rules will we apply in intergenerational relations? How will equity between generations be achieved? It is immediately obvious that we are dealing broadly with the conditions for truly sustainable development, which combines economic, demographic, ecological, social, and ethical considerations.

The calculations made by the task force clearly show that since the 1920s, the economic, educational, and material well-being of each new generation have risen above those of its predecessor. There has been a "generational contract," under which income has been transferred from the younger age groups to the older, and each generation has received more from the system than it has contributed.

The future—up to the end of the next century—will be different. If today's generations live out their lives according to present commitments and income transfers, and economic growth is slow, future generations will not achieve the current level of material well-being. Financial responsibility for the welfare system would fall to future generations.

Under conditions of moderate growth (1.5 percent per capita per annum), the problems of intergenerational income distribution can be solved only if present generations pay higher taxes and cut benefits. Under conditions of continuous rapid growth (3.0 percent per capita per annum), ecological sustainability becomes a problem. We would have to invest increasingly in technology that uses renewable natural resources and conserves materials; industry would have to operate with closed cycles. An increasing portion of this growth should thus be set aside to manage the consequences.

The assessments of experts therefore justify the questions of young people, which are both uncertain and aggressive. We indeed have a political and ethical responsibility for how we relate to change and to the issue of intergenerational justice that accompanies it. Government remains the guardian of future generations against present selfishness.

Proposed Actions

The status quo is overly represented in decision-making; virtually no one speaks on behalf of the future. Therefore, our first task is to put the future on the agenda by providing regular assessments of the sustainability of our rules, commitments, and models for society. These include, to mention a few examples from the Finnish experience, the Government's October 1993 report to Parliament on future options, as well as generational and environmental accounts published at regular intervals. Open public debate on the challenges of the future may lead to the social innovation needed to supplement technological renewal, as well as to new rules and new approaches for managing a common future.

Our public policy must abandon the illusion that good times are just around the corner. Our generational policy must prevent realization of the worst scenario, in which future generations are forced into an untenable situation. We must ensure them maximum latitude. Perhaps the world's richest generation lived at the end of the 1980s?

In applying this principle, our attention is naturally focused on saving and borrowing, expressed in the incomes and consumption of generations. We must reexamine and reassess the welfare systems of the developed economies in terms of sustainable development. This generation—my generation—must learn to live with less. But more important than incomes and consumption are the factors that affect the ability of future generations to produce economic values of their own. Therefore the state of our infrastructure—both mental and physical—is of primary importance. We must learn to think that if we do not provide the future generation with a good education and if we neglect our transport and communication systems, we will go into debt. If we protect the environment, even if it requires vast investment, we will probably save in the long run. Here we are speaking of real, not nominal, saving and borrowing.

Long-term mass unemployment, especially in Europe, has its greatest impact on the young. A significant proportion of the young, those who would presumably build our future societies, will be marginalized and unable to integrate through work with the rest of society. We must rapidly alter the rules of the labor market, so that firms can train and employ the young. Societies will otherwise pay a high price in community decay, alienation, human suffering, and, it must be noted, in a less efficient economy.

We must have the courage to invest in the ecological structural change through which we can adopt environmentally sound technologies, production methods, and consumption habits. I am well aware that all of this can be realized only through determined international cooperation. Here the front-runners will have the environmental markets to conquer. In Europe, it will be necessary to involve Russia and the new demo-

102   Esko Aho

cracies of Central and Eastern Europe in this cooperation. Implementation of a comprehensive environmental policy for all of Europe will require much sacrifice of short-term benefits for the good of future generations.

But it remains the duty of our generation to bear this responsibility.

-4-
The Increased Exclusion
of Young People

Franck Riboud

Description of Change

Over the past ten years, young people in industrialized countries have found it increasingly difficult to integrate into the work force. This problem is especially pronounced in France, with an unemployment rate of 23 percent in the 18-to-25-year-old age group, as compared with 5.6 percent in Germany. The only countries with a higher rate in this age group than France are Spain (34 percent) and Italy (32 percent), but the rate is high even in the United States (13.7 percent) and Great Britain (15 percent). During the past 20 years in France, the unemployment rate of young people has multiplied more than sixfold, as compared with three for the population as a whole. In disadvantaged social groups, the rate can be much higher; 66 percent of the young people in American ghettos are unemployed. This means that a large number of those who are supposed to ensure the future of our countries are being marginalized. A country cannot be competitive if its work force consists of untrained and inexperienced people, who have no notion of what constitutes a company and who can no longer integrate into society.

Consumer societies base their hopes on a future generation that will be better off, better trained, and better paid than the current one. Already, this is no longer true. A recent study in the United States shows that at the beginning of the 1980s one-third of those in the 22-to-48-year-old age group experienced decreased revenues, as compared with fewer than 20 percent in the 1970s. Among the untrained, the proportion who experienced decreased revenues jumped to 43 percent. We are creating, not without risks, a generation that feels tomorrow will be worse than today.

Reasons for Change

The reasons are well known. First, there is the slowdown in growth, but this is not a sufficient explanation. From 1986 to 1990, France experienced average growth of more than 3.5 percent per annum, yet the unemployment rate of the under 25-year-old age group never dropped below 19 percent. Competition required that companies cut labor costs by automating the manufacturing processes and relocating production facilities. In addition, productivity gains permitted enormous labor savings in industry, as was the case in the past for farming and will be the case in the future for services.

Another, more serious, reason is that exclusion leads to more exclusion. A young person who moves back and forth from a low-paying job to unemployment becomes more and more difficult to integrate. Exclusion is like cancer: the longer one waits to treat it, the more it becomes incurable. In a certain manner, this is the choice made by American society—the best get ahead and the others get charity. However, this has never been the European model, and it is very expensive from an economic standpoint.

Probable Consequences

The consequences are multiple. Exclusion fosters a parallel economy that is increasingly based on crime, particularly drugs. As a child in the Parisian suburbs observed: "Why should I work, when my brother earns more in one week dealing drugs than my teacher makes in a month?" The Manchester police estimate that a drug addict, with the exclusion of young people from the work force, will cost society more and more. Look, for example, at the cost of the Los Angeles riots.

Maurice Aubry, former Labor Minister, stated: "The social fabric is being torn apart, and soon we won't be able to patch it back together again." This prediction is all the more worrisome since, over the next few years and by reason of the demographic revolution, the productive effort will be borne by an increasingly smaller percentage of workers. By then, it will be too late to regret that the new generations were not better integrated.

Finally, and perhaps most serious, is that exclusion of young people increases their fear and worry when faced with progress and technology. There is a political risk involved, as can currently be seen in Germany, where the neo-Nazi movements are recruiting young people.

Proposed Actions

First, young people need not be excluded. Germany has survived an economic crisis with less than a two percent increase in unemployment among young people. Compare this with more than 10 percent in France. In the 15-to-24-year-old age group, the unemployment rates in 1979 and 1992 were 4 percent and 5.6 percent in Germany, but 10 percent and 23 percent in France.

The INSEE (French Institute for Economic Statistics) wondered in a recent study if, in the end, "in France, the hiring policies in companies and in the civil service administration, above all seeking to preserve the situation of adults, had not contributed to the externalization (if not the exclusion) of young people." Thus, there are two models. The French model uses less and less young labor. Exaggerating somewhat, it could be said that one generation is hoarding jobs at the expense of the younger generation. The German model, which in an almost regulatory manner uses professional training schools and apprenticeships, has organized the integration of young people.

In France, the application of the German model would shake up a number of current principles regarding labor costs (especially the burden of social security charges), rechanneling employment expenditures (current unemployment compensation, which is 300 billion francs, represents the equivalent of 3 million minimum wage jobs), developing new services, and upgrading the value of professional training.

In short, employment—especially that of young people—must take the forefront in social management, as was the case in the past for social protection in industrialized countries when one sought to avoid the exclusion of older and weaker individuals.

-5-
Overcoming Discrimination Against Women
Gabrielle Rolland

Description of Change

The transformation of the role of women is a major factor in this century. In industrialized countries, women have joined the ranks of public and professional life, forming the majority of workers in service industries and education. Those who have had equal educational opportunities at the school and university levels have experienced a slightly higher success rate on a global level than men. But the battle is not yet won.

Women may indeed form the majority in many sectors of the economy, but they are still a minority in the fields of power. Although some women have positions of responsibility that entail a short-term and immediate commitment, very few hold positions of power that involve anticipation of and commitment to the future. On the one hand, men have no reason to let go of such scarce positions. On the other, women are increasingly less interested in power.

Despite some major achievements, the situation of women, particularly in developing countries, is deteriorating. Women constitute half of the world population and perform about two-thirds of the work, but they receive only one-tenth of the income and own less than one percent of the property.

One major problem is the lack of adequate health care. In underdeveloped countries, which are experiencing an alarming increase in maternal and infant mortality, the main cause of female deaths is malnutrition. By the end of the twentieth century, the number of women infected by the AIDS virus could double. The World Health Organization has noted that this significant increase in mortality rates could annihilate the demographic progress recorded in certain parts of the world.

A second problem is illiteracy, which affects women more than men. The situation is conspicuously troublesome in Africa and Asia, where a girl is born in a world that does not expect her to succeed and thus prepares her for failure.

Reasons for Change

In industrialized countries, there are two main reasons for discrimination against women:

- The current speed of structural, technological, political, and sociological changes primarily undermine women because of their lack of experience in powerful positions.
- Women are physically and mentally exhausted after the age of thirty. Until that age, they enjoy a genuine period of equality. After thirty, however, when men have the luxury of specializing in their field of interest, women must manage two lives—one domestic and one professional. This dual effort exhausts women, making them less desirable and available. Thus isolated, women sacrifice the networks that pave the way to power for men.

In developing countries, where the position of women is tragic, current levels of poverty make them prey to and scapegoats for fundamentalists and nationalists. This is all the more dramatic since the Gulf War, when women lodged desperate and powerful protests against their status. Fatima Mernissi of Morocco wrote: "Women whether carrying the veil or not have taken initiatives of peace without waiting, as tradition has it, for the go-ahead of political leaders, inevitably male. In Tunis, Rabat, or Algiers, it was often women who were the first to improvise sit-ins and demonstrations that men . . . could not decide before having exhausted the eternal negotiations and bargainings between powers and minipowers."

Probable Consequences

To find solutions to the problems posed by globalization and to reconcile differences, whether between nations or clans, women must be included in the decision-making. Women no longer have to imitate men to be acknowledged; they can rely on their own identity.

In particular, women can suggest solutions to issues that concern them primarily; these suggestions will no doubt reflect the different outlook that women bring to problems. Unfortunately, there are few women in the political or international arenas with enough authority to tackle these problems directly. For example, educational policies are created by men even though the majority of teachers are women.

In developing countries, the education of women is a major key to progress. Often, leaders fail to realize that educating a women brings benefits to the entire family. A productive investment in the social and economic development of an entire society, it is the only way to democracy.

If women can provide innovative solutions to structural problems, then they can also transform the means and modes of exercising power. Women are less prone to see power as a way of balancing conflicts; rather they use power to reconcile and negotiate differences.

Proposed Actions

To cope positively with these changes, the international community should consider the following steps.

1. Entrust women with the establishment of innovative policies on such issues as work and employment.
2. Use the media to educate women.
3. Support the development of microsolutions to projects on issues such as education, where women throughout the world could devote one month in rotation to resolve problems. In short, apply the idea of *Médecin sans Frontières* to education.
4. Call on more women to participate in international organizations. Note that the number of women in positions of responsibility in the EEC is decreasing.
5. Promote a "cause of women," where women address other women on issues. For example, a world organization of women could hold meetings every ten years to share experiences and develop mutually supportive relationships.

The New Decoupled Elite
Ernst-Moritz Lipp

Description of Change

Globalization is producing an elite group of a few million people who live in a perfect international environment. They are part of, yet separate from, the four billion other people now inhabiting the planet. This communication elite is neither able nor compelled to take account of the major differences that exist in culture, living standards, and value systems throughout the world. French author Alain Finkielkraut wrote: "Modern man is accustomed to being a man of one world, so that the global village is his village and the videosphere his fatherland. Today he has cable where he once had roots, and he is incapable of imagining a life worth living outside the communication and consumption networks in which he moves and has his being."

Reasons for Change

Globalization takes many forms. Companies draw inputs from all world markets. Thanks to telecommunications, services can be performed at different locations around the world and then delivered to one central point. This is obvious, of course, with simple auxiliary services, such as maintaining company accounts or keeping bank accounts. But even complex engineering services can, for example, be produced in India, and then delivered to Europe or the United States. From there, the result can be dispatched around the world on diskette or an information superhighway. Today, only business acquisition and service networks still have to be geographically near their consumers—generally at expensive locations. Product development and manufacturing, however, can seek out inexpensive locations around the world. Certain industries, such as financial services, are now global in scale. Some staff are in closer contact with electronic partners around the world than they are with colleagues in the same physical location.

Televisions, computer screens, fax machines, satellite communications, data displays, teleconferences—these create the daily professional environment of a growing group of managers, political decision-makers, traders, analysts, journalists, and engineers who work all over the globe in such industries as financial services, media, telecommunications, and engineering. But basic industries, such as automobile manufacturing, the chemical industry, and electrical engineering, are also integrating their staffs into this global telecommunication system. In their daily jobs and in their private lives, people receive electronic information, images, and messages that have been processed and dispatched by other people with similar backgrounds.

Probable Consequences

The implications of this development are especially clear in the electronic media. Worldwide, a standardized language of picture and text is making greater inroads into the professional and personal lives of most people. Toda, information is processed for a world, not a regional, market. Less information than ever before has only a purely regional cultural reference. Viewers have access to events throughout the world, but are unable to relate them to their own environments. Information arrives in real time; news is live. For many people, only the items coming through by ticker tape from news agencies are really happening. Any event that is not included on the ticker tape does not exist in the world of telecommunications. In this respect, the few global agencies operating worldwide control the market. A case in point is a television team filming an interesting event in Panama, which will not evoke much interest in Washington or Hamburg until a ticker message draws attention to the event. Journalists know this, so the camera team will encourage a news agency correspondent on the spot to report the event worldwide. This is what turns the event into an interesting proposition for television stations. That is the peg that earns the film a slot, ensuring that viewers get to see it.

Worldwide information means not just standardizing the images, but also downsizing the language. Scripts for movies being produced in Japan, France, Germany, or Spain must be written so that they are easily translated into English. The language norm is English. This is not a statement of cultural chauvinism, but of fact.

Another implication is that the decisions made by members of the communication elite are based on incomplete data, even though their information looks perfect in view of the technology they use. This lack of information occurs because the elite has little or no contact with people outside the network. This explains their lack of knowledge of ongoing change in working conditions, social conditions, discrimination, values, and needs in different regions and among different social classes. They are deluded into believing that they have a truly international perspective. They do not, of course, since their partners in the electronic greenhouse around the world have a background similar to their own. This means that the providers of information convey only a small and very thin slice of the reality facing their countries, companies, and fellow citizens. The receivers of information are themselves taken in, believing that the information reflects conditions in the real world.

Proposed Actions

The telecommunications domain and its elite are part of our modern world; they are a fact of life. So the question is less about what we can change (technical progress will only accelerate the trend), than about how we can compensate for any adverse developments. Individual action could be taken on the spot. To ensure a better understanding of the world and improve decision-making by management, a career in business should start at an organization's grass roots. The career employee should be confronted with all living conditions and values. Such an evolution is preferable to a career at the Ecole Nationale d'Administration (ENA), France's elite university, that leads directly from an exclusive college to a top position in business or public service. The subsequent rotation of top managers among such top positions finally leads to isolation from social reality.

Sabbaticals, too, might be used to renew contacts with a firm's technical, economic, and human bases, and hence, contribute toward our knowledge of attitudes, values, and institutions in those countries and regions that are of strategic importance to the organization.

The risks of isolation in a telecommunications elite that loses contact with social reality might also be contained by having decisions made by people as low as possible in the hierarchy. Subsidiarity is a useful principle not only in state systems, such as the EU, but also in companies and organizations. After all, decisions made at the lowest possible level are least likely to come from decision-makers who have lost touch with the social and economic reality around them.

Chapter 4
Ensuring Sustainability in
an Overpopulated World

Introduction

George V. Vassiliou

The accepted objective of all governments is the search for sustainable development. The very concept of sustainability, as Sven Sandstrom points out, has significantly altered the way we look at global economic development. Despite the progress in recent decades, there are more poor people in the world than ever before, five million children die every year from easily preventable diseases, the world's resources are being rapidly depleted, threats to civil and political liberties are ever present, and military expenditures continue to exceed social spending worldwide. The threats from environmental deterioration, social and cultural degradation, and incompetent management of development projects are obvious. The answer can be found in what are called win-win policies, which benefit both the environment and GDP. These include investing in education, accelerating clean air and water sanitation policies, promoting agricultural research, implementing subsidiarity, improving the role of women, controlling population growth, encouraging free trade, and securing better resource management.

The question is how determined are the leaders and governments of the world to implement such policies? While we wait to find out, the problems increase. The prospect of a world with 14 to 15 billion people, as Sergei Kapitza estimates, requires that population growth be controlled by clearly defined demographic policies. As an example, U.V. Rao describes the successful approach adopted in Kerala, where population growth was lowered by improving the education of women.

In the search for sustainable development, all factors interact. Because population growth affects human consumption, they are both seriously endangering the Earth's atmosphere and resources. Therefore, Carl Sagan encourages the use of clean technology and of fission and fusion power, which do not contribute to global warming. Lester Brown warns of the impact of decreasing food production and the need for national assessments of carrying capacity and carefully articulated policies to avoid food shortages that would increase starvation, encourage mass migration, and intensify environmental problems. As Sandra Postel describes, the scarcity of water is already causing national and regional conflicts.

We must therefore change our attitude toward economic development. Economic growth must be made compatible with the protection of the environment. According to Robert Ayres, we begin using and recycling renewable resources more intensively. In addition to GATT, Lutz Hoffman suggests a general agreement on environmental protection and negotiations on mutual environmental measures. Within countries, writes Robert Stavins, governments need to adopt a new approach toward environmental protection. Instead of trying to regulate pollution and environmental destruction, they should encourage environmentally sound behavior among private firms and individuals through incentives, such as pollution taxes, "unit pricing," and tradable permit systems. Our attention should shift from policy formation and legislation to policy implementation, writes Philip Hildebrand. For this purpose, business and industry must be integrated into the environmental policy process by giving them a larger role in the management of the global environment.

Two other contributors further this argument. Steve Hanke and Fred Smith contend that scarce resources should be rationed through market prices and that GATT should not include environmental issues. They support a new environmental vision of ecological privatization, which would place more emphasis on market mechanisms than on government controls. Although many will not agree with this challenging view, it will help stimulate discussion on environmental policy. Scientists can play a very important role in this effort, writes Jeffrey Edington, if they learn to add social consciousness to their scientific and technological efforts.

After decennia of successful economic development for the affluent fifth of humankind, "more difficult times" are coming warns Jacques-Yves Cousteau. Pollution continues unchecked and population growth is greatest in the poorest countries. In addition, the market economy continues to base prices only on product demand, instead of including the amount of energy spent and the renewability or rarity of raw materials and resources used. Our leaders cannot remain passive about the future of our species. We must emphasize decent health care and high-level education. We need a carefully defined "sustainable social development." Any proposed solution is utopian, but Cousteau quotes Federico Mayor, who said: "Utopia today is reality tomorrow. So let us dream utopia."

-1-
The Global Environment
Carl Sagan

Description of Change

The global environment, on which humans and every other species is dependent, is in danger of precipitous change.

Reasons for Change

The exponential increase in the capability of modern technology, the fragility of the Earth's atmosphere, and the lack of foresight in national planning have all contributed to this change.

Probable Consequences

The most damaging effects of these developments are global warming, ozonosphere depletion, and pollution of forestland and groundwater. Secondary consequences include diminished capability for the human immune system, fundamental challenges to primary photosynthetic producers, declining agricultural productivity or the need for emigration of agriculture, accelerated deforestation, eventual inundation of islands and coastlines by rising sea levels, and massive increases in environmental refugees.

Proposed Actions

Future policy must take into account the fact that effluents injected into the atmosphere continue to affect the environment for decades or centuries. Thus, prudent preventive measures should be taken before the impact of these environmental factors grow more obvious. As with military strategy, you should plan for the worst an enemy is capable of and not its likeliest course of action.

Under the Montreal Protocol and subsequent international agreement, the use of CFCs and other principal depletents of the ozonosphere are being phased out. Next, we need to develop technologies for the more efficient use of fossil fuels and for alternative energy sources, particularly solar electric converters, wind turbines, hydrogen fuel, and biomass converters. Such steps have many subsidiary benefits, including the elimination of oil spills. But these policies are difficult to implement because of the economic and political power wielded by the fossil fuel (coal, oil, natural gas) and allied (automobile, chemical) industries in all industrial nations. In addition, although fission and fusion power are energy technologies that do not contribute to global warming, the first is considered dangerous for other reasons and the second is unlikely to be commercially available before greenhouse warming has serious global consequences. A related issue, in developing countries, is the need to develop appropriate nonpolluting technology.

-2-
The Evolving Concept of Sustainability

Sven Sandstrom

Description of Change

The concept of sustainability has significantly changed the way we look at global economic development in both richer and poorer countries. Since the late 1980s, there is a growing awareness of the importance of promoting lasting development that takes into account the needs of the future as well as the present. At the Earth Summit in Rio, the phrase sustainable development became a vital instrument in focusing attention on the need for better environmental stewardship. The concept of sustainability, however, goes well beyond the protection of natural resources. It also encompasses human welfare in the broadest sense, including education, health, equality of opportunity, and political and civil rights. Economic growth, of course, remains fundamental to development, but we must be more aware of issues pertaining to the quality—and therefore the sustainability—of growth.

Reasons for Change

We are now able to analyze what has and has not worked and what challenges remain. Sustainability looms large as we look back and forward:

- In the past generation, many more people have been lifted out of poverty than in any equivalent period in history. And yet, the dramatic increase in population growth has produced more very poor people than ever before in history.
- Average life expectancy has increased more in the past forty years than in all of previous human history. And yet, five million children still die every year from easily preventable diseases.
- Food production worldwide has doubled in the past 25 years (something never before achieved). And yet, it needs to double again in the next forty years—and almost all experts believe this will be an even bigger task.

- During the past decade, clean water has been brought for the first time to more people (more than one billion) than in any decade in history. And yet, with the wasteful use of water and rapidly rising unit costs, the number that remain unserved (one billion) may rise.
- The unprecedented growth of industry and energy use has improved living standards for most of the world's population. And yet, more than 1.3 billion people suffer from dangerously high levels of air pollution, and we may well raise the average temperature on Earth over the next century.
- Democracy is now enjoyed by more countries than ever before, with potential benefits to human welfare. And yet, the threats to civil and political liberties are as great as ever, and global military expenditures continue to exceed social spending.

Probable Consequences

If these and other issues related to sustainability are not addressed, long-term global economic and social progress will be jeopardized. In particular, there are three major threats:

- The threat from environmental deterioration. Too much of our increased income has come at the expense of depleted and degraded natural resources. Sustainability argues that exploitation of natural resources should be conducted so that vital ecosystems are preserved and the overall productive capacity of an economy continues to rise. Research is shedding important insights on how this can be done.
- The threat from social and cultural degradation. Too much economic growth has come at the expense of local community structures and values. Although the rights and values of local people are more respected than ever before, this process needs to be greatly expanded and accelerated. A more participatory form of development is vitally important. Put simply, people need to be given more of a voice in development. Figuring out how to do this effectively—how to assess the social, economic, and environmental aspects of development projects and policies remains an important task for the coming decade.
- The threat from what we might term "weak ownership." Many development projects have started well, but did not last because of a lack of commitment and ownership on the part of local communities, governments, and development agencies. At the project level, this is well documented. Whether in water sup-

ply, transport infrastructure, irrigation, or health investments, the lack of follow-through (including basic operation and maintenance work) is a primary explanation of project failure. But this is also true at the macroeconomic policy level. Although some argue that the market-friendly reform programs of the 1980s and early 1990s failed, evidence suggests that they have succeeded when systematically implemented. Where they have failed, lack of follow-through is almost always the cause.

Proposed Actions

There is a growing consensus on the policies required to move us in the direction of sustainability. These are sometimes called win-win policies in that they benefit both the environment and income growth. They are easy in the sense that they are clearly desirable, although sadly they are often not followed in practice for various political and financial reasons. Such policies include:

- Investing in education, particularly the education of girls in the developing countries.
- Accelerating the provision of clean air, water, sanitation, and health services to improve living standards.
- Promoting agricultural research and extension, which can boost productivity in environmentally sound ways.
- Empowering and involving local communities so that they can participate in the decisions and investments affecting their long-term interests.
- Promoting the role of women, so often the principal managers of resources.
- Implementing programs that slow the population growth rate, which is placing unsustainable pressure on natural resource use.
- Removing price distortions, including subsidies, that encourage overconsumption of natural resources.
- Opening economies to freer trade to encourage clearer, more productive technologies.
- Clarifying property rights as an incentive to better resource management.

In the past, the big question used to be: Can development be sustainable? Now that everyone agrees that it can be, the question is: Will development be sustainable? The answer will depend on the political and financial commitment of both the developed and developing countries. Increased international cooperation is the key to success.

The Impact of the
Demographic Transition

Sergei Kapitza

Description of Change

Of all global issues, those of demography are of primary significance. All of the factors that contribute to our development are reflected in the numbers of people in their world and their movements among nations and regions. Thus, demographic data express in a concise and quantitative way the results of all of the social, economic, and cultural processes that comprise history. The message of these numbers must be read carefully, if we expect to understand both our present predicament and our future in terms of development, environmental impact, and stability.

For several generations, the world's population grew so rapidly that it constituted a demographic explosion. Although some alarmists have an image of seemingly unlimited growth with apocalyptic scenarios for the future, what in reality is happening is a demographic transition. The present world population of 5.7 billion is growing at a rate of 1.7 percent per year. In a decade, the absolute annual growth will reach an expected maximum of 100 million per year; this will be followed by a rapid decrease as the population explosion comes to an end. In the next one hundred years, the world's population will grow and then stabilize at 13 to 15 billion people. This transformation, accompanied by the rapid growth of towns, has already occurred in the developed countries and is now taking place worldwide. In our modern interdependent and interconnected world, this transition will occur even more rapidly than it did in past, as, for example, in Europe, when it started at the beginning of the nineteenth century.

If human history is viewed in terms of millions of years of growth, the fundamental pattern of development is now changing. Probably never before has humanity, as an entity, experienced such an event.

Reasons for Change

These gross changes represent a systemic change in the paradigm of human population growth. It is guided by the invisible hand of social, economic, political, and environmental factors. This universal change from rapidly accelerating to decreasing growth rates happens in all populations when the relative growth rate reaches a certain maximum value. For the global population, this transition is the culmination of very long-term growth. A simplistic Malthusian explanation of this transition in terms of limited resources is not tenable. Today, this transition is at the core of demographic studies and requires intensive interdisciplinary study and worldwide debate.

Probable Consequences

As developing countries experience the stage of rapid growth, its younger and active members can be either the instrument for economic development or a force for social instability. When the now-developed countries passed through this stage, the economic development of Europe led to massive waves of emigration to the New World. In his seminal study, "The Economic Consequences of Peace" (1920), Keynes argued that Europe's rapid population growth was a major contributing factor to the instability that led to World War I. Today, such tensions are growing in the developing world and can similarly become a menace to global security.

As the developed world experiences the later stage of the demographic transition, the age structure drastically changes. With the decline in the birth rate and the growth of life expectancy, the population is to a great extent dominated by the older generation. This places increasing burdens on social and medical services. The profound change in the age profile, along with massive urbanization, led to major changes in values, family life, and criteria for growth and success in society.

Finally, the rate of change during the transition is so rapid that neither the individual nor society has time to adapt. This is the basic reason for much of the strain and strife in the modern world.

Proposed Actions

The demographic indicators are a message for action. In the first place, appropriate demographic policies should be defined and pursued as part of national social and economic development. At present, most governments do have such programs, but a detailed discussion of these issues is beyond the scope of this paper. The cases of India, China, and Indonesia show the results of these programs. As seen on a long time global scale, both food and energy are growing faster than the population. The available resources of land and energy, in spite of all inequalities in distribution, are sufficient to support at least 20 to 25 billion people, more than the 15 billion expected. In this stabilized world, sustainability will ultimately depend on the security of societies, rather than their resources.

Ethnic upheavals, economic and social crises, local famines, instability and conflicts—even wars—are probably unavoidable, although all should be done to mitigate them. The international community must prevent these local conflicts from escalating into large-scale regional or ultimately global conflicts, as happened previously in Europe. Although the end of the Cold War meant that an immediate global all-out conflict had been avoided, a major conflagration in the developing world is still possible. The demographic pressures exerted on Europe by the countries of North Africa and the Near East are of concern. With its rapid and often disparate growth, Africa is heading for a period of turmoil, where tribal and ethnic differences are gaining ground.

Demographic factors are having a profound effect on social and economic conditions in the former Soviet Union. As its population has stabilized, Russia is presently experiencing a pronounced drop in the birth rate. This is enhanced by the economic crisis, the deteriorating environment, and inadequate health services. Thus the life expectancy for men has dropped to less than sixty years. The demographic situation is further complicated by influxes of ethnic Russians from former Soviet Republics and economic and political refugees.

When a population passes from growth to a stabilized limit, new criteria and values emerge toward consumption and the environment. This problem of socially relevant aims should be recognized, interpreted, and acted upon. As an example, the military establishments must think in terms of quality rather than sheer numbers. Educational and health systems are challenged by the need to improve as the quality of people's lives becomes the dominant factor in the foreseeable future. Of growing importance is the responsibility of the media.

Giving such prominence to demographic factors may seem to be a one-sided—and even simplistic—approach to complex social and political events. But for many years, demography was not discussed in debates on global problems. Today, this attitude has changed. Demographic factors reveal the powerful external forces that collectively have a great influence on regional development and, hence, our attitude toward the growth of each country. In our interconnected and interdependent world, no one can escape from the impact of our surroundings; this is what really leads us to recognize that we now all belong to the same global village. We have to understand and take into account this new connectedness. It is simple minded to imagine that the course of events can be fundamentally changed; their magnitude is too great and the speed of occurrence alarming. But we can and should ensure global stability during these imminent changes.

Of all long-term issues, global security is the primary one. It should be of special concern for the international community. Only when the demographic security of the world can be ensured, can issues of development and sustainability, of environmental impact be dealt with, for only in a stable world can these common long-term problems be properly resolved.

-4-
Population Control:
A Critical Factor in
Economic Development
U.V. Rao

Description of Change

Today's most important challenge is sustainable development. Unbelievable and unprecedented events have torn the fabric of history. Radical political changes, the end of the Cold War, and widespread improvements in economic policies have led to globalization.

Unfortunately, the reform process in developing countries has not yet addressed the issues of education, health care, and most importantly, population explosion. Rapid population growth is a crucial concern in developing countries, which are caught in a Malthusian trap—the population has overtaken the Earth's ability to meet its needs.

The world's population has doubled since 1950; the proportion living in the poorest developing regions rose from 33 percent in 1950 to 75 percent in 1985. The average population growth rate in developing regions in the period from 1950 to 1975 increased to more than 2 percent, twice that of the developed world. By the year 2015, nearly 84 percent of the world's population will be living in developing countries.

Reasons for Change

Population growth in the developing countries was fueled by rapidly falling mortality rates and improved life expectancy; both resulted from better living conditions. Although rising incomes and falling mortality are incentives for lowering fertility and slowing population growth, this demographic transition is not always orderly. Differences in the age structure between the industrialized and the developing worlds contribute to further disparity in population growth. In the developing countries, far more people are in the young age group, which swells the number of children born every year.

Probable Consequences

Large populations and poverty reinforce each other in a number of ways. Low wages, inadequate education, high infant mortality, high fertility—all of these factors lead to rapid population growth. Just 15 percent of the world's population enjoys 72 percent of the world's wealth. Despite the vast opportunities created by the technological revolutions of the twentieth century, more than one billion people, one-fifth of the world's population, live on less than one dollar a day, a standard of living that Western Europe and the United States attained two hundred years ago. Today, nearly 80 percent of the world's population contributes less than 20 percent to global output; their share in world trade is just 17 percent.

Rapid population growth has caused serious concern about the outlook for economic growth, human development, and the environment in developing countries. Although not a threat in every country, it is a critical issue for many developing countries.

The effect of population growth on the natural environment is another problem. Rapid population growth burns nature's candle at both ends—generating more consumers while reducing natural property. The pressure of population can raise agricultural demand, which leads to the abuse of marginal land and other natural resources, deforestation, congestion of urban areas, and pressures on the urban infrastructure.

Statistics recently released by the Worldwide Fund for Nature show the extent of the problem. During the mere 12 days of the ECO conference, 600 to 900 plants and animal species became extinct around the world and the world's population grew by 33 million people.

Proposed Actions

What must developing countries do if the productivity and well-being of their people are to increase rapidly during the coming years?

Family Planning

There is a consensus on the need for birth control and safe contraception. Some progress in this area has already been achieved. Effective family planning programs can make people aware of the private and social costs of high fertility and encourage couples to reduce family size. However, it is necessary that these measures reach the lowest strata of population in remote villages.

Female Literacy

Equally important is augmenting female literacy and pushing towards a radical change in the power equation in man-woman relationships.

Women have always been treated as reproducers; their independent individual identities have been ignored. Empowerment for women should include the right to make decisions about reproduction and the right to parental and spousal property. Evidence from India shows that high literacy rates, especially high female literacy rates, are associated with low rates of population growth, infant mortality, and maternal mortality, as well as a higher life expectancy.

Kerala Example

Kerala, the southern state of India, illustrates the importance of education in population control. Kerala has achieved an unusually high literacy rate. This, coupled with almost total female literacy, resulted in delayed marriages, control of marital fertility, and the consequent adoption of a two-child norm. This led to lower population growth than the national average of 2.1 percent from 1981 to 1991.

Infrastructure Development

The biggest obstacle for the poor in gaining access to health services is the lack of infrastructure, especially in rural areas. The urban bias affects both quantity and quality. This requires shifts in spending priorities; greater efficiency and better targeting of expenditures, and, in some cases, greater resource mobilization. The challenge to policy makers is to exploit the complementarities between state and market.

Resource Mobilization

Various avenues must be tapped to improve resources for population control programs. In view of the paucity of domestic resources, vigorous efforts are necessary to attract external and private sources for financing educational programs, especially priority programs, without compromising a country's basic population policies.

Summary

For the developing world, the task is formidable. Decades of rapid growth will be needed to make inroads on poverty. Yet the opportunity for rapid development is greater today than at any time in history.

Insufficient Grain
and Food Resources

Lester R. Brown

Description of Change

The rate of growth of the world's grain harvest has slowed since the mid-1980s. Between 1950 and 1984, world grain production expanded 2.6-fold, outstripping population growth by a wide margin and raising the grain harvested per person by 40 percent. It rose from 247 kilograms per person in 1950 to 346 kilograms in 1984. Since 1984, however, grain output per person fell by 11 percent, and there is no evidence of growth returning. It was back down to 318 kilograms in 1993.

Grain is by far the most important good, amounting to more than half of all human caloric intake when consumed directly and an even more significant amount when also used as animal feed and then consumed as meat. Growth in the harvests of other foods has slowed as well. From 1950 to 1979, the soybean harvest multiplied more than fivefold, expanding at nearly 6 percent per year. But during the following 13 years, output expanded little more than 1 percent per year. Soybean output per person tripled between 1950 and 1979; since then, it has remained below the 1979 level.

Similarly, meat production per person has remained stable. For the last seven years, it has remained at about 32 kilograms per person. Compare this with the previous four decades, in which growth in world meat production had been one of the most predictable trends. And the most dramatic slowdown of all has come in the world's fisheries. After constant growth from 22 million tons in 1950 to 100 million tons in 1989, the catch seems to have hit a ceiling. Indeed, marine scientists had long ago warned that such a limit would eventually be reached. Today, all 17 of the world's major fishing areas are harvested at or beyond their capacity; 9 are in decline.

Reasons for Change

In the early 1950s farmers in most countries began to make use of long-standing agricultural technologies. In the past four decades, however, no new technologies were developed to provide further quantum leaps in world food output. The pipeline of new yield-raising agricultural technologies has not run dry, but the flow has slowed to a trickle.

The engine driving the rise in grain yields from mid-century onward was the expanding use of fertilizer—specifically, the synergistic interactions of rising fertilizer use, expanding irrigation, and the spread of grain varieties that were responsive to ever-heavier applications of fertilizer. From 1950 to 1984 fertilizer use climbed from 14 million to 126 million tons. During this time, each additional ton of fertilizer applied boosted grain output by nine tons.

But 1984 was the last year in which a large increase in fertilizer use led to a comparable gain in world grain output. During the next five years, farmers continued to use more fertilizer, but their crops did not respond as much. Each additional ton of fertilizer used raised grain output by less than two tons. Given such a weak response, applying more fertilizer was clearly not a money-making proposition. Farmers' reaction, both predictable and rational, was to use less. Between 1989 and 1993, they cut fertilizer use by 12 percent. Even excluding the precipitous drop in usage in the former Soviet Union following economic reforms, usage elsewhere dropped by 3 percent.

The phenomenal growth in fertilizer use from 1950 to 1984 was the result of record growth in irrigation from 1950 to 1978. Since then, however, irrigation has expanded at scarcely one percent per year. And we have not developed newer varieties of grain that respond to even heavier applications of fertilizer. Restoring rapid, sustained growth in fertilizer use and, hence, in the world grain harvest, is not likely unless someone can develop varieties of wheat, corn, and rice that are far more responsive to fertilizer than those now available.

In addition to the drop in food production, water is growing more scarce. Today, 26 countries, home to some 230 million people, are water scarce—their populations have surpassed the level that can be sustained comfortably by the water available. Some are using groundwater from "fossil" aquifers, underground reservoirs that today receive little replenishment from rainfall. Thus, they are essentially nonrenewable. Since current irrigation systems were built or placed near the most easily accessible water sources, future additions must come from less accessible and more costly sources. Moreover, each year some irrigated land is lost to salting and waterlogging.

Probable Consequences

Food prices are likely to rise over the next few decades. From late August to early November of 1993, for example, the world market price of rice doubled. Wheat and seafood prices have risen as well. Such trends will shift consumption away from meat, which requires several kilograms of grain as feed for each kilogram of meat produced. More seriously, however, rising prices will diminish the ability of the poor to afford adequate diets.

Imports of grain will become a basic source of nourishment for large numbers of people. For some countries, such as Egypt, this is logical, since the thin ribbon of arable land around the Nile is not enough to sustain that country's large population. But even though the situation may be logical, it is likely to be threatening, especially if competition for exportable supplies tightens.

Others have already noted that if China experiences a 10 percent drop in its rice harvest, no country in the world can supply exports of rice to make up the difference. Indeed, China's grain consumption will increase as the population increases by 490 million people by the year 2030 and as economic growth leads to increased affluence that enables people to buy more meat. Industrialization there is transforming croplands into buildings, roads, and pavement, with the amount of grain-harvested land currently falling at one percent per year. Since grain yields per hectare are already quite high—in fact, Chinese rice yields are almost as high as those of Japan—little increase may be possible. It is therefore quickly evident that China may not be able to support its own food needs. With its population headed past a billion and a half people, its import requirements could surpass all of the world's current exports of grain. If grain exports become scarce, it could induce outflows of refugees from food deficit countries, exacerbate environmental problems as farmers bring marginal land into production, and result in widespread hunger.

Proposed Actions

There is an urgent need for national and global assessments of carrying capacity. Each country will depend on that assessment to know how much it to import. Otherwise, there is a real risk that countries will blindly overrun their food carrying capacity, thereby developing massive deficits that will collectively exceed the world's exportable supplies.

Further, given the limits of the Earth's carrying capacity, every national government needs a carefully articulated population policy, one that takes into account its carrying capacity at whatever consumption level citizens decide on. With adequate supplies of food essential to the security both of individual people and national governments, agricultural and population policies are very much within the domain of national security policies; they may, in fact, be moving to the center of security issues. It is time to elevate population policies and carrying capacity assessments in national capitals everywhere.

-6-
Insufficient
Water Resources

Sandra Postel

Description of Change

Water scarcity is rapidly emerging as a serious constraint to raising living standards and meeting human needs in many parts of the world. Signs of scarcity and unsustainable water use are becoming more prevalent, even as human demands on water resources—for food, material goods, and household uses—rise inexorably. Globally, water use has more than tripled since 1950, and the answer to this rising demand has been to build more and larger water supply projects, especially dams and river diversions. This approach has created an illusion of plenty, even in water-short areas, and encouraged highly unsustainable levels of consumption.

One of the clearest signs of impending water problems is the increasing number of countries in which the population has surpassed the level that can comfortably be sustained by available water supplies. Water is a renewable resource, but it is also a finite one. The hydrologic cycle makes available only so much in a given location. As a result, the amount of water available per person decreases in direct proportion to population growth. Globally, for example, per capita supplies are one-third lower today than in 1970, strictly due to the 1.8 billion people added to the planet since then.

As a general rule, hydrologists consider countries water scarce when the amount of water made available by the natural water cycle drops below 1,000 cubic meters per person per year. Below this level, water becomes a severe constraint on food production, economic development, and the protection of natural ecosystems. Countries in this situation may also become heavily dependent on rivers flowing in from upstream neighbors, potentially giving rise to regional tensions or conflict.

Already, 27 countries fall into the water-scarce category, excluding the newly independent countries of the former Soviet Union. Africa currently has 12 such countries, the most of any continent. The Middle East is the most concentrated region of water scarcity, with 9 out of 14 countries in the water-scarce category. Moreover, the populations of 17 of the 21 water-scarce countries in Africa and the Middle East are projected to double within 30 years, greatly compounding water-scarcity problems.

In addition to the population-water balance, there are many physical signs of water scarcity and overuse. Falling water tables from the over-pumping of groundwater are now pervasive in many parts of the world, from the north China plain to the valley of Mexico and parts of Thailand, India, Indonesia, north Africa, the western United States, and the Middle East. In some areas, water use depends on mining fossil aquifers, underground reserves that may be hundreds or even thousands of years old and that receive very little replenishment from rainfall today. Saudi Arabia depends on fossil groundwater to meet 75 percent of its water needs, and hydrologists project that these sources may be depleted within 50 years. In the Great Plains of the United States, many farmers depend on Ogallala, a fossil aquifer that is also undergoing depletion in some areas. Texas farmers have depleted their portion of the Ogallala by 75 percent.

Finally, a sadly deteriorating aquatic environment signals that human use and management of water has greatly overstepped nature's limits. Wetlands are disappearing, fish and wildlife are declining in numbers, and many unique natural areas, such as south Florida's Everglades, Central Asia's Aral Sea, Spain's Doñana wetlands, and Brazil's Pantanal, are greatly at risk from existing or planned water development.

Reasons for Change

For most of modern human history, water policy, planning, and engineering were based on a strictly supply-side approach to water management. A need for more water was created or perceived and the task then became how to find new supplies to fill that need. Governments abetted this basic approach by heavily subsidizing water development. Although large dams and river diversions were often built at taxpayer expense, the beneficiaries of these projects repaid only a tiny fraction of the cost. As of the mid-1980s, for example, farmers in California's rich agricultural heartland had repaid only 4 percent of the total capital cost of the federally built Central Valley Project. Similarly, in developing countries, farmers rarely pay more than 15 percent of the real cost of the water they use.

Such undercharging encourages overconsumption, the planting of water-intensive crops in water-scarce areas, and neglect of water-conserving practices. A host of more efficient irrigation, industrial, and household water-use technologies and methods exist, but there is little incentive to use them when water is underpriced.

Equity concerns have also played too small a role in water development and use. All too often, water development has benefited the rich more than the poor, and sometimes has even occurred at the expense of the poor. As a result, vast discrepancies in water use exist between rich and poor, both within and between countries. A family in the western United States, for example, may use 20 times more water than a family in rural Kenya, even though the two live in equally dry climates.

There are also ethical roots to present water problems. Modern societies have disconnected from water's basic attribute as the source of life on Earth. By and large, we have come to view water strictly as a resource to be dammed, drained, and diverted for human consumption. There has been little recognition of the need to live within water's limits and to protect the integrity of the aquatic environment that all life depends on.

Probable Consequences

Water scarcity and the failure to live within water's limits will have serious consequences for food production, economic development, and the environment. Already, a historic reversal has occurred in the relationship between population and irrigated area. For most of modern history, irrigated areas grew faster than did population, helping food production keep up with rising demands. But per capita irrigated areas peaked in 1978 and have been falling more or less since then. Rising costs for expanding irrigation capacity, spreading salinization of cropland, groundwater depletion, and mounting environmental concerns have slowed irrigation's expansion to a rate below that of population, a trend that is unlikely to reverse any time soon. With irrigated lands accounting for more than one-third of the global harvest, this raises serious concerns about future food security.

With new water supplies becoming increasingly scarce, national and regional competition for limited supplies will increase, possibly turning water scarcity into a source of conflict. Tensions over water are high in all three of the major river basins in the Middle East—the Nile, the Tigris-Euphrates, and the Jordan—and as populations and demands for water continue to rise, those tensions will likely worsen. A less-talked-about hot spot is Central Asia, where five countries—newly independent from the former Soviet Union—must not only deal with the Aral Sea crisis, but reallocate and equitably share the scarce waters in that basin.

Cities and farms in the same region will increasingly compete for water as well. Active water markets in the western United States are now transferring water between sectors, typically from agriculture to the cities, where water prices are higher. Although a good bit of this reallocation makes economic sense, no built-in mechanisms ensure either that too much valuable farmland is not removed from production or that the environment will be allocated enough water to remain healthy.

Rising water prices are, of course, an inevitable consequence of increasing scarcity. This will have the beneficial effect of encouraging conservation and greater efficiency. Farmers will adopt more thrifty irrigation techniques and shift their cropping patterns to remain profitable. Cities and industries, which will turn to recycling and reuse, will adopt more efficient management practices. A possible consequence of rising water prices as well, however, is rising food costs that could further harm the one billion poorest people, who attempt to survive on scarcely one dollar per day.

Proposed Actions

In a world of increasing scarcity, sustainable water use hinges on greater efficiency, equity, and ecosystem protection. In addition, efforts to slow the growth in both per capita water demand and the size of the human population will be critical to achieving water balance. Some key steps toward these ends include:

- Greatly reducing water subsidies so that water users begin paying prices that reflect the water's true value. As long as water costs remain artificially low, water users will have little incentive to invest in conservation and efficiency measures.
- Making the protection of aquatic ecosystems a central goal of water development and management. In most cases, this will involve setting minimum flow requirements for rivers and streams, and ensuring that those levels are met.
- Ensuring that new water development projects benefit the poorest of the poor in the region concerned.
- Enabling markets to help reallocate water to achieve more economically rational patterns of water use. Maintenance of the health of the aquatic environment, however, cannot be left to the marketplace alone.
- Setting water-efficiency standards for various uses of water in agriculture, industry, and households.
- Placing strategies to manage water demand through conservation and efficiency on an equal footing with those to increase the supply. Saving water through increased efficiency, in effect, creates a new source of supply, and in most cases is now more economical and environmentally sound than new water development projects.
- Promoting greater public education and awareness about water problems and issues, and ensuring that those affected by water projects are included in the planning process from the outset.

- Promoting cooperation and the development of water-sharing agreements among nations within water-scarce river basins.

Water scarcity and the growing imbalance between human demands and available supplies pose multiple threats to human well-being. The basic security provided by adequate food, safe drinking water, a healthy environment, and peace with neighbors are all at risk as water scarcity and the consequences of management unfold. Serious and collective action is urgently needed to achieve more sustainable patterns of water use.

-7-
Overcoming the
"Cowboy Economy"
Robert U. Ayres

Description of Change

The "cowboy economy," which is based on exploitation of nonrenewable natural resources, is no longer viable. It will be replaced during the next half century by a "spaceship economy." This will be based on far more intensive use of existing—already mined—stocks of nonrenewable resources, which must be reused and recycled far more efficiently than is now the case. In addition, this new economy will eventually depend largely on renewable resources for energy. The strategy for economic growth will necessarily shift from increasing labor productivity to increasing resource and capital productivity.

Reasons for Change

Until the present century, there were still vast underpopulated areas in the world, including Africa, the Middle East, Australia, the Western Hemisphere, and Siberia. These areas still had easily exploitable natural resources that permitted rapid economic growth. Inexpensive resources were used to increase labor productivity. The short-term objective of economic development was conquest and exploitation of nature for human purposes. The private sector could be relied on to cut forests and clear land for agriculture and to find and utilize mineral resources for short-term consumptive purposes. The most effective economic development strategy for governments was to underwrite education and to encourage resource discovery and exploitation by the private sector, using tax policy and direct subsidies, and to build harbors, canals, railways, and roads, More recently, governments also provide electric power and telecommunications services to remote areas. This syndrome has been called, rather simplistically, the "cowboy economy."

However, since the middle of the twentieth century, most of these empty lands have been settled; those that remain are inhospitable, being either too cold (Canada, Siberia), too dry (the equatorial deserts, central Australia), or too fragile and infertile (the tropical rain forests) to support large human populations. Already, it is estimated that humans utilize directly, for economic purposes, more than 50 percent of all global biomass. The unexploited fraction consists largely of tropical rain forests and oceanic flora. Neither is readily usable as such, albeit both are critically important for biodiversity, sustaining the global climate, and recycling scarce nutrient elements, such as nitrogen and phosphorus. In short, the potential for further global economic growth along "cowboy" lines is extremely limited.

To make matters worse, the "northern" development strategy of using cheap resources to increase labor productivity has backfired. Europe is in the throes of an unemployment crisis. Generous social programs have been funded by taxes on income, consumption, and, above all, on labor. In short, everything except natural resource use and pollution is heavily taxed. Some macroeconomists still believe that the problem is temporary and that increasing world trade will create more jobs everywhere. But the evidence is clear that manufacturers are shifting investment and employment very rapidly to Southeast Asia. While the markets for goods and services in Asia will undoubtedly grow rapidly for some time to come, there is no credible evidence that any significant share of this demand will be met by exports from Europe or the United States. On the contrary, Asia confidently expects to continue its economic growth by exporting more and more consumer goods to the West, displacing even more manufacturing workers in the process. Capital goods needed by China and Southeast Asia will be supplied increasingly by Japan and Korea. The shift of manufacturing employment away from Europe is virtually inevitable, given the existing labor costs and tax structures.

Medical advances and improved public health have reduced death rates everywhere. But human fertility remains high, and the population in the poorest countries continues to grow much too fast. Direct government intervention, as in China, depends on very strong and virtually totalitarian central authority. Most major religions still encourage unrestrained childbearing. The only viable global strategy for population control, barring a global plague comparable to the "Black Death," is voluntary restraint. This would automatically result from higher standards of education and increased economic security. The latter requires continued economic growth in the so-called Third World.

To grow, the developing and less developed countries will need immense amounts of capital for infrastructure, especially roads, water supply, sewage disposal, electric power, schools, and health services for their exploding populations. It must be remembered that the school-age population rivals the working population in some of these countries. This needed capital will not be available from private investors (at least under current conditions). A radically new economic development strategy for both developing and industrialized countries is needed.

Probable Consequences

Although the private sector can still be relied on to find and exploit any remaining unexploited stocks of natural resources for short-term benefit, the resource-exploitative "cowboy" model is no longer a sufficient basis for sustained long-term economic growth, either for firms or nations. In the rich industrialized West, it will be necessary to sharply reduce the per capita use of land, water, biomass (e.g., wood), mineral fuels, and other extractive resources. Experts who have examined these issues, most notably the members of the World Commission on Environment and Development, now believe that to allow some room for increased per capita use of these material/energy resources in the poorer countries, the rich industrialized countries will have to cut back aggregate use by as much as 90 percent over the next half century. This implies either a reduced standard of living or a truly radical change in the structure of demand and a sharp increase in the efficiency of materials and energy use.

This is the "green challenge." It is not an impossible goal, given the political will to succeed, but it cannot be met by "business as usual." It means that many existing materials-intensive industries and firms will have to change direction in fundamental ways. Emphasis on maximizing the production and sale of material products—and, especially, of mineral fuels—will have to give way to emphasis on maximizing the production and sale of nonmaterial services, with minimal consumptive use, and consequent emissions and losses of energy and materials. Companies will increasingly learn to retain title to their ever more valuable material resources and capital equipment, and to sell services, rather than products. Extractive industries will necessarily become far less important. In the industrialized world, they will have to "extract" most of their material input requirements from renewable resources or from recycling their own worn-out products or former wastes. Agriculture will have to become much more conservationist and less chemical intensive. All sectors will become much more knowledge intensive and much less energy/materials intensive.

Proposed Actions

Firms, especially multinationals, can begin to restructure themselves to fit better into this long-term picture. The use of "risk-benefit analysis," life-cycle analysis (LCA), and materials balance accounting (MBA) methodologies will help identify "win-win" opportunities. Governments can, and must, create appropriate ground rules and incentives to provide more opportunities for firms to do what needs to be done. For instance, the present governmental pattern of heavily taxing labor to pay for social services and subsidizing materials/energy extraction and use must be altered. It has encouraged enormous increases in labor productivity over the past century, but the growing unemployment problems suggests that this mode of taxation is unsustainable. Business must persuade governments to finance necessary social services not by taxing labor, which discourages job creation, but by taxing energy and resource use, which will encourage increased resource productivity. In short, business should support increased resource/energy taxes and the elimination of energy subsidies.

Other government actions are also needed. Trade barriers may be required to encourage environmental protection, despite contrary pressures from free traders. Utility regulation must be altered to encourage resource conservation. By the same token, domestic transportation and utility services, even at the household level, should be provided by a combination of competitive on-call service firms, rather than by private ownership of cars and major appliances. This trend could be encouraged by a mix of road taxes, energy taxes, vehicle licensing, insurance regulation, emissions controls, and other means. The purpose is to emphasize efficient system design that minimizes lifetime energy and materials costs, including waste disposal costs.

In the long run, of course, the concept of disposing of wastes will have to change. The private sector must give in to source reduction, rather than waste treatment, burial, or disposal by even less acceptable means. Source reduction begins with product design. Rather than designing products to be sold (for others to use and dispose of), the entire life cycle of the product must be taken into account. In summary, although manufacturing firms are not yet required to "take back' their worn-out products, there is increasing pressure to legislate and enforce this approach. Those firms that prepare soonest for taking full life cycle responsibility for their products will survive and prosper in the coming decades. Those firms that try to resist the tide, like King Canute, will be overwhelmed.

-8-
Making Ecology and Economy Compatible
Lutz Hoffmann

Description of Change

Although environmental degradation is a worldwide process, only recently did we learn of its extent in the former socialist countries. Progress in international understanding and agreement on joined action to protect the environment is very slow, yet the implications for humanity become progressively more severe.

Reasons for Change

The lack of joint international action on environmental issues is a result of the misconception in both industrialized and developing countries that economic growth and preservation of the environment are incompatible. The gap between action necessary to contain environmental degradation and the preparedness to implement that action is ever widening.

Probable Consequences

The lack of action on environmental issues is similar to using a company's capital stock without reinvestment. At some point, production will falter and the financial burden of rebuilding the capital stock will be too high. The company will go bankrupt. Similarly, the world economy will experience major difficulties if the environment is not continuously restored. Eventually, environmental degradation will become so extensive that significant reductions in consumption will be necessary to rebuild a viable environment.

Proposed Actions

All nations must realize that degradation of the environment makes all economic growth illusionary. The international community should follow the GATT model by establishing a general agreement on environmental protection (GAEP) and entering into negotiations on mutual measures. Many of the principles of GATT, like reciprocity, most favored nation rules, or arbitration could be applied in such a system. Action is urgently required. Because the effects of environmental degradation only become visible years after the problems begin, the situation may already be more severe than we know.

-9-
The Greening of GATT: A Conflict of Visions

Steve H. Hanke
Fred L. Smith

Description of Change

The rules or guidelines for conducting most international commercial relations are codified in GATT, whose underlying tenets are the efficacy of an unimpeded market economy and thus, free trade. Under GATT, trade can only be restricted by a tariff that is imposed on a geographically nondiscriminatory basis. In short, the tariff rates offered to the most favored nation should be offered to all. This is the most favored nation (MFN) clause.

Two exceptions to the MFN clause are permitted: the customs union and the free trade area. The customs union is an institutional arrangement in which members do not impose tariffs on trade with other members, but all members impose a common tariff vis-à-vis nonmembers. The free trade area is similar to the customs union, except that there is no requirement for a common external tariff vis-à-vis nonmembers.

The Uruguay Round represented the eighth GATT-sponsored multilateral trade negotiations. With the 116 countries that make up 85 percent of world trade participating, the Uruguay Round was effectively completed on December 15, 1993.

GATT members agreed not only to lower tariffs on merchandise trade, but also to integrate into GATT areas of trade and investment that had not been subject to effective GATT discipline. These include agriculture, textiles, trade in services, investment, and intellectual property rights. The Uruguay Round also made progress in reforming multilateral dispute settlement procedures and other multilateral trade rules, including those dealing with nontariff measures. In addition, members of GATT agreed to establish a multilateral organization, the World Trade Organization (WTO), to enforce these new agreements.

The successful completion of the Uruguay Round's trade liberalization initiatives will result in a major boost to the world economy. Preliminary studies suggest that the benefit to the U.S. economy alone will amount to one percent of GDP after all the Uruguay Round tariff cuts are phased in.

If this were the end of the GATT story, it would indeed be blissful. After all, the benefits of international specialization, which Adam Smith enumerated in *The Wealth of Nations* (1776), would be further realized and international competition would be enhanced.

Reasons for Change

Alas, that is not the end of the story. In recent years, trade and environmental issues have become intertwined. Indeed, trade sanctions are sometimes used—or threatened—as a way to enforce environmental agreements. For example, the 1987 Montreal Protocol, which seeks to reverse the depletion of the upper-atmosphere ozone layer caused by the release of chlorofluorocarbons and other chemicals, requires trade actions against countries that do not abide by the environmental standards in the agreement.

A second example is the Convention on International Trade in Endangered Species of Wild Fauna and Flora (CITES), which aims to protect endangered species of wildlife. During 1993, CITES recommended the use of trade sanctions for environmental purposes—once to stop Chinese and Taiwanese trade in rhinoceros and tiger parts; once, under the Pelly Amendment, to stop Norway's violation of the International Whaling Convention's moratorium on whaling. In both cases, however, sanctions were deferred.

Trade restraints are not the best solution to environmental problems. If the environmental problem is limited to one country, then domestic policies, not trade protection, should be employed to correct it. If pollution or other environmental problems spill across borders, international rules and cooperation will be necessary. But, here again, trade protection is not the most effective remedy.

Unfortunately, the door has been left open for trade and environmental issues to become intertwined in the WTO. Indeed, the preamble to the agreement establishing the WTO recognizes the importance of environmental concerns. Moreover, the WTO negotiators have agreed to develop a work program on trade and the environment to ensure the responsiveness of the multilateral trading system to environmental objectives. This potential "greening of GATT" will jeopardize the enormous benefits promised by the Uruguay Round.

Probable Consequences

The cause of the trade-environment conflict is transparent: the basic tenets of the GATT agenda and the current agenda of the modern environmentalists are in sharp conflict. The GATT vision is solidly based on the tenets of an extended, liberal economic order. Hence, free exchange based on private property rights is desirable because it promotes public prosperity and welfare.

The GATT vision is, therefore, opposed to mercantilism, whose ultimate objective is to enhance the power of the state. Not surprisingly, mercantilism was originally espoused not by disinterested philosophers, but by cabinet ministers, administrators, government advisers, merchants, lobbyists, and adventurers.

In contrast to the GATT visison, the green vision is solidly based on the tenets of the "market failure" paradigm. This leads to assertions that markets do not work because environmental resources are either underpriced or unpriced. Hence, environmentalists find the free-market system undesirable; it negatively affects the attainment of prosperity.

The market failure paradigm motivates virtually all environmental policy initiatives. Market-based economies have used it as a rationale for the massive expansion of regulatory controls and interventions. As with mercantilism, the ultimate objective of the green vision is, therefore, to enhance the power of the state. For example, under an "ideal" green-dictated system, no new technology could be introduced and no economic activity could proceed unless a green bureaucracy deemed them "safe" for the environment.

The United Nations-sponsored Earth Summit in Rio de Janeiro is a perfect example of the pervasiveness of this kind of green thinking. The market failure paradigm was used to rationalize extending the power of the state for purposes of controlling resource use. Participants failed to acknowledge that environmental problems were invariable spawned when property rights in environmental resources were absent or controlled by the state. Consequently, there was virtually no discussion of extending private property rights to protect natural and environmental resources.

It is important to stress Nobelist Ronald Coase's point that the market failure paradigm floats in the air. It is as if a medical doctor set out to study the circulation of blood without having a body to examine. Coase himself never commits this error. The careful observation of markets and governments, which has been his life's work, discloses the robustness of markets and the fragility of government. Indeed, when private property and contract rights are established, market prices effectively ration scarce resources. Consequently, Coase insists that in evaluating the case for state intervention, one must compare the possibility of real markets with real government, rather than real markets with ideal government assumed to work not only flawlessly but without cost.

The fundamental conflict between the GATT and green visions brings to mind the work of another Nobelist, Jan Tinbergen. His analysis suggests that when two visions conflict, we have a classic "policy assignment" problem. Even though trade policy can be used to serve environmental objectives, another set of policies would be more cost effective. Trade policy should be the exclusive domain of a GATT regime that is capable of securing enormous gains from free trade. The temptation to make trade policy captive to sundry objectives, unmindful of the benefits and costs of alternatives, must be rejected. Indeed, when stripped of its noble rhetoric, the environmental language in the preamble of the agreement establishing the WTO is nothing more than a protectionist ruse that will crush competitors from the developing nations.

Proposed Actions

If environmental problems are to be excluded from the GATT regime, then how should they be dealt with? We propose a new environmental vision, one that relies on extending the liberal economic order, not the power of the state.

To appreciate the attractiveness of extending the liberal economic order to the environment, consider that in America, for example, private homes and backyards are beautiful, but government owned and operated parks and streets are in a state of disrepair. For some environmentalists, the answer is to raise taxes to better support the "cash starved" public sector. For other environmentalists, the answer is more stringent regulations covering every aspect of modern society. A better approach would be to discover what makes homes and backyards beautiful. Rather than increasing the power of the state and bureaucratizing the environment, we should privatize natural and environmental resources. In other words, environmental values must be fully integrated into the free-enterprise system. One might say that trees should not have legal standing, but behind every tree should stand a private steward—a private owner who is willing and legally enabled to protect that resource.

This new environmental vision of ecological privatization may sound radical, but it promises lasting success in dealing with the ever-changing circumstances of human interaction with the natural world. Not only is this vision applicable to environmental protection, it is compatible with respect for individual liberty.

Current environmental policies are based on the false assumptions associated with the market failure paradigm. Markets based on private property and contract rights work to protect resources. It is state ownership and management that fails to protect resources and promote prosperity. One only needs to observe the legacy of socialism's environmental disasters and the poverty in postcommunist countries to appreciate this fact. To avoid such a legacy on a worldwide scale, we must eschew the greening of GATT.

-10-
Harnessing Market Forces to Protect the Environment
Robert N. Stavins

Description of Change

Public concern over environmental issues has risen dramatically over the last two decades. As a result, governments are increasingly pressured to develop reasoned responses to a variety of environmental problems. These problems include localized issues, such as contamination of potable water supplies and clean-up of toxic waste dumps, and environmental problems that transcend political boundaries, such as acid rain, stratospheric ozone depletion, and global climate change.

Until recently, the predominant approach to environmental protection by governments around the world has been "command-and-control" regulations—technology standards and performance standards—that tell private firms how much pollution to control and how to control it. Although these approaches have sometimes been effective, they have been exceptionally costly. For example, a law may require that power plants use scrubbers to reduce air pollution, regardless of whether another technology or a process change might more cheaply achieve the same level of air quality. Now, the incremental cost of environmental protection is mounting at an ever faster rate around the world.

Beginning about four to five years ago and accelerating internationally is a growing recognition of an alternative approach to environmental protection. This approach would enable us to achieve our goals at significantly lower aggregate costs by harnessing market forces to protect the environment. By providing incentives for firms and individuals to "do the right thing environmentally," environmental protection can be achieved without sacrificing desired public goods, such as education, health care, and national security, or private goods, such as a reasonably priced food supply.

Thus, the environment can be effectively protected by giving firms and individuals a direct and daily interest in doing so. In this way, market-based policy instruments will strengthen environmental protection by changing the financial incentives that millions of people face when deciding what to consume, how to produce, and where to dispose of their wastes. As a result, market-based policies, which include green charges, tradable permit systems, and a range of other approaches, offer many important advantages. They enable private industry to comply with environmental protection policies at a lower cost to themselves and, thereby, to consumers. They also give firms a constant incentive to find new and better technologies for combating pollution, rather than locking one kind of pollution control technology into place. They make the incremental costs of environmental protection more visible, and thus can focus public debate on the most efficient ways to protect the environment, rather than simply on the evils of pollution, Finally, because some market-based approaches such as pollution charges raise substantial revenues, they can enable governments to reduce "distortionary" taxes—those that reduce market efficiency by taxing desirable activities, such as investment and labor—and replace them with levies that discourage socially undesirable behavior, such as pollution and degradation of natural resources.

Several industrialized nations have enacted laws and regulations that utilize these market-based instruments, and there is increasing interest from the emerging market economies and developing countries as well. In the United States, a tradable-permit system was used in the 1980s to phase out leaded gasoline; the estimated savings was $250 million per year. In 1990, a similar approach was adopted for limiting acid rain. It could save society as much as $1 billion annually when compared with a conventional command-and-control approach. Several European nations, including France, the Netherlands, and Germany, currently use water pollution charge systems. And a frequently discussed potential application in many countries is a tax on the carbon content of fossil fuels to help address global climate change.

Reasons for Change

These changes have been brought about by a variety of factors, including the increasing costs of environmental protection that have made cost effectiveness an important criterion of new policies; the new economic climate in which the burdens of regulation are increasingly important; a more favorable view, in general, of using the market to address a variety of social problems; and a new set of environmental problems that cannot be adequately addressed with yesterday's policy approaches.

Probable Consequences

Although it is too soon to tell, the result may well be a major shift in the way we address environmental problems around the world, particularly as more and more nations recognize that market-based policy instruments ought to be within their overall portfolio of potential approaches. The result will be more environmental protection with less sacrifice of other legitimate social and private goals. Eventually, this will mean that environmental protection can be provided without the rancor and divisiveness that is part of the adversarial system that dominates this area today.

Proposed Actions

The United Nations through its environmental program should begin to provide technical assistance to emerging market economies and developing nations. They can then decide which, if any, of this new set of environmental policy approaches is appropriate for them. Each country should not have to reinvent the wheel of environmental policy reform. Rather, through the clearinghouse of the UN, countries can learn from each other.

In many nations, governments should consider the application of market-based approaches to a variety of environmental challenges, including municipal solid waste, recycling, hazardous waste disposal, air and water pollution, and international environmental threats, such as global warming and the loss of biodiversity. Specific policies that may merit serious consideration, depending on the economic, political, and cultural context, include:

- National deposit-refund systems for lead-acid batteries and some solvents. By applying this approach, which is already used by a number of countries for beverage containers, to the health threat posed by the illegal disposal of lead-acid batteries, we can reduce significantly and cost effectively the number of batteries that wind up in landfills and incinerators.

- "Unit pricing" for trash pickup at the local level. By charging households more if they produce more trash, municipalities can reduce solid waste disposal costs, encourage recycling, and reduce the use of virgin materials, while preserving a high degree of individual choice.

- Tradable permit systems to promote solid waste recycling and to reduce water pollution and other environmental challenges. Generally, by using this policy instrument to allocate the pollution-control burden among firms, the total costs of control can be reduced dramatically.

- Carbon charges enacted at the national level, with revenues recycled to consumers by lowering other taxes, if needed to achieve internationally established and enforceable long-term goals for controlling greenhouse gases.

These economically rational policies do not represent a laissez-faire, free-market approach. They recognize that market failures are at the core of environmental degradation. At the same time, incentive-based policies reject the notion that such market failures justify scrapping the market and dictating the behavior of firms or consumers. Instead, they provide freedom of choice to businesses and consumers in determining the best way to reduce pollution. By ensuring that society's environmental costs are factored into each firm's or individual's decision-making, incentive-based policies harness rather than impede market forces and channel them to achieve environmental goals at the lowest possible cost to society at large. No single policy mechanism can be an environmental panacea, but market-based instruments can provide more cost-effective solutions for some pressing environmental problems.

-11-
International Environmental Policy: From Formation to Implementation

Philipp M. Hildebrand

Description of Change

The two decades between the 1972 United Nations Conference on the Human Environment in Stockholm and the 1992 United Nations Conference on Environment and Development in Rio de Janeiro have been marked by a formidable expansion of international environmental regulatory initiatives. In 1972, at most a few dozen international multilateral environmental agreements were in force. International environmental law was a discipline in its infant stages. Twenty years later, according to one recent survey, the international politics of the environment are regulated by more than 900 international legal instruments that either fully address environmental issues or have more than one important provision addressing them.[1]

This growth of international legislative initiatives has had significant effects on global sociopolitical and economic relations. A wide range of international institutional arrangements, both formal and informal, have emerged to address international environmental degradation. The scientific community has penetrated the international political arena in an unprecedented way. International environmental negotiations have become important items on the agendas of national governments and administrations. Finally, and perhaps most importantly, international environmental issues have become inseparably linked to the international political economy.

---

[1] Edith Brown-Weiss, Daniel B. Magraw, and Paul C. Szasz, *International Environmental Law: Basic Instruments and References.* New York: Transnational Publishers, 1992.

Reasons for Change

This fundamental change in the position of international environmental affairs is a result of many factors. First, after the initial postwar economic growth period, it became apparent that the future required "decisive political action now to begin managing environmental resources to ensure both sustainable human progress and survival."[2] Second, international organizations and other international institutional actors came to view the environment as a new issue providing them with opportunities for institutional growth and political leverage. Third, most governments judged it to be in their interest, albeit for different reasons, to involve themselves in the emerging international politics of the environment. Finally, environmental nongovernmental organizations and popular advocacy groups encountered fertile ground for their activities and became a crucial force in continuously strengthening the momentum of this new domain of international law and politics.

Probable Consequences

Ironically, the international politics of the environment is in danger of becoming a victim of its own success. The effectiveness of international regulatory efforts is threatened by a widespread implementation deficit. Unevenly applied international environmental norms are a significant corollary of this deficit. Implementing international environmental agreements is a costly process for countries. They are reluctant to bear the cost if, as a result, they find themselves at a relative competitive disadvantage with regard to countries that sidestep implementation.

Proposed Actions

If sustainable development is to become a global political and economic reality, the international community needs to shift attention from negotiation to effective implementation of international initiatives. Agenda 21, a nonbinding instrument that was agreed on at the 1992 UNCED Conference, strikingly illustrates the need to give practical effect to broad policy objectives. In a text that exceeds 800 pages, it sets forth strategies for addressing the complex objective of reconciling development and environmental protection. By themselves, these strategies will

---

[2]World Commission on Environment and Development, *Our Common Future.* New York: Oxford University Press, 1987, p. 1.

not be sufficient. Administrative, technological, and intellectual resources need to be harnessed to determine how the broad policy objective of sustainable development can be realized in a world of scarce resources and competing political interests.

One of the most important elements in this process is the integration of business and industry into the environmental policy process. The UNCED Conference took an important step in the right direction. There, perhaps for the first time, the business community found an independent and coherent environmental voice to recognize that the dialogue among industry, business, and governments needs to be enhanced and refined. Industry and business sector-by-sector analyses must be undertaken to assess how each sector can give meaningful and long-term effect to existing and future initiatives. The dialogue among business, industry, and governments must be strengthened and, in some cases, further institutionalized in order to design an optimal regulatory environment. During recent years, considerable efforts have been undertaken to harness market forces for the benefit of the environment rather than to rely exclusively on traditional command-and-control measures. These efforts must be pursued. In fact, market forces may well be the most effective process by which business and industry can be more firmly tied into the difficult process of creating a globally sustainable economy. Creating environmentally sustainable industrial processes can be technologically demanding and financially burdensome for certain industrial activities. The industry-government dialogue therefore needs to address capacity-building measures for particularly problematic and damaging industrial and business processes.

Industrial and business activities can and do have an impact on the environment. At the same time, and partly as a consequence, industry and business are the most important actor groups to give ultimate effect to existing and future international efforts to manage the global environment. The international community has begun to recognize their relevance. Perhaps more importantly, industry and business have come to appreciate the crucial position they occupy in the quest for sustainable development. Important foundations have thus been laid. What is needed now are specific interdisciplinary strategies that elaborate on the future course of action for a wide range of industrial and business activities. Only then will it be possible to circumvent the looming threat of a widespread implementation deficit in the international politics of the environment and to convert formal objectives into practical achievements.

-12-
The Sustainability of Scientific Progress

Jeffrey Edington

As a scientist and a business executive, I approached the challenge to redefine the basic assumptions of the global economy from the viewpoint of Descartes, who in his 1639 *Discourse on Method* said "It is not enough to have a good mind; the main thing is to use it well."

Description of Change

We are still at the dawn of the technological revolution. More than 90 percent of the scientists and engineers who have ever lived are alive today; they and their immediate successors will have an enormous impact on future global production, consumption, and standards of living.

Reasons for Change

A major force is the need for world's economies to grow in order to improve living standards and social services for all people. This will ensure a stable, evolving, and improving sociopolitical system. Trade and commerce, the bricks of our global economy, have been developing for centuries, but the mortar produced by the current technological revolution is just being formed. During the last century, the OECD countries used technology to create manufacturing industries that generated wealth and national economic growth. Recently, technology has also become the basis of new service industries, including finance and entertainment (through the electronics revolution) and health care (through the drug and pharmacology revolution). The formation of mortar will continue as the human mind inexorably advances technology more rapidly than ever. Its growth will be enhanced by the globalization of industrial production and education, and with it, the worldwide mobility of technology.

Probable Consequences

As a result of the ongoing technological revolution, the world economy will continue to grow. This will lead to a reasonable amount of universal prosperity and international political stability. However, technologists must also ensure that future growth is sustainable; we cannot bequeath to our descendants a world with depleted resources and global pollution. Industries, consumers, and nations (both rich and poor) must use technology so that its impact on production and consumption leads to greater cooperation in minimizing pollution. Products should be redesigned so that they are longer lasting, reusable, smaller, lighter, and made of recyclable material, but with no loss in quality. These goals can be achieved, and there is every incentive to create win-win policies that benefit both income growth and the environment.

Proposed Actions

Creativity, innovation, and confidence—all widely dispersed across national boundaries—are the keys to future success. Education should be broadened so that scientists and engineers seek more than one solution to a problem. We can no longer accept the kind of thinking that was epitomized in a profile of Bill Gates, the 38-year-old multibillionaire chair of Microsoft Corporation (*The New Yorker,* January 10, 1993). In the article, a high-tech software executive is quoted as stating: "You know Mother Teresa is not going to build the broadband network of the future." I believe that the people who will build the broad band network of the future should think a little like Mother Teresa, but they will have to be educated to do so.

We can no longer afford to say "science for science's" sake. Science must take into account its impact on society. Indeed, we must have science for the world's sake. In order to do so, we should:

- Shift scientific education from the analytical to the holistic approach, so that solutions to society's problems are globally sustainable in the long term. Education in only narrow scientific disciplines is inadequate. We must understand the central concerns and theories of a broader range of disciplines—their major insights and their areas of ignorance. By teaching broader societal values, technical people will better understand and assume responsibility for the long-term implications of their actions and for explaining them simply and clearly to others. An essential ingredient of success will be the ability to assume a world view. To contribute at the top level, people need to focus on each other, on work, and on words and ideas.
- Educate the general public in the basics of technology so that they can deal knowledgeably with the increasingly difficult issues that will arise from future advances in such complex

fields as the information highway, medical science, biotechnology, and environmental protection.

- Broaden access to education by strengthening the fledgling Western university undergraduate programs in the developing world.
- Expand the infrastructure for education, particularly in science, engineering, and vocational skills.
- Recognize and advocate the place of science and technology in society and their contributions to the generation of wealth and economic sustainable growth. This should help counter the antitechnology lobbies, particularly in the OECD countries.

National governments, UNESCO, and regional groupings, such as the European Union, NAFTA, and APEC, can contribute to these actions.

Clearly, cooperation between governments and between governments and international companies can create the basis for a sustainable growth based on the application of knowledge. This can have a positive impact on many of the problems outlined elsewhere in this book—problems caused by globalization of the world economy and the emergence of dynamic economies in Asia. Of particular importance are the widening income gaps between the least developed countries and the OECD countries, as well as among the OECD countries themselves.

-13-
A Laborious Future
Jacques-Yves Cousteau

Description of Change

For many decades, the free-market economy resulted in successful economic development for one-fifth of the world's population. At the same time, life was very different for the poorest 5.6 billion people. Now, however, warning signs announce more difficult times even for the affluent nations. These include minimal progress in the implementation of Rio's conventions and Agenda 21, the explosion of unemployment, desertification, exhaustion of resources, and a quasigeneralization of ethnic, tribal, and religious conflicts.

The final victory of free trade over planned economy has considerably exaggerated our arrogance and our confidence in a system that is far from perfect. Inevitably, the world has to change. We can no longer tolerate discrimination between rich and poor countries, particularly when the minorities in rich countries are growing larger and more destitute.

Reasons for Change

Radical changes in the structure of our global society will soon become mandatory for two main reasons—overpopulation and inadequacy of the market economy. In no more than forty years, the world's population will reach at least 10 billion, three-quarters of whom will live in the poorest areas, such as Africa. No world leader, no serious geopolitician, has ever talked about this tidal wave; even the preparatory Commission of the Cairo Population Conference is trying to sidestep the issue. We avoid realistic discussions of the upcoming population explosion, for which our economic system offers no solution. Any allusion to the problem is ironically referred to as a Malthusian theory, as if Malthus was anachronistic.

The market economy, in the meantime, continues to price goods only on the basis of demand. This camouflages the real value, which also includes the cost of energy spent and the renewability or rarity of raw materials and resources used during production.

Probable Consequences

The passive attitude of our leaders may have two intolerable consequences—either a formidable genocide triggered by famine, jealousy, and violence, which might be crowned by the use of atomic weapons, or a progressive accentuation of the division between the rich and the poor—two different groups of humanity sharing the same planet and constantly fighting for survival.

If neither of these possibilities is acceptable, then what is? Today, any proposed solution is utopian. But, as Federico Mayor says: "Utopia today is reality tomorrow. So, let us dream utopia."

Proposed Actions

We must first answer the difficult question: What are we on earth for? The answer is simple: Life is worth living if every human being has access to dignity and the joy of living. These two goals can be reached only in the absence of need, with decent health care and high-quality education. It has nothing to do with—in fact, is even impaired by—wealth, waste, and worries. Any kind of sustainable economic development is impossible for a world of two, five, or ten billion people. We must carefully define sustainable social development. We must hope that the upcoming World Summit for Social Development, planned for March 1995 in Copenhagen, will help radically change the structure of our economic civilization.

Chapter 5
Living in the New
Information Society

Introduction

George V. Vassiliou

The information revolution is radically changing our lives and creating a new business and political environment. We are flooded daily with information that we were never trained to cope with and assimilate. The process, instead of slowing down, is accelerating. Joël de Rosnay writes: "As we enter the digital age, we are in transition from energy-intensive societies and infrastructures to information-intensive societies and infrastructures. From pyramidal, vertical, specialized, Taylorian organizations, to networked, decentralized structures within which information flows naturally. One does not replace the other. The two will coexist."

People have externalized their methods of communication, but this externalization has accelerated beyond recognition. Five thousand years ago was the age of writing; five hundred years ago the age of industrialized writing by printers; fifty years ago the age of audiovisual techniques and computers, and five years ago the age of digitization in commercial networks.

The catalyst in this revolutionary change was the unforeseen and mind-boggling evolution of microprocessor capacity, of digitization and data compression, of the hybridization of communication, and of the interphase between computers and communications as well as the development of computer networks and electronic highways.

This revolution had a dramatic effect on business. Vertically integrated corporations are giving way to closely knit groups of smaller firms in complex business relationships, writes Craig Fields. Outsourcing is not only possible, but necessary. In the new environment, where people, ideas, and technology are continuously mobile, competition is no longer based on long-term uniqueness of products and services, but rather on such attributes as time to market, price quality, and variety. The new digital highways affect not only the business environment, but also education, entertainment, and culture. CD-ROMs have revolutionized the way information is accessed and used.

This revolution was made possible by American telecommunications companies, which were quick to see the potential for their networks and pioneered the switching of large packets of data. The merging of the computer with telecommunications and entertainment suppliers is creating new "edutainment" industries, as Colin Chapman calls them.

The information and telecommunication revolution will certainly create new business opportunities and generate employment in many fields, help to link the world closer together, and make information accessible to millions of people. However, it causes many problems that need to be addressed. Ownership of the information society will be controlled by privately owned transnationals; information itself will be controlled by media giants. Society and governments need to find ways to regulate these companies without hindering them. The flood of information, Neil Postman points out, does not necessarily mean better understanding. In addition to conveying a glut of information and photographs, one needs a way to put the information into perspective.

Those who have access to this information, or control it, enjoy advantages that can be dangerous in a democratic society. This is why Robert Dilenschneider urges democratic societies to foster legal and market environments that will discourage manipulation. To prevent countries in the South from being left behind in this new digital age, technologically advanced countries should help them master these new techniques so they can participate in this new world.

Even greater emphasis must be placed on training and education. In the future, more than ever before, the differentiating national assets will not be minerals or land, but the skills of the people and their ability to master the new information. Eiichi Itoh believes that the creation of a global information society will lead to greater world peace and prosperity, but he advocates the establishment of an international forum for planning, organizing, financing, and operating a universal information infrastructure. This is related to the need for common standards. Several contributors emphasize the need to promote standards that will enable everyone to have access to information and communications systems. Simultaneously, we must respect and protect the cultural identity of the various nationalities. Media owners and leaders, writes Chapman, should be encouraged to work in a framework that takes account of national and cultural differences.

The challenge we face, according to Alan Kay, is whether we will appropriately use the potential of the computer and digital revolution to develop a global civilization or whether we will continue to work and think as before. The computer has a special domain of representation and argument that qualitatively transcends what can be mustered by natural language and classical mathematics. Kay warns that to make use of this capability and learn "twenty-first century thinking" requires a fair amount of effort, and the will to put forth effort usually comes from placing a high value on what is to be learned. The result of the discovery of the printing press was modern civilization. Not just science and technology, but new ways of thinking about politics and human rights. The computer and digital representation should open unforeseen vistas.

-1-
The Challenges of
the Information
Technology Superindustry

Colin Chapman

Description of Change

The difficulties of even a well-disciplined authoritarian state to exercise control over information and communications was demonstrated by the collapse of the Soviet Union. But newer, inexpensive innovations in information technology are forcing a convergence of global industries, such as computers, telecommunications, entertainment, and publishing, whose ownership is predominantly in the private sector.

The leading computer corporations are based in the United States. U.S. telecommunications companies have been very aggressive in developing digital highways that will soon deliver previously unimaginable choices of information services, educational material, entertainment, and culture to anyone with a telephone or a television set. Telecom giants outside the United States, following the example of Britain's BT and Japan's NTT, are being privatized. The entertainment, publishing, and growing "edutainment" industries, which are almost all privately owned, are allying themselves to these giants. The South is barely represented in any of these ventures.

The dynamism of an information technology superindustry developed swiftly by private capital will power the greatest change since Guttenberg's printing press started the unstoppable growth of literacy and mass education. The rapid development of this society challenges social, political, and cultural boundaries.

Reasons for Change

The new information society has been created by a series of accelerating technological innovations, almost all of them pioneered by private companies in the United States. New silicon chips have increased the amount of information that may be stored on devices of ever-decreasing size that can be accessed in microseconds. At the same time, digitalization of the media, particularly moving pictures, and the technology of digital compression means that new worldwide distribution systems for both textual and printed material are potentially a much cheaper way of accessing consumers than producing hard copies of printed works or videotapes and shipping them out via retailers. The new digital highways will allow medical students, for example, to access the equivalent of a textbook, such as *Gray's Anatomy,* with illustrations and videoclips, in seconds. For those who need portability, CD-ROMs, which can now be bought for as little as $150, already offer these benefits. An American mail order group will today ship the entire 21-volume *Grolier Encyclopedia* on CD-ROM anywhere in the world for $99. Newspaper groups, such as Knight-Ridder and the *Washington Post,* are planning to deliver an interactive newspaper electronically to a flat form pad about twice the size of a clipboard. Readers will be able to see videotape of important news items, such as presidential speeches and press conferences; advertisers will be able to offer interactive services.

American telecom companies, quickly recognizing the potential for these networks, pioneered the switching of large packets of data. Their interest in developing digital highways was further accelerated by the potential challenge from cable and satellite television to their core business. Conversely, because they enjoyed monopolistic positions in telecommunications traffic, many European and Asian public telecom companies were slow to grasp these new opportunities. That, however, is changing, as most of these companies approach privatization.

Probable Consequences

The consequences, which are many and varied, raise different issues.

1. Stable, advanced economies will benefit first. Because creating information highways requires investment and the prospect of a reasonable return, the new information society is being created first in the United States, and then will quickly spread to other English-language countries, such as Australia, Britain, and Canada, before establishing itself in the G-7 non-English-speaking nations.

   The laying of millions of miles of fiber and the installation of new equipment will create tens of thousands of jobs for some time to come, and act as a substantial economic stimulus ($50 billion forecast for the United States alone in the four years to 1998). It is likely to reach the less-developed countries last, but when it does, it will bring them rapidly to the international standard, leapfrogging previous developments, particularly in broadcast television, data processing, and media.

   It will be very difficult for authoritarian governments to resist these changes and still remain part of the world community. The parallel here is with the arrival of the printed word. Even in villages where individual access to telephones and television is limited, access to the information society will be possible via community groups. The risk is that national and local cultures will be usurped and subverted by a McDonald's information and entertainment culture.

2. Ownership of the information society will be controlled by privately owned transnationals. This will raise two separate issues. There will be concern that organizations created from what are primarily computer and telecom companies have access to excessive profit power on the global scale. In the United States, this will be restricted by antitrust laws, but in many other countries anticompetition policy is weak. Some countries may attempt to limit overseas ownership by insisting on local partnerships, but this may restrict the development of the local information society.

   The greater concern is that the information itself (the content or software) will be controlled by media giants. Of those with substantial libraries of software—and the ability to produce more—only a handful are in the public sector. They include the BBC, which has formed an alliance with Pearson, a British plc; NHK of Japan, and the Australian and Canadian broadcasting corporations. This could lead to political concern as to the individual power of such media giants as Time Warner, News Corporation, Paramount, and Bertelsmann.

3. If mass media is no longer dominant, the advertising industry faces a global crisis. Until the 1990s, most consumer products were marketed through the mass media. In most countries, the dominance of one or two terrestrial television channels, along with a limited number of newspapers and magazines, meant that the consumer could be reached inexpensively. However, a multichannel television environment combined with a wide range of visual materials available via digital highways means audience fragmentation. Inevitably, the cost-per-thousand of reaching consumers will rise, leaving advertisers to seek new ways of reaching the consumer.

4. The ease and speed with which individuals can access information means that in many occupations, particularly in the professions, it will be possible to work anywhere. Telework, which is working at home or in small remote communities, will be easy. Much routine processing work formerly carried out in London is now done in Poland and Bombay, at a fraction of the cost. This has severe implications for jobs in expensive service centers in G-7 economies.

5. The operations of the information society, particularly the global digital highways, may prove to be even more difficult to regulate than the financial markets. Some of the business leaders involved have already been quoted as saying the industry is now "beyond regulation."

6. The new information society will open up opportunities for new goods and services that at present do not exist. Initially, the principal beneficiary will be the United States.

Probable Consequences

Countries that are likely to be left out of the information revolution need financial and technological assistance to ensure that they too can build digital highways and access the global information society. It is unlikely that this will be achieved without the creation of a special fund, perhaps under the auspices of the United Nations. Those who are most likely to benefit from the spread of the information society—computer hardware and software manufacturers, telecommunication companies and consultancies, and the media—should bear a substantial proportion of the cost.

Educators worldwide need to be adequately informed about the potency of the information society and trained to use it. Otherwise, the quality and spread of education will be uneven. Governments also need to inform their people about the impact of the changes and to prepare societies for the new jobs that will be created. This suggests detailed forecasting work should be conducted by the 24-nation Organization for Economic Cooperation and Development (OECD).

Media owners and media leaders (editors, producers, and software designers) need encouragement to work in a framework that takes account of national and cultural differences.

The Digital Revolution
Joël de Rosnay

Description of Change

As we enter the digital age, we are in transition from energy-intensive societies and infrastructures to information-intensive societies and infostructures. From pyramidal, vertical, specialized Taylorian organizations to networked, decentralized structures within which information flows naturally. One does not replace the other. The two will coexist.

People have externalized their methods of communication. Even before writing, people manipulated symbols. Then, they developed the ability to store text and images using external media. Television is the long-distance eye; radio the long-distance ear. Computers are the external part of memory. The acceleration of externalization is represented by the following figures: 5,000 years ago was the age of writing; 500 years ago the age of industrializing writing by printers; 50 years ago the age of audiovisual and computer technology; and 5 years ago was that of digitization in commercial networks.

We are now entering an "explosive" phase, in which networks will deliver information over great distances (using cable, satellite, television, and computer networks). A complex network that resembles a global nervous system is emerging. Receiving information, circulating it, and manipulating symbols touches our daily lives. I call this "explosive" phase of media developments the "mediamorphosis."

The mediamorphosis is shaking industrialized societies through decentralization, the acceleration of time, and the shrinking of space. Small new ventures are threatening large industrialized groups in the data processing and publishing sectors. Mergers and acquisitions are changing the map of the multimedia sectors (cable, telephone, television, publishing, software, home shopping, and videogames). The market of communication systems and products is exploding. Governments are trying to capitalize on such developments or to protect national industries in the communication sector.

Reasons for Change

Why such a mediamorphosis? What are its catalysts? Why is this global system in the process of accelerated development?

Microprocessor Improvements

The first catalyst of rapid change in the digital age is the microprocessor. Dating back some twenty years, it has changed everything. It
continues to destabilize some leading enterprises, shake top executives,
and question the survival of some 50,000 information technology companies worldwide.

It is found everywhere, from telephones to televisions, not to mention
videoplayers and portable microcomputers. The microprocessor power (8
bits, 16 bits, 32 bits) is currently changing by an order of magnitude.
The generation of the 64-bit microprocessor has already been launched.
One indicator of this change in scale is the DEC Alpha microprocessor
with 64-bit words, which permits 18 billion billion addresses. It processes information at 150 MHz (2½ times the average microprocessor)
and supports 140 million instructions per second (MIPS). The power of
a Cray One computer at the beginning of the 1980s is available today on
a desktop computer for one thousandth of its price. This gives some idea
of the potential for processing information, not only alphanumeric
information, but also images and sound, thus enabling voice and pattern
recognition.

Digitization and Data Compression

Whatever its origin, a signal contains a large proportion of useless or redundant information. Compression algorithms can be used to reduce the
quantity of information by a factor of as much as one hundred. A television signal of 25 million bytes per second can be compressed to 4 million bytes per second (high-density television) or even 1 million bytes
per second. A stream of coded information compressed at the input and
decompressed at the output allows the passage of extremely dense
information via the telephone. These techniques of compression already
.exist. MPEG, the recently adopted international standard, is already
challenged by fractal and holographic compression techniques.

Hybridization of Communication Technologies

Several elements converge into a single device. In the digital age, it
becomes pointless to use a fax, a scanner, a laser printer, a telephone
answering machine, and a computer. It is better to use the scanner as the
"reading fax," or the laser printer as the "printing fax," thus constituting
a single device for a lower price. The notepad, a personal digital
assistance (the portable computer that includes a telephone), is another

example of hybrid equipment. Hybridization of communication technologies is a powerful factor of change in this field.

Computers and Communication Interfaces

People/machine interface has constantly improved during the last ten years. The tradition input/output devices, like keyboards and cathode ray tubes for computer screens, are being replaced by mouses, scanners, voice input devices, pens, flat LCD color screens, virtual reality headsets, and data gloves. In the future, biosensors will directly feed information from the brain into the computers.

Computer Networks and Electronic Highways

Large computer networks, such as the Internet, link millions of personal computers around the world. Commercial services allow connection with large databases. Electronic highways based on ATM technology, videoservers using parallel computers permit the transfer of considerable amounts of multimedia information and the emergence of interactive television with thousands of services.

Probable Consequences

What effect will these changes have? The following are among the consequences of the digital revolution.

Convergence of Industrial Sectors

Catalysts of the digital age, such as microprocessors, new software, and communication systems will lead to the convergence of industries. Four spheres of activities are merging because of digitization: editing (printed text, magazines, and books); audiovisual (video, television, and cinema); microcomputers and software; and telephone and communications networks. Merging text and telephone produces the fax; text and computer produce the word processor. The three together (text, computer, and telephone) generate videotext. Telephone and video produce the videophone, but the combination of telephone, video, and computer produces what I called "videomatics," a new sector where still and moving pictures are carried by networks in addition to text and graphics. For industries, the convergence of these four sectors is triggering mandatory mergers and huge reengineering adaptations.

Opening of New Multimedia Markets

Today, we receive television broadcasts via radio waves, satellites, or cable. In France, the Minitel is transmitted only via telephone lines and information is in the form of alphanumeric characters and a few graphics. The screen definition is not excellent, but the use of the keyboard and standard menus permits the access to numerous (8,000) information services. Thanks to compression of data, digitization of information, and the presence of terminals everywhere (television and telephone), interactive multimedia television brings high-resolution color television via normal telephone lines without interrupting telephone usage. We are entering an era when home television will be not only an entertainment device, but also a business tool. In two or three years, 500 services will be at our disposal, first in the United States and then perhaps in Europe—a hundred channels with movies, ten educational channels, ten sports channels, and ten shopping channels. With a remote control device, everyone should be able to have access to these services.

Impact on Organizations and Reengineering

The centralized structures of the industrial age are challenged by the new networks. The flow of information in digital networks, its processing through personal computers, and the possibilities of groupware are creating the opportunity for virtual enterprises. Telework is a reality for many workers in the computer, banking, and insurance sectors. Traditional hierarchical and Taylorized structures are replaced by "flat" organizations with reduced levels of hierarchy. The digital revolution creates a reengineering need in many giant firms and public organizations.

Risks and Constraints

The increased complexity of computers and telecommunication networks creates a risk of fragility. Breakdowns, computer viruses, sabotage, privacy intrusions are all consequences of such rapid developments. There is a "big brother" risk created by the need for control and surveillance of the exchange in such networks for security purposes. Individuals can also find themselves isolated in their "electronic bubble" with reduced face-to-face communications. "Couch potatoes" will spend time ordering products on their interactive television or playing electronic games with multiple partners. Education will be important if people are to master these complexities. A new economic gap might form between the information rich and the information poor. For developing countries, the digital age is a chance and a risk. A chance because it will help them catch up with major advanced industrialized countries, particularly in the fields of education and health. A risk because countries that are unable to adapt will find the information gap growing and see their intellectual resources drained away by the international economy.

Proposed Actions

The following actions are recommended to maximize and equalize the benefits of the digital revolution.

- Adapt regulations to cover the growing sector of international communications. FCC regulations, national PTT monopolies, and European regulations are not adapted to the free flow of information between enterprises and individuals. Equipment agreements will have to be eased to allow freer access to the networks.
- Promote standards. New technologies are born with their own standards. Engineers tend to fight over the best-suited standards and try to influence politicians. This, in turn, slows down the development of new communication technologies. International standards for data compression and transmission, digital television, memory cards, sound and speech processing equipment, and telecommunication software are needed. Recent history shows that the public only invests when standards are mature, thus lowering costs and complexity of use.
- Catalyze mergers and regroupings between companies. Alliances between American and European companies are needed to compete with major Asian players in communication equipment and program development.
- Promote laws to protect intellectual property. Intellectual creation will represent one of the most important assets in the coming century. Intellectual products should be allowed to cross international borders freely without technical obstacles. Such laws would have to be harmonized between countries.
- Help the Third World. Technologically advanced countries should help developing nations to master the techniques of the digital age, giving them a chance to enter the international competition and opening new markets for the future.

- Protect privacy. Public networks, access to databases, group-ware, telework, cellular phones, personal digital assistant, agent software, interactive television and home shopping all create opportunities for infringement of privacy. International rules and regulations should protect individual freedom and privacy in the digital age.

- Avoid protectionism. The digital revolution creates a nervous system at the planetary level that involves every nation. Traditional protectionism will be counterproductive in the transitional stage to the wired society.

- Invest in education. Education in order to master the new information and communication tools is essential for every individual. It will become one of the major societal goals for the next century. The digital revolution provides powerful tools to meet such a challenge: CD-ROMs, A/V computers, interactive multimedia television, telematics, and networks. New "navigation rules" should be established to help the younger generation navigate through hypermedias. "Edutainment" should replace most of the videogames currently on the market.

Conclusion

The digital age represents a unique opportunity for a new model of economic development. Beyond the concept of sustainable development, the digital age offers the possibility of an adaptive self-regulated development that is needed to reconcile economy and ecology.

The Impact of the Information Glut

Neil Postman

Description of Change

Information was once a resource that helped people solve specific and urgent problems by increasing their knowledge of the physical and social environment. Although there was a scarcity of information in the Middle Ages, its very scarcity made it important and usable. In the late fifteenth century, this began to change when a goldsmith named Gutenberg, from Mainz, Germany, converted an old wine press into a printing machine. In so doing, he created what we now call an information explosion. Forty years after the invention of the press, there were printing machines in 110 cities in six different countries; fifty years later, more than eight million books had been printed, almost all of them filled with information that had previously been unavailable to the average person. Nothing could be more misleading than the idea that computer technology introduced the age of information. The printing press began that age, and we have not been free of it since.

Reasons for Change

But what started out as a useful stream of information has turned into a Niagara of chaos. In the United States, for example, there are 260,000 billboards, 17,000 newspapers, 12,000 periodicals, 27,000 video outlets for renting tapes, 400 million television sets, and more than 500 million radios (not counting those in automobiles). There are 40,000 new book titles published every year (300,000 worldwide), and every day in the United States 41 million photographs are taken. Just for the record, more than 60 billion pieces of advertising junk mail come into our mailboxes every year. Everything from telegraphy and photography in the nineteenth century to the silicon chip in the twentieth century has amplified the din of information. Matters have reached such proportions that for the average person information no longer has any relation to the solution of problems.

The tie between information and action has been severed. Information is now a commodity that can be bought and sold, used as a form of entertainment, or worn like a garment to enhance one's status. From millions of sources all over the globe, through every possible channel and medium—light waves, airwaves, ticker tapes, computer banks, telephone wires, television cables, satellites, and printing presses—information pours in. Behind it, in every imaginable form of storage—on paper, on videotape and audiotape, on discs, film, and silicon chips—is an ever-greater volume of information waiting to be retrieved. Information has become a form of garbage. It comes indiscriminately—directed at no one in particular, disconnected from usefulness; we are swamped by information, have no control over it, and do not know what to do with it. And the reason we do not know what to do with it is that we no longer have a coherent conception of ourselves, our universe, and our relation to one another and our world. We do not know where we came from, where we are going, or why we are going there. We have no coherent framework to direct our definition of our problems or our search for their solutions. Therefore, we have no criteria for judging what is meaningful, useful, or relevant information. Our defenses against the information glut have broken down; our information immune system is inoperable.

Probable Consequences

One serious consequence is a growing sense of impotence. We are told by news media about the problems in the Middle East, in Northern Ireland, in Yugoslavia. We are told about the depletion of the ozone layer and the destruction of the rain forests. Is there something we personally are expected to do about these problems?

For most people, there is nothing they can do about them. And so, there grows in people a sense of passivity and ineffectualness, leading inevitably to a preoccupation with self. If you can do nothing about the world, you can at least do something about yourself. You can become thinner, or change the color of your hair, the shape of your nose. It is a kind of egotism that results from knowing of a thousand things and being unable to affect any of them. But even worse, most people continue to believe that it is information and still more information that is what people mostly need, and that will be the backbone of our problem-solving efforts.

But our most serious problems do not arise from having inadequate information. If a nuclear catastrophe occurs, it will not be because of inadequate information. Where people are dying of starvation, it does not occur because of inadequate information. If families break up, crime terrorizes a city, and education is impotent, it is not because of inadequate information. It happens because of an inadequate sense of meaning.

Proposed Actions

For people to have a sense of the meaning of things, they must have a believable narrative. By narrative, I mean a story of human history that gives meaning to the past, explains the present, and provides guidance for the future. It is a story whose principles help a culture to organize its institutions, to develop ideals, and to find authority for its actions. Information by itself is no narrative and in our present situation only serves to disguise the fact that most people no longer believe in any story. Of course, the major source of the world's greatest stories has been religion, as found, for example, in Genesis or the Bhagavad-Gita or the Koran. There are those who believe, as did the great historian Arnold Toynbee, that without a comprehensive religious narrative at its center a culture must decline. Perhaps. There are, after all, other sources—mythology, politics, philosophy, and science, for example—but it is certain that no culture can flourish without narratives of transcendent origin and power to help people sort through and assess information and decide what more they need to know.

This does not mean that the mere existence of such a narrative ensures a culture's stability and strength. A narrative provides meaning, not necessarily survival. There are destructive narratives, as for example, the story provided by Adolph Hitler to the German nation in the 1930s. Drawing on sources in Teutonic mythology and resurrecting ancient and primitive symbolism, Hitler wove a tale of Aryan supremacy that lifted German spirits, gave point to their labors, eased their distress, and provided explicit ideals. The story glorified the past, elucidated the present, and foretold the future, which was to last a thousand years. The Third Reich lasted exactly 12 years. There are many reasons why the story of Aryan supremacy could not endure. Among them is that its assumptions were demonstrably false. Its implications were lethal to those who did not accept it. And it gave to humans a godlike omniscience that, as the great Greek storytellers warned, could only lead to doom. But we may also learn from the German experience that cultures must have narratives and will find them where they will, even if they lead to catastrophe. The alternative is to live without meaning—the ultimate negation of life itself.

Of course, we may well wonder what will happen to those nations that once organized themselves around the great narrative known as Marxism. That narrative postulated that the great revolution in 1917 was part of history's plan and that history was moving inexorably toward the triumph of the proletariat. Does anyone still believe in this story? And if they do not, what new story will give purpose to their lives? I might add that Americans have a somewhat similar problem. We used to believe that our great revolution in 1776 was not merely an experiment in governance, but was part of God's own plan. Not many Americans, I am afraid, believe this any longer. And we wonder, as do both Eastern and Western Europeans, where we will find a narrative to give meaning to our culture. I fear that I cannot answer this question. I know only that the plague of information that our new technologies have visited upon us is not a blessing, but a tyranny that blocks us from constructing life-enhancing narratives and does so by diverting our attention and depleting our energies from that important task.

I also know that those geniuses of information technology are not the people to whom we can turn to find new and life-enhancing narratives. They will give us artificial intelligence and tell us that this is the way to self-knowledge. They will give us instantaneous global communication and tell us this is the way to mutual understanding. They will give us virtual reality and tell us this is the answer to spiritual poverty. But these are only the ways of the technician, the fact monger, the information junky, and the technological idiot.

Here is what Henry David Thoreau told us: "All our inventions are but improved means to an unimproved end." Here is what Goethe told us: "One should, each day, try to hear a little song, read a good poem, see a fine picture, and, if possible, speak a few reasonable words." And here is what Socrates told us: "The unexamined life is not worth living." And here is what the prophet Micah told us: "What does the Lord require of thee but to do justly, and to love mercy and to walk humbly with thy God?" And I can tell you—if I had the time (although you all know it well enough)—what Confucius, Isaiah, Jesus, Mohammed, the Buddha, Spinoza, and Shakespeare told us. It is all the same: There is no escaping from ourselves. The human dilemma is as it has always been, and we solve nothing fundamental by cloaking ourselves in technological glory. Even the humblest cartoon character knows this, and I shall close by quoting the wise old possum named Pogo, created by cartoonist Walt Kelley. I commend his words to all the technological utopians and messiahs. "We have met the enemy," Pogo said, "and he is us."

-4-
The Gap Between
the "Knows" and
the "Don't Knows"
Robert L. Dilenschneider

Description of Change

In the twenty-first century, the world will be dramatically enhanced by instantaneous communications. News and other media, using technological tools not yet invented or refined, will offer sophisticated individuals a wealth of information on which to base judgments and decisions. At the same time, this development offers unscrupulous individuals an opportunity for massive distortion that could negatively affect social, political, and economic spheres. Pressure groups in the developed world, as well as nations struggling to establish themselves, may utilize these same information channels to create short-term distortions.

Reasons for Change

Technology will continue to develop tools that make ever-greater amounts of information available to millions of people. Sophisticated individuals, however, will have special access to this information. Using this same technology, senders of information can pinpoint sociodemographic targets and transmit their messages to precisely defined groups and individuals.

In addition, national laws and international pressure for disclosure will disseminate even more information. Peoples will find unique ways to receive, handle, and manage all these data.

Probable Consequences

In many ways, the consequences are positive. In general, people will be better informed, thereby having more information on which to base their decisions. Life will be better, waste will be cut, new ideas and inventions will flourish, and better ways of performing work will be employed. In short, the world will enter a new era of modernity that is driven by access to, and employment of, the information.

However, if one country, one power bloc, one individual, or group of individuals seeks wealth and control over others, these methods can be used against the public good. This, plus the possible spread of conflict in the future, creates significant possibilities for major dislocation.

Proposed Actions

Established institutions in democratic societies should foster legal and market environments that allow the new communications technologies to maximize the enhancement of the intellectual and material wealth of their peoples. At the same time, these societies need to guard against those segments of society seeking to advance their own agendas in lawless ways. In furthering their causes, these groups can manipulate modern communications technology. A few voices will sound like millions of voices and people who are susceptible to doubts about the existing order may become converts to these causes.

Leaders in democratic societies cannot assume that the values and traditions of their societies will prevail. The enormously powerful economic wrenching currently sweeping through the industrialized world has profoundly affected the economic well-being of large segments of the population, making them vulnerable to simplistic solutions proposed by those whose agendas are not in the population's best interests. There will be new responsibilities and demands placed on leaders. They must not only be persuasive about the values of existing society, but must also devise plans and programs to ameliorate the effects of negative economic forces and redirect economic activity toward the goal of higher levels of prosperity in real terms.

Market economics has permeated much of the world, but has not always been accompanied by the infusion of democratic values. In the somewhat distant future, this will present an even greater challenge to leadership, whose populace may witness a nation with an autarkic government ruling over great prosperity.

Leaders in democratic societies need to confront directly the reality of the economic success of Third World nations, where relatively low levels of compensation and lax or nonexistent regulation on environmental and other matters results in low costs of production. These are, in effect, export subsidies. Whether through the United Nations or a reformulation of GATT, access to the markets of the industrialized world needs to be curtailed to those Third World nations whose social responsibilities and environmental regulation, among other concerns, are not consonant with the national disciplines in these areas in the developed nations. We need to create a level playing field of competition among nations by returning to the laws of comparative advantage that once prevailed.

-5-
Information Technology and Economic Success
Craig Fields

Description of Change

Industry worldwide is undergoing a radical restructuring, reengineering, and reinvention that can be fairly characterized as this century's industrial revolution.

Vertically integrated corporations are giving way to closely knit groups of smaller firms in complex business relationships. Companies are outsourcing any and all functions that are not differentiating core competencies. These include the traditional areas for outsourcing—MIS, telecommunications, media, public relations, document publishing, mailroom—as well as less traditional areas—design, manufacturing, human resources, legal activities, and even sales and marketing. Corporations are spinning off entire divisions and departments as separate companies. Customers are forging closer links with their suppliers, involving joint design, coordinated scheduling of shipments and inventory control, and much more. Relationships go beyond purchasing and payment to, say, sharing of profit or exchange of equity. The brand name on the outside says little about the source of value added on the inside.

Competition and differentiation is based less on having a unique product or service, and more on rapid introduction of new products and services into the marketplace, value derived from quality and price of the product and accompanying customer service, and the ability to provide such a variety of offerings that the customer perceives a custom product at a mass production price. The business system has become so "nonlinear" that small advantages in time to market, price, quality, or variety can be magnified into large advances in market share.

The distinction between service companies and manufacturing companies is becoming blurred. Nine out of ten employees in many manufacturing companies provide service—general management, design, purchasing, human resources, office work, sales, marketing, and other activities. When these functions are outsourced, they are considered service; while inside the product company they are considered manufacturing. Products are increasingly becoming a packaged value of contributing services.

In short, we are rapidly evolving toward an industrial fabric with many more small- and medium-sized service firms working closely together to gain even small advantages in time to market, price, quality, or variety, and sharing in the business success enjoyed by the alliance—the virtual corporation. This is occurring on a global basis—engines designed in England; automobile bodies designed in California; software written in India; health care information digested in Puerto Rico; telemarketing from Ireland. More and more of the value of transnational trade is in the form of information.

Reasons for Change

Irrespective of age-old academic social and economic debate, intense competition seems to lead to superior performance. Firms providing a specialist service in competition with their peers achieve unparalleled excellence, or perish. Those same services in the protective environment of the vertically integrated corporation rarely reach the same level of performance. Thus an efficient alliance of "survivor" service firms will oftentimes outperform the sheltered community of divisions and departments within a large company.

The key to that efficiency is just now becoming commonplace, namely an effective information infrastructure of high-speed telecommunications; software for electronic mail, electronic funds transfers, automated buying and selling, and joint design and decision-making.

Continuous mobility of people, ideas, and technology leads to competition based not on long-term uniqueness of products and services, but on other differentiating attributes of offerings, like time to market, price, quality, and variety. The continuing automation of the mechanical functions of manufacturing is shifting the balance toward the service contributions to production.

Probable Consequences

Nations with an educated and motivated work force that is overqualified for locally available jobs and is willing to work for lower wages will benefit from the international free trade in information-intensive services. Just as the global transportation infrastructure, developed over thousands of years, made possible free trade in goods, so the global information infrastructure, developed over decades, is making possible free trade in information-intensive services. As the transnational transfer of value is in the form of coded data, monitoring, let alone controlling, is difficult or impossible. Duties, quotas, and tariffs will become increasingly impractical instruments of national will.

Nations can overcome the penalty of distant location with the skills of their people and the power of global telecommunications. Regions with an information infrastructure sufficiently sophisticated to support electronic commerce in information-intensive services will demonstrate disproportionate economic development, export knowledge-intensive services, and attract investment.

Proposed Actions

Regional actions will focus on promoting growth in the information infrastructure by direct investment, regulatory incentives, and support of business applications that can serve as catalysts by demonstrating the benefits of the technology to industrial access.

International action should focus on establishing standards to enable interoperability of information systems. Countries failing to achieve international interoperability for their information infrastructure will be cut off from much of the global commerce in information-intensive services, in much the same way that closed borders, or even inconsistent rail systems, have impeded trade in times past.

The highest priority for nations will be the lifelong training and education of every citizen, who will be faced with developing four or five or even six sets of skills during their working careers. The differentiating national assets will not be minerals, harbors, forests, or farmland, but the skills of the people.

-6-
The Universal Information Infrastructure

Eiichi Itoh

Description of Change

The world is about to ring in the long-awaited information society (société globale informatisée). In this new era, information will most likely be at least as important as other business resources, such as materials or financing. The potential danger is, however, that only the developed countries will reap the benefits of the information society.

In the advanced countries, which have already plunged into the information age, information-related industries account for more than 50 percent of the total GNP. A desirable cycle is developing, in which international competitiveness is enhanced by information, which, in turn, is creating the basis for further advancements toward a more affluent society in the next century.

On the other hand, the developing world is splitting into countries which are adapting themselves to the information age and countries which are not able to jump on the bandwagon. The former countries are expanding their industries in all three sectors, while the latter are spiraling into a vicious circle of lack of information, loss of competitive edge, and contraction of their industries. The facts show, alarmingly, that this dichotomy is in danger of worsening.

The obstacles of time and distance can now be surmounted with the introduction of high-capacity, high-speed, two-way communications systems. For instance, information transmission, which has traditionally been broadcast by a limited number of companies, assumed that people were passive recipients of information. This system is now being replaced by a "converged system of broadcasting and telecommunications," where anyone can freely supply and consume information. This change, in turn, is expected to enhance the understanding of various cultures and beliefs around the world and contribute to forming a peaceful global community.

The benefits of developing and introducing a multimedia information infrastructure, which include more job opportunities and increased social welfare, are not necessarily recognized in the developing countries. Undoubtedly, establishing an information infrastructure is of grave importance for developing countries seeking to take off. The second industrial sector, for example, is becoming more and more market and consumer oriented, requiring intensive information in order to produce small quantities of a diverse array of goods. Similarly, the first industrial sector, and the agricultural sector in particular, must increasingly rely on the universal information infrastructure for such information as fluctuations in demand and supply, weather forecasts, environmental changes, soil improvement, and prevention of damage from harmful insects. This is necessary to increase productivity, in terms of both quality and quantity, and to enhance the market value of its products. A universal information infrastructure will not only realize such economic benefits, but may also eliminate distance as an obstacle to developments, thereby drastically improving, in every corner of the world, education, medical treatment, and social welfare, just to mention a few examples.

However, inadequate one-way communications that are excessively commercially oriented may only stimulate demand for goods in the developing countries without increasing productivity and may also result in a lopsided flow of culture.

Reasons for Change

The economic and technical conditions necessary for the convergence of various media have now been achieved. In particular, the increased transmission capacity of fiber optic cables, along with the development of mobile communications, has introduced flexibility and the ability to surmount the obstacle of "distance."

As deregulation progresses, competition is being introduced both on a country-by-country basis and on regional bases, thus bringing about changes in the structure of industry. For example, "a society with energy and competitiveness in the 21st century," as envisaged in Japan by the Enhancement of Info-Communications Systems or in the United States by the National Information Infrastructure, is being created on a national level. With the conclusion of the GATT Uruguay Round and the establishment of the World Trade Organization, an economic environment for establishing a borderless global community has been formed.

Probable Consequences

If a truly universal information infrastructure is established, impediments of distance and national borders will be surmounted. In addition, inequalities between urban and rural areas and between advanced and developing countries will be overcome, particularly in such fields as education, medical treatment, and employment. The swift and free exchange of information will result in the efficient movement of people, materials, and money, thereby enabling the pursuit of prosperity on a global level.

However, if that information infrastructure is established only among urban areas or among advanced countries, the disparity between the "haves" and "have nots" of information will only be aggravated. Having or not having information is potentially a defining factor, possibly more important than the "missing link" of telephone service in the past, for production efficiency and increasing per capita income.

The development of a universal information infrastructure will not only positively affect the first, second, and third industrial sectors, but will also result in strong cultural, social, and political impacts. The potential scope of these impacts is significant. We must therefore note that although a truly universal information infrastructure will contribute to establishing a global community, if individual countries invest in information infrastructures for the sole purpose of improving their competitive edge, this will adversely affect the world community at large. It is necessary, therefore, to devise methods to promote the positive consequences and minimize the negative consequences as much as possible.

Proposed Actions

The creation of a global information society—enabling people around the globe to access, use, and provide information on an equal basis—will lead to greater world peace and prosperity.

We should establish an international forum for planning, organizing, financing, and operating the universal information infrastructure. Its responsibilities would include the implementation of measures to coordinate national or regional infrastructures into an international infrastructure that would contribute to the development of society and the economy on a global scale.

The national or regional mechanisms used to provide information services to people in rural and/or remove regions should be applied globally. To provide truly universal services and to develop a global universal information infrastructure, the world community must assist in training and developing human resources, securing financial resources, and transferring technology and know-how.

-7-
Global Village or
Global Civilization?

Alan Kay

Description of Change

Most people and businesses use computers to automate accounting and writing—activities that were formerly done with paper. Since the first known uses of writing on cuneiform tablets were for counting the King's jars of grain and wine, followed centuries later by the first attempts to transcribe poetry, the current use of computers seems to be the latest chapter in a grand tradition. The printing press was first used to automate the production of Bibles and indulgences; many thought it was a harmless addition to the Holy Roman Empire that could only strengthen the faith. Five hundred years later, one of the most frequently printed books is still the Bible, not to mention the modern versions of indulgences! Were they right in their basic assumptions?

The parts of history that interest me most are those in which people found more than a better way to continue the past—they discovered that new tools can often lead to completely new ideas about thinking and doing. When alphabetic writing was invented by the Phoenicians, it should not surprise us that for hundreds of years it was used to transcribe and support oral tradition. The Ionian Greeks, on the other hand, were taken with the efficiency of representing hundreds of thousands of words with just 23 symbols. This led to the idea that the world itself might be understood as being made of simpler parts. And that led to new ways to think about the world, and to think about thinking.

About fifty years after its invention, the printed book came into its own with the "Portable Library" of Aldus Manutius, the Venetian printer who measured saddlebags to determine the most useful dimensions for books. Dimensions which, by the way, are still the most frequently used. More importantly, his books were not particularly about the established religion, but about everything. His press published thousands of titles by as many authors both ancient and contemporary. And he was not alone. There were more than 20,000 presses in Europe around the year 1500, and most of them were not printing Bibles. The result was modern civilization. Not just science and technology, but new ways to think about politics and human rights.

This happened in the midst of most people thinking "old thoughts." Most still do, and will. In the United States, fewer than one percent invent and discover, and fewer than three percent grow all the food, which is the largest export. On the other hand, substantial portions of U.S. citizens are "fundamentalists." They believe literally and dogmatically in the tenets of their religion—often to the point of refusing medical treatment for sick children. Almost worse, many nonscientists who "believe in" science (and a few scientist too!) believe in it "fundamentally"—it has been reified into dogma. It is not so odd that our minds work as they did tens of thousands of years ago—we are set up biologically to absorb and deeply believe the view of our cultures about the world. What is unusual is that very different and powerful ways of thinking can be invented—examples are science and democracy—and learned by enough people to make radical changes in the way we live.

Reasons for Change

What we want to ask about computers, then, is not so much how they will be reused as old media—they will—but what properties do they have that are so special and powerful that the shape of society will once again be changed?

The first property is that all previous marking and symbol systems can be subsumed by digital representations. The implications of this become really interesting when the second property is added: that stable digital representators can be inexpensively made in astronomical quantities. Third, the representations can be transmitted to everyone in the world very rapidly and at low cost. Finally, the digital representations are active and reflective—they can read and write themselves at great rates of speed. These four properties easily account for the imitation of the old media that has blossomed so strongly in the last few decades. (It also sounds a bit like a new disease!) How are they also the hidden powers that make the computer qualitatively different from all previous media?

Every medium of expression also brings forth new ways to argue. Printing brought forth the essay which begat both modern science and modern democracy. Both require giving up absolute notions of truth and dogma in favor of flexible multiviews. These are bolstered by careful and special forms of argument that have been best carried by printed text and distributed widely. As important as the chance to argue, dialogues—both intertwined as in Galileo and essay versus essay as in the debate over the Constitution—capture the nondogmatic and high-content multiview nature of modern discourse.

Every medium of expression is better at describing certain areas than it is for others. Thus, each has a silent bias that leads discussion in certain directions and away from others. Mathematics became the important language of science because its biases, ways of representing and arguing, have a good fit—make good maps—to gross physical phenomena. Bertrand Russell noted that "language serves not only to express thought but to make possible thoughts that would not be possible without it."

Computers-in-networks extend the notions of library and sending messages in important ways and extend twentieth-century notions of nontrivial argument by being able to find analogies, examples, and counterexamples, as well as to solicit the opinions of colleagues.

More important is that the computer has a special domain of representation and argument that qualitatively transcends what can be mustered by natural language and classical mathematics. These include complex nonlinear dynamic system ecologies, which include the biosphere, epidemics, population explosions and famine, pollution, human health, and twentieth-century physical science.

$E = mc^2$ is compact, astounding, literally earthshattering, and difficult to briefly explain just why the relationship holds. Similarly, the reflective ability of computers to simulate and view arbitrary symbolic systems is compact and astounding, will be earthshattering, and is difficult to briefly explain so that the implications are clear and the emotional impact deep. It is not that system ecologies cannot be talked about in language and classical math (I am doing so right now). It is that making good arguments and, more important, substantiating them, is almost impossible without the ability to simulate the system to determine if it meets all the claims about it. In particular, complex systems are often chaotic; small changes to initial conditions can produce wildly different evolutions over time. Because this is very difficult to spot in most static descriptions, empirical experimentation is required to get some sense of the balance between stability and instability.

The dynamic nature of the computer leads to a natural simplification of representations and descriptions of complex systems. For example, although Newton's laws are simple and express the gravitational relationships between any number of bodies, in classical mathematics it is generally intractable to deal with more than two. Many adults, especially politicians, have no sense of exponential progressions, such as population growth, epidemics such as AIDS, or even compound interest on their credit cards. In contrast, a 12-year-old child in the fine lines of LOGO can easily describe and graphically simulate the interaction of any number of bodies, or create and experience firsthand the nonintuitive swift exponential progression of an epidemic like AIDS. Speculations about weighty matters that would ordinarily be consigned to common sense (the worst of all reasoning methods), can now be tried out with a modest amount of effort, particularly if qualitative intuition is most needed. People who can act heroically during a disaster, but do nothing earlier when it could have been prevented, were not able to imagine.

Another very special property of computers allows different parts of knowledge to be related and compared in ways not feasible in the physical world. We are all used to footnoting and other forms of reference and have well-used thumbs (and sometimes feet) to find these references elsewhere. The computer can simulate a world in which the representations of all related ideas are in the "same place," hyperlinked, even though this is not directly possible in our three-dimensional world. Moreover, there can be many ways to view and compare the ideas simultaneously. And finally, the ideas can be in the form of dynamic and interactive simulations. The first computer systems to create these new ways to represent and think appeared in the early 1960s. Thus I believe it is significant that thirty years later almost no commercial systems hyperlink ideas or use dynamic simulation. This is because most commercial systems are made in response to perceived market needs. The current day mass marketplace is still too unsophisticated to demand real power from their computers, and most vendors do not understand it either or are too timid to try to create a market based on value rather than ignorance. The gap between what computers can do and what most people want from them is critical.

Probable Consequences

McLuhan predicted that speed of light transmission would replace the cool "Gutenberg" sequential discourse of high civilization with a fragmented return to a global oral tradition. Forty years of experience with American television and about one decade with access to computer networks seems to bear him out. Indications are that most people will use computer media and networks for old-style business, new-style social interaction, and lowest common denominator entertainment. This is comparable to the use of printing for accounting, romance novels, trash exposés, and comic books: twinkies for the mind. In short: Junk.

By "junk," I mean stuff that is advertised to be a particular kind of thing—one whose main selling points are convenience and low cost; that often contains substances or processes for which humans have no built-in defenses; and which on close examination turns out not to be the thing that is claimed after all. Business, by means of advertising and exploiting the lack of sophistication among buyers, has successfully introduced junk in most areas of life, including food, housing, possessions, theater, entertainment, literature, education, rights, sports, music, art, money, knowledge—and computing. This is not new: the main complaint in *Madame Bovary* was about junk romance novels, and one of the many complaints of Socrates about his times was that the Sophists were teaching the youth how to win arguments (via rhetoric) without need or concern for the "truth." I will leave it as an exercise for the reader to apply the above criteria to identify computer junk that is on the market today. (As a greater challenge, the reader should try to find the few products on the market today that are not junk!)

The real barriers to the development of a global civilization are the forces and values that are leading most people to join the global village instead. Will this trend continue? Or will more and more people start to use the new communication systems to learn "twenty-first century thinking?" The reason I feel pessimistic is that learning ideas that we are not strongly "prewired" for requires a fair amount of effort, and the will to put forth effort usually comes from putting a high value on what is to be learned. In a world that is increasingly about entertainment and the replacement of high-value goods and ideas by junk, it is hard to see from just where the new and needed upsurge in valuation is going to appear.

Powerful ideas create needs only they can solve. This is what is meant by a paradigm shift; not just the beliefs, but the very priorities of a belief system are replaced. Note that addictive substances and processes also create needs that only they can solve. A perceived need does not automatically mean "valuable." It just means there are powerful forces at play with our belief systems. McLuhan's observation that the Greek roots of "Narcissus" and "Narcosis" are the same is particularly germane here.

Proposed Actions

It is hard to decide early on just how pernicious a new belief system is likely to be; even harder to pull back after the belief system has established itself. I am indebted to Neil Postman for drawing my attention to *Giving Up the Gun,* by Noel Perrin, a fascinating account of the Japanese adopting cannon and musketry for war and then giving it up a century later because it undermined their notions of bravery and honor. Its fascination lies in part in the rarity of humans pulling back from any tool that conveys a large advantage on its users. If we had the chance would we give up science and modern medicine for the belief of assured eternal paradise after death? We cannot venture an answer because of the skepticism inherent in our age. We cannot really know what it was like to believe without any hint of doubt. Since our nervous systems are set up by evolution to jump to conclusions and believe deeply with little evidence—imagine conducting a scientific experiment into possible danger when being charged by something big—the best we can do with the new is to learn to make softer landings into the new belief structures so that we can enjoy them without blindly committing our entire being to them.

Chapter 6
Keeping Pace with a
Globalizing Economy

Introduction

George V. Vassiliou

The global economy has attained a standard of universality inconceivable a decade ago. At this moment, only a few relatively insignificant economies lie outside the world market for goods and services, and flows of international capital are expanding exponentially. No serious ideological dissension exists from a belief in market-based capitalism as the motivating force in economic policy, and rigorous liberalization and restructuring have become macroeconomic benchmarks worldwide.

The globalization of the economy is one of the most remarkable changes facing us as we near the end of the twentieth century, writes J.E. Andriessen, the Minister of Economic Affairs of The Netherlands. The most important effects of this globalization process are:

- In an ever-increasing number of sectors a truly global market is evolving, and globalization leads to an even greater degree of specialization and a more highly differentiated division of labor among countries. Specialization is expressed more in terms of parts of production processes than in products. Hence the familiar phrases, "made in Switzerland," "made in the USA," to which we have all become accustomed, are no longer relevant. In the case of more and more products, a very significant part is manufactured in other countries (Andriessen).

- Globalization is not confined to the production of goods, but also occurs in the service sector. On the demand side, too, forces are contributing to the emergence of a true global market. The explosion in international communications has to a certain degree resulted in a convergence of tastes and preferences of consumers in various parts of the world and the emergence of a "world consumer" (Andriessen).

- Let us not hurry, however, to bury local consumers and national habits. The convergence of taste is destined to coexist for many decades with significant differences in local habits and preferences.
- David de Pury points out that because of the globalization process, there will be an increasing trend "from hardware related value creation to software added value." The international distribution of wealth will begin to shift. Countries that are capable of adapting more quickly to the new environment and of mobilizing the innovative and creative speed of their people, will gain; those that are slow to change will lose. But according to George Shen, in some countries the existing social welfare system makes change and adaptation even more difficult.
- Increasing competition will tend to strengthen protectionist voices, but protectionism has to be resisted. All contributors agree that, whatever the problems, the answer does not lie in new protectionism but, on the contrary, on the even faster removal of barriers and the increasing liberalization of world trade. Furthermore, DeAnne Julius argues that we must also assure free market access for services. This is important because growth in services can relieve the pressures from loss of employment in the manufacturing sectors.
- The ever-strengthening global character of the economy conflicts with the fact that policies are formulated at national levels. This conflict needs to be addressed, among other ways, by creating global rules of behavior. In this respect, the establishment of the World Trade Organization is a very important step forward.

  To meet the demands of the globalizing economy, we are moving from "shallow integration," that is, from the removal of all barriers, tariffs, and quotas, to "deep integration," which will lead to a "harmonization and reconciliation of domestic policies," predicts Robert Z. Lawrence. "The challenge for policy makers," he continues, "lies in achieving the appropriate balance between international harmonization and local autonomy."
- The real globalization of the economy is an objective which is proceeding in parallel with the regionalization of the world economy. Regional integration should not be at odds with multilateral liberalization, argues Jaime Serra Puche, but Philip Bowring believes that regionalization is a trend that is already too strong to stop. We must acknowledge its existence and try to regulate it. In that way, it will contribute to the development

of a real global economy, rather than degenerate into regional economic wars.

- Globalization will also require the real global corporation. Despite the fact that, with few exceptions, most multinational corporations are presently operating on a worldwide scale, all corporations still have roots in one nation and one culture. This background is evident in the top management of these corporations. Haruo Shimada provides in this respect the interesting concept of backyard strategy for companies located in the three major industrial pillars of the world economy.

Paul Walsh looks at the globalization process from yet another angle. He reflects that the strengthening of the borderless corporation undermines the policy making ability of the nation-state and leads to increasing conflict between national policy making and multinationals. Governments must create the conditions necessary to effectively control world corporations by adopting similar and compatible processes and procedures.

Globalization means increasing competition in every respect. Thus, F. Romeo Braun points out, competition will not only be between products, but also between countries. Each will devise new rules and regulations to attract more foreign capital.

"To remain sustainable, " Wolfgang Reinicke states, "globalization must be politically accountable, legally accessible, and socially justifiable." Existing international institutions should be overhauled to create a new balance between private interest and public good in the international community. National policy making needs to be supplemented by decision making and control at a multilateral level.

This is the argument made by the German State Secretary, Gert Haller, who examines the policy implications of the globalization process. In this new environment, international cooperation is a must. For problems that have to be solved at home, such as rising inflation, medium-term monetary policy, and macroeconomic strategy, each country has to formulate its own policies, but they must always take into consideration possible repercussions on partner countries. Another wide-ranging set of issues, however, has to be tackled on a multilateral level, and each of the international forums—G-7, the World Bank, the IMF, the WTO—has to implement its own mandate and responsibilities.

-1-
The Globalized
Economy Is a Reality

J.E. Andriessen

Description of Change

The most remarkable changes facing us at the end of the twentieth century are:

- The disappearance of communism as a social system.
- The emergence of dynamic economies in Asia, particularly in Southeast Asia and China.
- The globalization of the economy.

Reasons for Change

Communism collapsed in the former COMECON states because the leadership's reforms were ineffective and could not overcome the population's desire for freedom, wealth, and democracy. Once the reformists gained power, the difficult process of transforming centrally planned and autocratically governed societies into market-oriented democracies started.

At the same time, the Asian "newcomers" have maintained impressive economic growth rates. Their success is based on good macroeconomic management, good education policies, and outward-looking development strategies. Other factors, particularly a flexible social system, low labor costs, and increasing organizational and technological capability, also played an important role.

In a growing number of sectors, a true global market is evolving. This phenomenon is caused by a combination of rapid technological progress and far-reaching socioeconomic and institutional reforms in several parts of the world. As a result of new technologies, such as information technology and computer applications, entrepreneurs can divide integrated production processes of goods and services into several subactivities. These subactivities can be carried out at a greater number of locations, as more and more countries are opting for a market economy and opening up their markets to foreign investment and technology.

Therefore, the strong increase in the international mobility of capital has also contributed to the globalization of the economy.

Probable Consequences

The collapse of communism and the subsequent end to the East-West confrontation fundamentally changed international relations. Concepts, like the First, Second, and Third World, have lost their meaning. Two rival socioeconomic systems are no longer striving to expand their spheres of influence in the Third World. Moreover, the Third World itself is no longer a homogeneous group of poor countries, but rather a highly differentiated one. A nation's future role on the world stage will be determined more by the economic power it generates and less by its relation with one of the superpowers.

The emergence of dynamic economies in Asia indicates that the postwar bipolar world order, led by the United States and the USSR, and the economic dominance of the United States, the Economic Union, and Japan, is making way for a new, perhaps multipolar, world order. Some newcomers intend to play a major role. Hence, new growth poles and power bases emerge, not only in Asia, but also in Latin America.

Globalization will lead to a more highly differentiated division of labor between countries and specialization in parts of production processes instead of in complete products. Thus, products are no longer "made in the Netherlands" or "made in Switzerland," but consist of components that have been manufactured in various countries. Assembly of these components, as well, can take place at numerous locations. As a result, industries have become more and more "footloose."

Further, globalization is not confined to the production of goods, but also occurs in the services sector, where, for example, administrative work can be contracted out. On the demand side, too, forces are contributing to the emergence of a true global market. To some extent, the explosion in international communication has resulted in a convergence of consumer tastes and preferences in various parts of the world (the emergence of a "world consumer"). In such a globalized economy, competition for markets will intensify.

The globalization of the economy, with its inevitable increase in the interdependencies among national economies, seriously curtails the ability of national governments to carry out autonomous policies and to implement effective national regulations. Another consequence of this growing interdependency is a more complex definition of national interest. Regional cooperation and integration can be seen, in part, as a response to these realities.

Proposed Actions

The reality of a globalized economy has strengthened and extended multilateral cooperation and furthered the liberalization of international trade and investment. Clearly, a globalized economy will need a more international and comprehensive regulatory framework. Therefore, the world community must design and implement multilaterally accepted minimum rules and principles that facilitate global interchange. A well-designed regulatory framework will enable national realization of the full benefits of deregulation and liberalization. It will also provide a stable and transparent environment for private economic decision-making. Thus, the globalized economy will function more efficiently and equitably.

The impending creation of a World Trade Organization (WTO), one of the main results of the Uruguay Round, is an important step forward in the direction of such a global and comprehensive regulatory framework. The WTO is an adequate forum for addressing many of the necessary regulatory issues relating to international economic exchange. However, further progress has to be made, especially in the establishment of rules and principles governing competition policy, foreign direct investment, and environmental measures.

In principle, the industrial countries, especially in Europe, have two ways to respond to the challenge of a globalizing economy. They can respond conservatively by withdrawing into their own fortresses, thereby attempting to protect home markets, give preferential treatment to home-based industries, and defend their costly postwar welfare state. Or, they can respond progressively by making structural adjustments that will strengthen their competitiveness. The conservative response denies the nature and scope of the globalization process. Networking between enterprises in various continents has developed to such an extent that withdrawal into one's own fortress is no longer a feasible proposition. Opting for such an inward-looking and defensive strategy will in the long run irrevocably lead to loss of prosperity. What remains is the more promising progressive response. That route is certainly not an easy one; it involves far-reaching and painful structural adjustments in numerous sectors of society. In some cases, even the socioeconomic order will require a substantial overhaul.

Industrial countries choosing the progressive response should first try to eliminate those rigid policies that hamper the functioning markets (not only in the goods and services markets, but also in the labor and capital markets). This approach boils down to deregulation, incorporating more incentives on the supply side, reducing the excessively high labor costs associated with the modern welfare state, and stabilizing the environment through the appropriate mix of macroeconomic policies.

Another important element is the improvement and strengthening of the so-called public supply side of the market; this involves such issues as increasing technological and innovative capability, improving the physical infrastructure, and improving the quality of education and training. The action program should also fight against the sluggishness of public decision-making and the concomitant high decision-making costs.

In summary, the challenge of a globalizing economy can be met by a combination of strengthened multilateral cooperation, continued liberalization of international trade and investment, and consistently carried through structural adjustments, especially in Europe. The implementation of such a strategy requires strong leadership at the national and international levels.

-2-
Abundant Human Resources and Technology

George Shen

Description of Change

In recent years, foreign direct investment (FDI) has enabled many developing countries to establish export-oriented manufacturing operations, with products aimed mainly at markets in developed countries. The combination of abundant human resources in developing countries with capital and production technology from advanced countries has led to many changes. Among them, the following are the most noticeable:

- Increasing competitiveness, market share, and thus profits for producers who have set up off-shore operations through direct investment overseas.
- Structural adjustment in the advanced countries, causing unemployment and protectionist sentiments.
- Accelerated pace of economic development in countries hosting these manufacturing operations.

These changes show that when resources are more productively deployed, the production of goods and services becomes more efficient, benefiting both producers and consumers. Technological advancement in manufacturing and management operations, as well as in information processing and communications, has not only ushered in the postindustrial society, but also given birth to the global village. Production operations are no longer necessarily performed by blue-collar workers, and parts and components of a finished product can now be made and assembled in different parts of the world. To many developing countries, the combination of domestic human resources with acquired technology has helped their economies take off. Although the changes that hasten economic development do have side effects that create social, economic, and even political problems, people in the developing countries have generally welcomed and quickly adapted to such changes.

Unfortunately, advanced countries have found it more difficult to cope with the changes arising from the new international division of labor. They are confronted with the loss of comparative advantage and unemployment. How to adapt and benefit from such changes is the main challenge facing many advanced nations today.

Reasons for Change

For decades, manufacturers in industrialized countries have kept their products competitive by shifting production operations to developing countries, where wages are low. Countries in East and Southeast Asia, including China, have therefore attracted large amounts of foreign capital both from outside and within the region. Not content with performing only labor-intensive operations, these countries have eagerly absorbed new technology and know-how in order to make products with more added value. Some of them have even gone one step further by nurturing their own research and development capabilities.

As a result, some of these developing countries have newly industrializing economies with much higher annual growth rates than the developed world. Although the improved standard of living has expanded their demand for both capital and consumer goods from the advanced countries, their manufactured products have also gained larger market shares in advanced countries. This has provided consumers in the advanced countries with more goods at lower prices, but has also aggravated unemployment and related problems.

Thus, although the globalization of industrial production should theoretically benefit all nations, some advanced countries feel that the benefits derived by their competitors have created economic and social predicaments at home. These problems are particularly difficult to cope with in times of economic recession and serve as hotbeds of political debate among pressure groups with vested interests. For instance, textile manufacturers and workers have long resorted to imposing quotas on exports from developing countries, domestic electrical appliance makers have accused foreign suppliers of dumping, and even governments have joined the chorus in attacking Third World countries for violating human rights by not paying their workers wages according to international standards. In short, instead of making efforts to restructure their economies, some advanced countries have sought refuge behind the shield of protectionism to resist such changes.

Structural changes are never easy, but the advanced countries have found it extremely difficult to restructure their economies by shifting the workers from traditional to high-tech jobs or by retraining blue-collar workers for the service sector. The cause is a social welfare system that negates any incentive for workers to adapt to changes. Unlike the vast majority of workers in developing countries, who are eager to find work and anxious to learn in order to free themselves from hunger and poverty, those in advanced countries fall back on social welfare and resist change. Many developing countries are experiencing the painful process of economic restructuring, with their people enduring all sorts of hardships, including unemployment. At the same time, the advanced countries are complaining about unfair competition caused by cheap labor and imposing trade restrictions on developing countries in an effort to protect their sunset industries and to feed an idle work force with tax-payers money.

The combination of advanced technology and abundant human resources should provide better and cheaper goods and services for the benefit of all people, yet many advanced countries are sufficiently preparing themselves to reap the due benefits. It is really a pity that the ones who initiated the link between technology and human resources are the very ones having difficulty with the results.

Probable Consequences

For advanced countries, the main concern has been the "hallowing" of the manufacturing sector and the "exportation" of jobs to developing countries, which has caused structural adjustment problems, notably unemployment. In contrast, many developing countries in East Asia have experienced high rates of economic growth and rising shares of GDP contribution by the secondary and tertiary sectors.

But the most significant consequence is the integration of the economies of many developing countries into the global village. China and India, for example, two of the world's most populous countries, have now adopted an outward-looking policy. During their transition from a closed to an open economy, these countries have already provided vast opportunities for trade and investment not only to the advanced countries, but to their developing neighbors. The impact on the world economy is already quite significant.

Proposed Actions

The top priority in both advanced and developing countries must be human resource development to cope with the changes. In advanced countries, workers who lost their jobs because of economic restructuring should be retrained for work in the postindustrial society. To encourage them, the welfare system should be reformed to ensure that unemployment benefits do not negate incentives to find work. Employers and employees should find ways to reduce costs, thereby rendering their goods and services more competitive. In short, international market forces should be allowed to determine prices. Advanced countries, which are losing their competitive edge in certain sectors of manufacturing and/or service industries, should either improve their competitiveness or hasten economic restructuring. Recent attempts by the French government to allow trainees to work at lower wage levels represented a step in the right direction, but unfortunately it failed because of student demonstrations.

In addition, many developing countries objected to the demand made by certain advanced countries that world trade should be linked with the observance of specific labor standards. They fear that this might be protectionism in disguise. This does not imply that workers' rights should be ignored in developing countries. Apart from the right to work, the vast work force in developing countries needs training to adapt to new technology and to shift to higher value-added jobs. They need access to markets in advanced countries through trade, so that the products they produce can earn precious foreign currency that will quicken the pace of economic development of their countries. They also need to share with fellow workers in advanced countries the benefits of economic growth through the efficient international division of labor.

Thus, trade barriers need to be further lowered to ensure the free flow of goods and services among all nations. This will also facilitate the free flow of technology, which developing countries need to produce goods and services at optimal costs and productivity. The successful conclusion of the Uruguay Round is an important step in this direction.

A spin-off of the human resources and technology link is that China's dependence on world trade is quickening the pace of economic reform, which will eventually lead to political reform. The advanced countries should therefore encourage China to participate in world affairs more actively, with a view to encouraging China's peaceful evolution from an authoritarian to a democratic society.

-3-
Open Regionalism and Multilateral Liberalization

Jaime Serra Puche

Description of Change

In recent years, international businesses have expanded around the world. Partly because of the progress in telecommunications and transportation, world flows of merchandise, services, finance, investment, information, and people have expanded. Year after year, business operations across international boundaries have been growing. These are the underlying technological and human forces that, in today's world, gradually push countries toward globalization.

Reasons for Change

These trends constitute a new reality for governments. On the one hand, the fast pace of international business represents an opportunity to access new markets, access additional financial sources, acquire enhanced technologies, and forge strategic alliances with foreign companies. On the other hand, the interrelated nature of these transactions means that if international exchanges are not liberalized, there are fewer benefits for countries considering the possibility of reciprocal liberalizations. For instance, potential profits for countries that only liberalize their trade in goods, but not in services, will be lower than for countries that liberalize the full spectrum of their transactions.

A multilateral agenda to liberalize merchandise, trade, services, and investment is clearly a first-best scenario. However, consensus on such an agenda is virtually impossible in a "once and for all" negotiation. Although governments find it appealing to consider broad agendas when engaging in international negotiations, agreements are difficult to reach when issues are diverse and interrelated. International negotiations are intrinsically more complex. Each country must have the internal political consensus to support any resulting agreements. These difficulties increase considerably when a large number of nations are participating in the process. The increased complexity of international economic linkages was evident in the recently concluded Uruguay Round negotiations.

Probable Consequences

Not surprisingly, a growing number of countries, on all continents, have designed formal and informal formulas to increase national competitiveness through regional integration. Faced with the complexities of multilateral or universal "one and for all" negotiations, these countries are relying on regional economic agreements, which include trade in goods and services, investment, and technology licensing under adequate intellectual property protection, for economic success.

Regional integration should not be at odds with multilateral liberalization; quite the opposite should be true. Regionalism can support further progress on the multilateral front. In fact, it would be a serious policy mistake to design regional agreements that are incompatible with the ongoing globalization trends that will, sooner or later, increase potential profits from universal or multilateral economic transactions. That is, if regional agreements do not take multilateral liberalization into account, most countries will eventually lose an increasing number of opportunities for mutually beneficial exchanges. Furthermore, if regional agreements become closed trading blocks, the result will be greater economic imbalances, greater income disparities, and tensions that could threaten world stability and peace.

Mexico, for example, is aware that regional trade liberalization can both raise the competitiveness of participating countries and help to generate global trade, but it must be consistent with the multilateral spirit, as formulated in Article XXIV of GATT. These conditions are met in NAFTA and in agreements Mexico has negotiated with Latin American countries.

These features reflect consistency of regional agreements with the spirit of multilateralism. Thus, regional economic spaces and multilateralism are not developments that oppose each other. On the contrary, they constitute simultaneous processes that should be harmonious and complementary.

Proposed Actions

The new multilateral trade organization, created as a result of the Uruguay Round, will play a key role in the supervision of the multilateral agenda and in imposing consistency on regional agreements vis-à-vis that agenda. On the other hand, organizations or institutions, such as UNCTAD and ALADI, will have to be restructured. In addition, artificial economic alliances that were born of the previous global geopolitical arrangements will definitely dissolve.

In short, to efficiently face globalization and to complement regionalism with multilateral liberalization, all regions must implement an open door policy. Only through open trade spaces that contribute to the expansion of world exchanges, can the current evolution of science, technology, and ideas contribute to development, fair distribution paths, and higher living standards in the world.

-4-
Regionalism, Not Internationalism

Philip Bowring

Description of Change

Contrary to received opinion, globalization of the world economy is not inevitable. Indeed it may now be at a high water mark; nationalist and regionalist sentiments are beginning to reassert themselves. The notion of a global corporation with no ultimate national loyalty was always a myth.

For now, the GATT Uruguay Round has shored up the global trading system and eased pressures for giving priority to regional blocks, whether in Europe, North America, or East Asia. The internationalization of the service sector has provided a bigger marketplace for accounting, retailing, and insurance. However, GATT is about mechanisms, not fundamentals. To understand where we are going, we have to understand where we have come from and why.

The spread of globalization in the past decade is illustrated by the surge in international capital movements. These were characterized by international investment in countries that combine cheap labor with reasonable organizational levels, the extension of international brand names such as Coca Cola and Toyota to most countries of the world, including China, Russia, and India, and, most recently, the flood of portfolio capital from developed to emerging markets.

Reasons for Change

This international movement is the result of reductions in trade barriers; the desire of companies in mature markets to find faster growth elsewhere; competition between firms in developed countries that are transferring technology to younger economies; the decline of socialist economic and political thinking; technological changes that make it more difficult for governments to control capital movement; and—the sine qua non of it all—the existence of large capital surpluses in mature countries caused mainly by demographic factors.

However, none of these factors is permanent. The savings transfer will probably slow over time as the population bulge in OECD countries moves from high-saving middle age to low-saving old age. The reaction against socialism may be cyclical as well as structural; a bad accident in international capital markets—for example, over derivatives—may reverse enthusiasm for the free capital movement; unemployment in the developed world, which is already a severe constraint on freer trade, could get worse.

Probable Consequences

Most important, the political conditions for global trade are withering. Globalization was a creation of post-World War II institutions, such as IBRD and GATT. They operated under the U.S. umbrella and with the communist threat holding the United States/Western Europe/Japan alliance together. Recently, the former or quasicommunists have moved closer to, but not quite into, the global system. Yet while economic globalization appears to continue, at the political level fragmentation is apparent, enhanced by the end of the superpower duumvirate and also by the proliferation of nuclear weapons, which is virtually unstoppable as technology is disseminated.

The upsurge in United States-Japan trade tensions so soon after the Uruguay Round is less a product of trade issues than a sign of the declining political rapport based on mutual need. As for China, it currently has need of foreign capital and markets to develop its industries. But the benefits of the open door policy has been so ill distributed that its survival is not assured. Economic nationalism not only has deep roots, but may make sense for a country that is huge but not at the forefront of applied technology. That applies to China and to Russia, which has even less of a foreign trade tradition.

Nor should one assume that the global spread of brand name manufacturing will do more than marginal good for either free trade or internationalism. Multinationals have, in fact, been the major beneficiaries in the past of high cost, import substitution regimes, from Australia to Argentina. Ultimately they too reflect the national interest—in a broad sense—of their country of origin. Foreign subsidiaries may have much autonomy. Parent company boards may have a sprinkling of foreigners. Their global interests may be traded on foreign stock exchanges. But ultimately (with a couple of Anglo-Dutch exceptions to prove the rule), they have their roots in one nation and one culture, from which come the majority of their shareholders and their top management. It is also the primary center of their research, development and funding.

If some Western multinationals have fallen into woolly thinking about being above nationalism, the newest entrant on the multinational scene has certainly not. Korea currently has an official globalization campaign that is all about increasing the global impact of Korean firms, not becoming less Korean.

While multinationalism remains a half truth, there is political as well as economic impetus behind regional concepts. Hispanic/Latin issues are a gradually growing factor in U.S. domestic politics. NAFTA will expand because of Latin America's disenchantment with economic nationalism and U.S. disenchantment with the Pacific. Asia's need for the U.S. military presence will fade, while U.S. concerns about technological competition from Japan and later Korea will grow. Its relations with China will continue to oscillate between missionary zeal to convert it to Jeffersonian democracy and fear of its numbers and potential power.

Meanwhile, East Asia, excluding China, has good geographical as well as purely economic reasons for favoring open trade. Led by Japan, it will continue efforts to expand regional trade and investment as its relationship with the West gradually dwindles. At some point, a trade grouping linking developing Southeast Asia into an enlarged ASEAN dominated by Korea/Taiwan/Japan is likely to emerge. However, a continuing upsurge of Chinese assertiveness might split East Asia into allies of either China or Japan respectively. Japan's natural allies would be the 250 million Malay-speaking peoples and the Vietnamese.

In general, medium-sized countries will become more important relative to the regional leaders—thus Korea and Indonesia compared with Japan in Asia, Mexico and Brazil relative to the United States. Other lesser subregional groupings, all with their own preferential systems and political cement, may also emerge. Turkey, for example, may turn its attention away from the West toward Turkic-speaking former Soviet countries. India's development, indeed that of the entire subcontinent, may speed up to some extent with foreign capital. But it will remain detached from other groups.

Relationships within regions between more and less advanced nations will grow, as for in East Asia, where a symbiotic link exists between Japan, Korea, and Taiwan on the one hand, and their southern neighbors on the other. The latter are mostly pragmatic countries open to trade and investment and with younger but not oppressively fast-growing populations that are able to absorb north Asian capital and skills.

The United States-Latin America relationship is now on a sounder footing, although geography is not as favorable to regional trade as in East Asia. The big problem is Europe. West as well as East is old. They both need to invest in populous neighbors to the south and east, just as Japan is investing in Southeast Asia. But relations will remain tense. On one side, fear of the demographic explosion in North Africa and the Middle East is adding to historical Islam-Christianity enmity. In those countries themselves, nationalism and archaic social systems have held back investment and development, thereby increasing hostility to the rich neighbors to the north.

Whatever happens to their relationship with Europe, unless the countries of the Middle East and North Africa do something very soon to reduce their very high birth rates (population growth in Iran, Iraq, Syria, and Jordan is over 3.5 percent per year, or double that of India), the region is likely to be the scene of even greater conflict than in the past. Water in these regions is especially scarce.

Every country is gradually becoming more aware of regional relationships and the problems and opportunities they present. In turn, national policies are beginning to give priority to regional over global issues. One current example is the determination of all the ASEAN countries to develop their relations with Burma regardless of United States and European attempts to isolate the regime on human rights grounds.

Proposed Actions

How should the world cope with these changes? First, while acknowledging that the global trading system is in theory preferable, political realities lean toward regional accommodations. Regional economic arrangements can help contain the economic disadvantages of political fragmentation. However, it is especially important to keep resources trade open on a global basis. Competition for resources is likely to intensify, so global access to the cheapest possible supplies will help mitigate conflict.

As for the specific regions, East Asia has done so well out of open trade that its benefits should need repeating. However, the strength of mercantilist attitudes in parts of Asia (especially Korea and Japan, where the spirit of Colbert seems stronger than that of Adam Smith) are souring attitudes elsewhere to free trade and will retard the development of regional trade. Without an institutional framework, the economic dynamism of East Asia could spill over into the destructive rivalries seen earlier in Europe, especially once the U.S. military has departed.

Europe should concentrate its attention less on Eastern Europe, whose return to the Eurofold is assured, and more on relations with North Africa and the Levant. Latin America should take care to realize that only through openness can it capitalize on its relations with both the United States and Europe.

It will also be important to recognize that the giant countries—Russia, China, and India—currently on the periphery of the world trading system are likely to remain so. Their trade to GNP nations (except perhaps China which may have peaked already) should rise in response to capital flow. But their size and the problems of internal transport will limit their role in world trade. They may want to buy technology, but capital and management systems are going to have to be locally bred.

Likewise it is important to acknowledge that all corporations, however international their operations, have national roots and goals. Trade and communication create common interests in maintaining peace and prosperity and have globalized inventions ranging from water closets to pop songs and soft drinks. Commerce and capital flows are beneficial, but they are neither a religion nor a cure-all. There is precious little sign in this century that they have done much to erode nationalism, except within such regional contexts as the European Union, or where there are existing cultural and linguistic ties to build on. The global village is a myth. It is either a utopian dream or a hegemonistic vision. If the best is the enemy of the good, the future lies with regionalism.

The "Backyard Strategy" of Old Economic Powers

Haruo Shimada

Description of Change

The old economic major powers, such as European countries (or the European Union), the United States, and Japan seem to be rapidly adopting and promoting what I describe as the "backyard strategy." By this I mean that they invest and develop production facilities in their hinterlands, just as they built factories in their backyards.

EU countries make direct investments in Eastern and Middle Europe and CIS areas; the United States does the same thing in Mexico, taking advantage of the NAFTA agreement, and tries to expand its scope to encompass the Pacific Rim areas resorting to the APEC network. Although its strategic intent is not clear, Japan also seems to be moving in a similar direction by investing vigorously in China and Southeast Asia.

Reasons for Change

There are several reasons behind this change. Corporations in the major economic powers find it increasingly less profitable to continue production in their home countries because of the high costs of production, including high wages, high taxes, and high expenses for social programs and environmental protection. Their direct investments in the hinterlands are also strengthened by a desire to escape from rigid institutional constraints, such as legal restrictions, policy regulations, and stubborn labor practices of home countries.

The contrast with less developed areas as well as excommunist and socialist countries is striking. Costs of production are much cheaper thanks to low wages and low prices of domestic commodities. Social conditions for production, such as labor practices, are much more flexible, and environmental regulations are much less stringent. People are excited to receive new technologies from advanced economies and are highly motivated to work with them. Moreover, currency exchange rates are relatively low when compared with their real domestic purchasing power. This enhances the export competitiveness of products produced in these countries and areas. Multinational corporations based in old major economic powers invest vigorously in these "backyard" areas in an attempt to take advantage of these favorable conditions to make better use of the productive resources of host countries and attain greater competitive advantages.

Such behavior necessarily intensifies competition among advanced economies, because these corporations compete among themselves by providing cheaper products produced in their backyard areas. Viewed from a global perspective, these developments also intensify competition between old major economic powers and newly evolving developing economies, particularly because the latter enhance their international competitiveness by taking advantage of technologies transferred from the former.

Probable Consequences

As products produced in backyard areas penetrate into the economies of home countries, prices of tradable commodities in home countries decline as a result of intensified competition. This makes competing businesses within home countries unprofitable and unsustainable. Faced with this difficulty, many corporations leave home countries searching for cheaper costs of production; others give up. Whichever reaction occurs, their home countries inevitably suffer from industrial hollowing and its concomitant, higher unemployment.

This is what happened in EU countries in recent years and it may explain a large part of the increase in unemployment. In the United States, employment opportunities are flowing out of country to Mexico and other foreign countries. Japan, which until recently enjoyed a high level of employment, is not an exception. In the short run, the shift of production facilities abroad does not seem to reduce domestic employment; there are off-setting increases in exporting capital goods. In the long run, however, it may very well increase unemployment.

In contrast, economies of backyard areas are receiving the benefits of industrialization. Thanks to technology transfers from advanced economies and increased exports, they enjoy higher incomes and can eventually develop their own industries. Such developments, however, run the risk of widening the gap between rich and poor, as well as destroying the natural environment. If proper policies are enforced to distribute incomes equitably among people and to protect the environment, backyard areas can really enjoy the merits of the backyard strategy of old economic powers.

MNCs or global corporations that promote the backyard strategy are the prime beneficiaries; they enjoy higher profits and prosperity by taking advantage of the large markets offered by advanced economies on the one hand, and the favorable conditions of production in backyard areas. In contrast, their home countries may well suffer from loss of industries, jobs, and government revenues. This may well trigger and encourage protectionist inclination in these countries.

Proposed Actions

Finally, let me propose some policy actions that can minimize the drawbacks and maximize the favorable consequences of these developments.

First, make the economic, social, and institutional conditions in home countries more attractive for global corporations, so that they are induced to invest at home. Such changes might include improvements to the industrial infrastructure, such as transportation systems and information networks, development of a human capital infrastructure, including education and training programs, reform of the legal and institutional systems, liberalization of rigid regulations, and modification of labor practices and labor relations.

Second, transfer useful technologies as openly and swiftly as possible from advanced economies to backyard areas, so that the latter can develop rapidly and enhance standards of living quickly. At the same time, be sure that the increased income is distributed among employers and workers as equitably as possible and that the environment is properly protected. The people and environment of backyard areas should not be abused or exploited.

With these policies in place, unemployment and industrial hollowing in old economic powers can be minimized and backyard areas can be enriched. Prosperity can thus be shared more equitably among old and new economic powers and also among countries, corporations, and people.

-6-
The Global Corporation and the Decline of Nation-States

Paul Walsh

Description of Change

National geographic borders are increasingly meaningless to the conduct of business by globally oriented corporations. Historically, the national headquarters of a corporation shaped its activities and its point of reference. An individual corporation operated primarily within the geographic boundaries of a specific nation, paid taxes to that nation, and looked to its government to protect its interests.

A change occurred with the emergence of multinational corporations—corporate entities that sold products and services and conducted business in a number of countries while still holding fast to a single headquarters country.

Today, however, many global companies operate around the world with major headquarters-type activities taking place in many countries. In some cases, foreign subsidiaries are larger and better known than their parent companies. In many ways, these subsidiary corporations act as domestic corporations. These truly multinational corporations have become stateless—or borderless—corporations.

Reasons for Change

As developed markets became saturated, and transportation and distribution became more global, successful corporations looked for new areas to produce and market products. The dramatic breakthroughs in global communications and computing power made the geographic place of business less and less important. Money, purchase orders, documents, and data all move around the world with the ease of a keystroke. Raw materials come from one country; initial processing is done in another country; and final processing is completed in one or several additional countries.

Also helping this trend is GATT and the recently concluded Uruguay Round. Although worldwide trade procedures remain unnecessarily burdensome and many trade barriers remain in place, the Uruguay Round will facilitate trade on a global basis. Corporations have found that skilled workers, talented executives, and growing markets are available worldwide. Country of origin for the product, and the national headquarters of a parent corporation, become meaningless concepts.

Probable Consequences

The borderless corporation will put increased pressure on the rationale behind current national economic, legal, and trade policies. How should nations tax goods that pass through their borders during a production process that begins and ends elsewhere? Is a product made within the borders of a country by a plant owned by a foreign corporation really different from a product made in a neighboring facility by a domestic corporation? Borderless corporations must know which national laws govern their behavior. Accepted business practices in one country may be considered illegal in another country. The ongoing legal battle between Volkswagen and General Motors concerning J. Ignacio Lopez de Arriortua only hints at the legal difficulties of true worldwide trade.

It will become increasingly difficult for a nation to determine what corporate activities are in its national interest and what activities are not. Countries currently have varying legal definitions of confidentiality and fair competition. International accounting rules may become outmoded. Technology developments will become increasingly global in nature. Work force and personnel patterns will change. Scientists from many countries can work for the same borderless corporation and develop technologies not possible within a single nation. This increased sharing of knowledge and skills with fewer barriers can lead to rapid positive change in the technology landscape, but it will also raise questions about national immigration and labor policies. National economic, trade, and technology policy will be increasingly shaped by the needs of borderless corporations. At the same time, nations will benefit from the jobs, technology, and capital offered by these same borderless corporations.

Proposed Actions

A new paradigm will need to emerge regarding national sovereignty and national self-interest. More cooperative forums for exchange of ideas between heads of state and heads of corporations must be developed and current forums must be enhanced. The World Trade Organization (WTO) should recognize its unique role and agree to serve as a forum for the discussion of how governments and corporations can begin addressing the issues surrounding global trade.

There is growing international commerce in ideas, processes, and procedures. Solution-oriented transactions will need new accounting definitions and new legal protections. This does not mean that corporations should ignore cultural and historical traditions of commerce. But governments must recognize and accept that a global corporation can change the way it does business far faster than governments can change public policy. Accordingly, governments should consider creating an official entity to interact on a formal basis with global corporations to address these new accounting and legal issues.

Simultaneous satellite transmission creates a borderless flow of news, data, and funds. New national and international laws and regulations, consistent across all markets, will be required to accommodate a growing number of borderless activities. Traditionally, corporations formed trade associations based on product lines (i.e., food association, automotive association, and telecommunications associations). Although bilateral associations (such as the British-American Chamber of Commerce) have become more proactive during the past ten years, there is now a need for a worldwide business association bringing together the capital and intellectual resources of today's truly global corporations. Working with the WTO, this partnership can have a real impact on the issues facing today's world economy.

-7-
Competition and International Trade

David de Pury

Description of Change

Wealth and prosperity will increasingly shift from countries with large natural resources to countries able to promote a competitive national economic environment that mobilizes the innovative and creative spirit of their people. Simultaneously, these countries will be able to successfully access the international trading system. The trend is thus from hardware related value creation to software added value and from national and regional markets to global markets.

Reasons for Change

The political and economic liberalization of the late 1980s has led to a more open and global world economy, as well as to fiercer competition. This competition has, in turn, accelerated technological innovation and the development of new products and new geographical markets. It is closely linked with what is referred to as the third industrial revolution (time-based management, lean production, and supply management).

Greater competition has also altered the employment equation. Unemployment has risen sharply in countries where the jobs eliminated by this third industrial revolution have not been replaced by new jobs created to accommodate new products and markets. As a result, the international distribution of wealth has begun to shift. Formerly rich nations, such as many industrialized nations, have become poorer; some former developing countries have become wealthier. These shifts are accelerating and are likely to continue to do so.

Probable Consequences

There will be an increasing struggle between nations that view increasing competition and trade as an opportunity for growth and nations that fear this competition and seek refuge in protectionism. This evolution presents the world economy with both opportunities and risks.

The risks lie in increased isolationism and protectionism fueled mainly by the recession and the problem of structural unemployment. Declining growth and social unrest will be the result.

The opportunities arise from the potential of sustainable growth. It lies in the revolutionary global economic adjustment already underway. The process can only be achieved through national and international economic frameworks based on the principles of competition and a free market. Trade should benefit both industrialized nations, which will increasingly focus on products and services with high value added, and developing countries, which initially will rely more on the transformation of natural resources, on primary products, and on hardware production. Industrialized nations facing stagnating demand at home need to invent new products and services and to access new markets; developing countries need full access to industrialized countries in order to reach new levels of development.

Proposed Actions

Competition, increasing global trade, and a free market economy will result in sustainable growth if there are rules to enforce the necessary international adjustment process. Without rules, freedom invariably turns into chaos and growth into stagnation and recession.

The successful completion of the Uruguay Round of GATT is a major step in the right direction. However, it would be fatal to believe that this result will suffice for the foreseeable future. It is just the beginning; immediate efforts are needed to at least intellectually prepare the next step. There should be a new Round or rather—because we cannot afford to wait another ten years—the launching of a permanent negotiation process. The objectives are as follows.

Ecology

Contrary to popular belief, there is basically no conflict of interest between trade and the protection of the environment. Underdevelopment and poverty are the worst enemies of the environment. Only trade is capable of producing the wealth necessary to invest in a cleaner environment. Also, free trade encourages the most efficient use of resources by removing tariffs and other barriers that distort prices. However, to promote truly sustainable economic growth, we need to operate within a framework that makes sure that trade policies and environmental protection are compatible. As concerns for the environment transcend national boundaries, environmental standards and legislation among countries need to be coordinated.

Direct Investments

Foreign direct investments were identified as one of the priorities when the Uruguay Round was launched, but in the final agreement little progress was made on this issue. GATT should follow the principle of national treatment, that is, foreign firms should be free to do what domestic companies are permitted to do. Keeping investments open benefits everyone, not just the country into which the capital flows. Major problems that need to be resolved in the area of foreign direct investments are trade balancing, the elimination of local equity requirements, and the issue of currency transfers.

Global System of Competition

A global system of competition should be developed, which takes into account the more international nature of competition. Why, for instance, should dumping be prohibited only if practiced by a foreign competitor in a country's home market? Today, most cases of dumping take place in third countries.

Private Sector

The private sector should have direct access to the GATT system. In a world in which companies are increasingly global and multinational, corporations and even private entrepreneurs should be given rights and obligations that today are only granted to nations. In a global world economy, the GATT system will need to be made directly accessible to the private sector.

National Technology Policies

Friction is likely to increase on the high-tech frontier as governments grow more inclined to support and protect their local high-tech industries. The Uruguay Round limits research and development subsidies to 50 percent on applied research and 75 percent for basic research. However, with national technology policies spreading, more comprehensive global rules and guidelines are called for. These could cover areas such as access to research universities, common rules for patent issuance, and compatible technical standards.

-8-
Global Shifts in Manufacturing and Services

DeAnne Julius

Description of Change

The world economy is experiencing two structural shifts. The first is a demand-driven shift in the rich (OECD) countries from manufacturing to services. The second is a supply-led shift of manufacturing production from rich countries to middle-income developing countries. These sectoral and geographic shifts reinforce each other, accelerating the loss of manufacturing jobs in the OECD countries.

The effect on employment will be similar to the shift from agriculture in this century. In 1900 farming employed 68 percent of the labor force in Japan, 44 percent in the United States, and 19 percent in Britain. Despite heavy protection of the sector in all three countries, job loss was universal. By 1990 the shares were 7 percent in Japan, 3 percent in the United States, and 2 percent in Britain.

Manufacturing employment is likely to show the same trend. Labor-saving technology will increase output. Because manufactured goods are highly tradable, incremental production capacity can migrate to low-cost locations. Thus, both account for a shrinking share of consumer spending as incomes rise. Thus we may expect to see:

1. Manufacturing employment continuing to fall in the OECD countries, reaching 10 percent or below in most in 30 years.

2. Faster job loss in those countries where manufacturing employment is currently the highest: Germany (currently 32 percent), Japan (24 percent), and Italy (22 percent). The biggest falls so far have followed this pattern. They have been in Germany and the United Kingdom, which were the two most industrialized countries at their peaks.[1]

---

[1]The rationale for these predictions is contained in Brown and Julius, "Is Manufacturing Still Special in the New World Order?" In R. O'Brien (ed.), *Finance and the International Economy.* New York: Oxford University Press, 1993, on which this article is based.

Reasons for Change

Over the long sweep of economic history, such shifts are more the norm than the exception. Examples of other geographic and sectoral shifts include the European emigration to the Americas, the industrial revolution, the abolition of slavery, and the decline of domestic service. It would be surprising indeed if the current period of unprecedented technological and political change did not produce something similar.

On the political front, the major catalyst has been the sudden collapse of the Soviet Union. That shook the last vestiges of belief in the centrally planned, closed economy model. As a result, radical policy change is underway, not only in Eastern Europe, but also in such diverse places as South Africa's ANC, Argentina's Perónist party, China's Communist party, and India's socialists. Not all of these can be traced to the end of the Cold War—some began long before 1989—but the spread of radical, market-oriented policy reform in the developing world is undeniable.

Less noticeable, but equally important, has been the slow but steady improvement in the skill base of developing countries. This means that the seeds of policy reform are falling on well-prepared soil. Between 1965 and 1988 secondary school enrollment leapt from 26 percent to 55 percent of the school-age population in the 58 middle-income developing countries. The skills gap is closing and productivity is rising.

Probable Consequences

This is pulling investment toward developing countries—both international direct investment (IDI) and portfolio investment via the many emerging market funds. In just 5 years, the share of IDI captured by the developing world jumped from 17 percent to 33 percent of the total. This is both cause and effect of the growing expectation that economic growth in the LDCs is likely to be in the 5 to 6 percent range over the next decade, compared with under 3 percent during the 1980s.

As this growth swells, the number of middle-income families in Asia and Latin America, their consumption of everything from color televisions to motorcycles to computers to cars will grow much faster than in the mature markets of the OECD countries. To meet that demand, companies that manufacture such goods will naturally build new plants there, where costs are lower and markets are booming. This will cause the center of gravity of global production of manufactured goods to shift from today's rich to today's poor countries.

Does this matter? In the paper cited earlier, the arguments are spelled out in some detail. The bottom line is that the loss of manufacturing jobs does not matter—and indeed is a healthy and welcome shift—as long as service sector jobs continue to grow and the OECD's service companies are able to compete internationally.

The first requirement poses little concern. In nearly every OECD country, job growth in services has been significantly faster than in any other part of the economy for a very long time already. It was services, not manufacturing, that absorbed the massive shift of labor out of agriculture after World War II.

The main force behind this job growth has come from the demand side. Across the OECD, the demand for services is growing faster than the demand for goods. Even for traditionally up-market goods such as VCRs and home computers, sales in recent years have grown more slowly than GDP, despite price declines. The sectors that are growing faster than GDP now are telecommunications, business services (design, advertising), health care, travel, and entertainment. There are also some supply-side drivers. Women are the fastest growing component of the labor market, and they have revealed a preference for service sector jobs. Such jobs are often more flexible and provide higher levels of worker satisfaction.[1]

The key question is who will supply the growing demand for services. This is where the importance of international competition and trade becomes critical. Traditionally, most service companies were restricted to their home market and, as a quid pro quo, were protected from international competition on their home turf. That was true of telecommunications, insurance, gas, electricity, and airlines. This cozy arrangement had the unwelcome effect of limiting both industry size and productivity growth. Economies of scale could not be sought beyond the home market and competitive pressures there were not sufficient to drive technological or managerial change. An erroneous belief was born that services were inherently less capable of productivity growth than manufacturing and thus could provide only low-wage jobs. The key to changing this is to unleash real competition and trade in services.

Proposed Actions

Effective market access is the essential basis for world trade in services, just as tariff reduction was the key to liberalizing trade in goods. Unlike goods, many services can only be produced where the consumer is. Unless foreign service firms have access to those consumers, trade in services cannot take place.

---

[1]Gallie, Duncan, and White, *Employment in Britain*. BEBC Distribution, June 1993.

The restriction of such access is still common in OECD and developing countries. Ask the insurance company that has to get clearance from 50 state regulators in the United States to do business. Ask the construction company bidding for a contract in Japan. Ask the airline trying to fly domestic routes in almost any foreign country. Most of the world's largest service companies still have no effective competition in their home markets.

The new Uruguay Round agreements contain a framework for trade in services and a much enhanced dispute settlement process. We must now build on that to negotiate effective market access across a wide range of service industries with their diverse regulatory barriers. Because of their diversity, this will have to be done sector by sector. And because access is often via direct investment, rather than trade, the new World Trade Organization (WTO) will have to expand its remit.

Multinational companies can contribute to this in two ways. First, they could become involved in the sectoral negotiations. Both their experience of operating under different regulatory regimes and their own interest in opening markets will often be broader than those of any particular home or host government. The WTO would benefit from involving them directly in setting the negotiating agenda.

Second, the time has come to grant multinational companies direct access to the dispute settlement process in the WTO. As international corporate citizens, they require an impartial judicial forum where disputes with governments that relate to international commercial transactions (trade, investment, and intellectual property) can be heard and where a case of law of such judgments can be built to guide future action. The current patchwork of bilateral investment treaties and the confidential nature of arbitration proceedings provide an insufficient base for the major expansion of IDI that is needed to make services fully tradable.

This task will not be easy. But we should not underestimate the very severe pressures that our economies will face if we fail. A major shift in comparative advantage is underway. Our choice is a stark one. We can try to slow the job loss in manufacturing—as we watch wages decline—or we can enhance job creation and productivity in services. The key to that is effective market access and dispute settlement. Our task now is to build the WTO into the driver for this new growth dynamic.

-9-
Global Competition
on Rules and the
Private Sector

F. Romeo Braun

Description of Change

New or accentuated trends in the world economy include globalization of trade flows, investment and finance, communication, and competition. More and more markets in developing countries are involved in this process of merging domestic and foreign markets. They can no longer be seen as niche markets (i.e., single economic and social units separated in various ways from the rest of the world) and dealt with by international companies on a country-by-country basis. The globalization of competition and demand has become a factor integrating developing economies.

At the same time, developing countries compete with other economies for private investment. In this new international market environment, the comparative advantage has become more important. This can best be shown examining the history of foreign investment. The policies of host countries in the postcolonial period can be divided into three major phases: aversion to FDI, attempts to selectively attract foreign capital using subsidies, and liberalization. The first phase ended in the 1970s, when the aversion to and distrust of FDI in numerous developing countries was gradually superseded by a desire to interest new investors. Government policies in this second phase consisted of attempts to accept only certain types of FDI, sometimes interfering with the investor's allocation decisions according to an often interventionist industrial policy set-up. Some host countries entered a "negative-sum game" of competing with each other for subsides by offering tax holidays and other advantages. In the third phase, which started in the mid-1980s, host countries competed for new investment by liberalizing and deregulating their economies.

Reasons for Change

A new and powerful engine for liberalization is at work today: global competition. A country with efficient, transparent, and stable framework conditions for private business is expected to attract a higher share of global FDI flows. Competition is no longer restricted to business; it has now entered the areas of economic policy, politics, and social systems. By taking this new trend into account, more and more countries make global competition work in their favor.

Probable Consequences

When looking at the outcome, country-by-country liberalization driven by competition on rules seems to provide as good or even better results than, for example, negotiating global rules. The new policies are well focused, and over the last several years, the opening of markets has accelerated. The governments know that the competitiveness of their countries is at stake. Instead of enacting fragmented policies, they have begun promoting well-coordinated programs. Transforming the economy is an internal process. It must be responsible to national aspiration and carried out under national leadership, following the priorities defined in a national long-term strategy. Completing this internal process of transformation successfully also requires a commitment from decision-makers and major social groups, as well as the will to change. Competition on rules will rapidly unmask mere window dressing. The competition on rules has led to a rise in the convergence of conditions that are relevant for private investment. There has been no mindless abandoning of basic principles nor of regulations that organize daily life and work; there has been a weeding out and modernization of rules and institutional arrangements. Rules have become simpler, more rational, and more goal oriented.

Liberalization driven by the competition on rules does not mean weakening government and state institutions. Governments in the developing countries will have to play a strong, albeit different, role than they played in the 1970s. Investors and citizens need a strong and efficient state that is capable of implementing the rules of the game coherently, of building up the infrastructure, and of organizing an administration that also work in rural areas. Transforming an economy also requires solutions to social questions.

Proposed Actions

As a result of this process of liberalization driven by the competition on rules, the private business sector is improving in social status and growing in strength; more scope of action is provided to private commercial initiatives, both local and foreign. The move toward a market economy in the developing world, with less restrictive regulations and a stronger private sector, creates efficiency and ultimately competitiveness and wealth. For the industrialized countries, this means that new opportunities and challenges of a strategic dimension (new competitors) are emerging; they must respond to them. The new trends also exert political pressure on industrialized countries. More and more the South is adopting what the industrialized North has been preaching for so long: open-door policies, adjustments with often very painful social consequences, and democracy. At the same time, there is still a large amount of immobility in the North; its economies are not willing or feel insufficiently able to adapt. In the developing world, a new political generation is coming to the fore, whereas in the industrialized countries, short-term thinking, backward-looking industrial protection, and lack of leadership are preventing the necessary change in policies. Governments in the North continue to apply protective measures (e.g., for agriculture and textiles); selective, sector-specific restraint on trade and investment, variable levies, voluntary export restraint agreements (VERAs), specific subsides, and administrative protection in the form of safeguard measures and antidumping action. There might be a new type of gap widening between North and South.

-10-
Integrating the World Economy: Economics Is Not Enough

Wolfgang H. Reinicke

Description of Change

Few if any would disagree that the world is engulfed in a dramatic period of change that is likely to continue into the next century. Although most attention is currently focused on the end of the Cold War and how this historic event will affect the international system, other changes in the international political economy, less visible and less noticed but no less dramatic, have taken place during the last two decades. One such change has been what is commonly referred to as the globalization or deep integration of the world economy. Indeed, as we have begun to analyze the complex pattern that explains the demise of the Eastern bloc, several causal factors in the collapse of the centrally planned economies have emerged: rapid technological innovations, the information revolution, and the increasing integration of market economies—all factors that are closely associated with the phenomenon of globalization and from which the former Soviet Union and for the most part Central and Eastern Europe had been excluded. As such, globalization may well be a primary cause for the end of the bipolar world and thus will be instrumental in determining whatever international structure emerges from it. As the threat of military confrontation on a global scale has receded, deep integration, or the lack thereof, will become the new driving force in shaping the world economy.

Globalization has long been an organizing principle for the private sector, but only recently captured the attention of political elites and the academic community that conceptualize the international system as interdependent. At the same time, however, it is important to recognize that the shift from an interdependent to a global world economy represents not another quantitative change, but a qualitative transformation. While interdependence was characterized by a world system of interactive, but

This essay is based on the author's current research project at the Brookings Institution, entitled "Global Public Policy: A Challenge for International Finance and Trade."

separate and, for the most part, externally sovereign states, deep integration will require new forms and structures of economic and political organization both outside and within the nation-state. Still, many would disagree over the precise meaning of the term globalization. More importantly, there is as yet no comprehensive conceptual framework that would enable decision-makers to consider the possible implications of deep integration for the conduct of public policy. This had led to a lack of policy prescriptions and an absence of political leadership that threatens to undermine the most basic principles of our societies.

Globalization is a complex and dynamic phenomenon that defies a comprehensive definition in the context of this essay. From the perspective of this volume, however, it is important to note that globalization originated as and remains a largely microeconomic process. In contrast to the era of interdependence, which is conceptualized mostly in macroeconomic terms, deep integration is driven by changing corporate strategies and behavior in response to heightened competition at home and abroad, leading to new developments in corporate and industrial organization coupled with the movement of increasingly intangible capital, such as finance, technology, knowledge, and the ownership or control of assets.

Reasons for Change

This microeconomic origin becomes particularly apparent when attempting a quantitative sketch of globalization. For example, international trade in goods and services, a mainstay of increased interdependence, has been overtaken by foreign direct investment (FDI) as the principal source of integration. Moreover, considering that in 1991 43.3 percent of imports and 32.6 percent of exports by the United States consisted of trade among units of the same corporate entity,[1] it follows that a considerable part of international trade is no longer an independent force, but is determined by the amount and destination of FDI. Where data are available, other countries exhibit a similar pattern. This raises questions about the continued usefulness of calculating the balance of trade in macroeconomic terms—that is, on the basis of national territory. For example, in the case of the United States, using a microeconomic indicator such as ownership about the continued usefulness of calculating the balance of trade in macroeconomic terms, that is on the basis of nation-

---

[1] U.S. Department of Commerce, *U.S. Direct Investment Abroad: Preliminary 1991 Estimates*, July 1993, and "Merchandise Trade of U.S. Affiliates of Foreign Companies," *Survey of Current Business*, October 1993.

al territory. For example, in the case of the United States, using a micro-economic indicator such as ownership rather than location, a $28 billion trade deficit in 1991 turned into a $164 billion surplus.[2]

Looking at developments in labor markets is yet another way to monitor deep integration. For example, U.S. affiliates of foreign corporations employed 12 percent of the manufacturing work force.[3] But while few would reject the above illustration as insignificant and temporary, deep integration for the most part has been confined to the level of industry.

The globalization of corporate activities, however, should not be misunderstood as the globalization of the market economy. Such a confusion occurs if one conceptualizes a market economy as an almost idealized state in which rational, self-interested economic agents interact free of constraints, be they legal, political, or some other form, and are minimally affected by social relations, their history, traditions, ethnic allegiances, and other factors. In this atomized, undersocialized, and depoliticized conception of human action, the market economy is a separate, differentiated sphere of modern society, unrelated to the broader historical, political, social, and ecological environment in which it is embedded. Economic rationality prevails over political, social, judicial, and ecological rationality.

Such a conception does not fully capture the complexity of a modern market economy and thus fails to suggest all the necessary policy initiatives required to establish a market system at the global level. A market economy is a complex organization based not only on the interaction of individual economic preferences, but also on social relationships and patterns of behavior, legal norms and mechanisms, political forces and institutions, and, increasingly, ecological and resource constraints, all of which interact in a structured manner to produce relatively consistent behavior characteristic of any large institution.

---

[2]Ownership-based calculations of trade balances vary. See "Alternative Frameworks for U.S. International Transactions." *Survey of Current Business*, December 1993.

[3]U.S. Department of Commerce, *U.S. Direct Investment Abroad: Preliminary 1991 Estimates*, July 1993; the numbers are even higher for other countries: United Kingdom 16.2 percent, France 23.8 percent, Argentina 32 percent, Mexico 21 percent, Ivory Coast 42 percent, Botswana 35 percent, Malaysia 27 percent, Singapore 58 percent. See United Nations, *World Investment Report 1992*, New York, 1992, and data supplied by national sources.

Probable Consequences

Given this conceptual framework, it becomes apparent that to date the debate over and action on globalization has been quite one-dimensional, focusing almost exclusively on the economic realm of market economies. The legal, political, social, and, to a considerable extent, ecological frameworks within which markets operate, however, have remained confined to the level of the nation-state. The subsequent imbalance between economic activity and other, but no less important, constituent elements of a market economy has put a severe strain on modern democracies and has begun to threaten the legitimacy of the political, legal, and social order. Most importantly, it threatens to undermine continued deep integration, as nationalism and cultural centrism provide an easy, but powerful, response to globalization. To remain sustainable, globalization must be politically accountable, legally accessible, socially justifiable, and ecologically viable.

Proposed Actions

These four dimensions begin to delineate an agenda that policy makers need to adopt if deep integration is to be successful. If implemented, this agenda will enable the international community to pursue at the global level not only private interest (characterizing the current state of deep integration), but also public interests. To establish a proper balance between these two is the central precondition for any market economy to function smoothly, be it local, national, regional, or global. It goes much beyond the scope of this essay to discuss each of these dimensions in greater detail. Suffice it to say that for each dimension the biggest challenge will be the establishment of appropriate networks that can link common interests across national borders while providing the appropriate structures for opposing interests to be resolved globally and without conflict.

But setting up what essentially amounts to a framework for global public policy will not only require engaging new actors and institutions, it will also compel the reform of the old ones. First, most international institutions (such as the International Monetary Fund, the World Bank, and GATT) were created with the goal of fostering and/or managing international independence. Indeed, the fact that industry has been able to move ahead into the new era of globalization is a reflection of their success. At the same time, however, the expertise they possess and power that their members have bestoed on them must now be geared toward sustaining globalization. Considering the four dimensions listed above, this will demand a considerable reorientation and may well require a revision of their charters. To some, such changes seem dramatic, even radical, but no more so than the changes in the world that call them forth.[4]

The political momentum for such reform will have to originate in the member countries and must be the second focus of attention of policy makers. Here the global economy will require greater flexibility in defining the goals of public policy and subsequently in implementing them. To achieve such flexibility any reform effort should keep several important considerations in mind. Two of them are briefly mentioned here. First, sovereignty is divisible. In other words, government can operate at different levels of social aggregation, be they local, national, regional, or global. Thus the above agenda does not require the establishment of a global government, nor does global public policy attempt to govern all aspects of social life. Its efforts are geared toward global markets.

Second, greater flexibility also requires new and innovative approaches in the pursuit of the public interest. One such approach should be based on the principle that governance, a social function critical to the operation of market economies, does not necessarily require government, where power and decision-making are often concentrated and removed from those affected by it. The dismantling of overly centralized and top-heavy decision-making structures and processes is therefore a necessary condition to meeting the goals of public policy in a global market economy, but it is not a sufficient one. Unless individuals and corporations are willing to acknowledge their responsibility and capacity in supplying and preserving the public interest—locally, nationally, regionally, and globally—such a reform effort will not succeed.

Finally, a word of caution. While the establishment of a global market economy may be possible in theory, it can be questioned whether it can be achieved in practice. The agenda outlined above must be implemented in order to stabilize the current level of integration and allow the international economy to continue on that path. But considering the political, social, cultural, ethnic, and religious diversity in this world, it is not inconceivable that there are limits to deep integration at the global level and thus to its role as an engine of sustainable growth. This caveat should not be dismissed easily, at the very least because it points to the urgency with which the issues raised in this essay should be addressed.

---

[4]The international trading system took a major step in this direction with the creation of the World Trade Organization (WTO). Moreover, the inclusion of such issues as international trade, the environment, and labor concerns in the WTO's agenda is, of course, an effort to balance private with public interests in the emerging global economy.

-11-
Trade Policy:
From Shallow to
Deep Integration
Robert Z. Lawrence

Description of Change

There are growing tensions between two fundamental features of the
world as it enters the twenty-first century. First, the world is organized
politically into nation-states with sovereign governments. Second, growing economic integration between nations is eroding differences among
national economies and undermining their autonomy. Hitherto, the world
has tried to balance these pressures with a strategy of "shallow integration." Nations have cooperated to remove border barriers to trade and
capital flows. They have also agreed not to discriminate against foreign
products and firms. However, governments have regarded other policies
as matters in which nations were sovereign.

Increasingly, however, the effective domains of economic markets
coincide less and less well with national government jurisdictions. Pressures are thus building for deeper integration—that is, the harmonization
and reconciliation of domestic policies. Product standards, labor practices, environmental policies, and competition policies, all once thought
of as matters of purely domestic concern, are coming under international
scrutiny.

This new emphasis is clear in:

- Bilateral agreements such as the Structural Impediments Initiative (SII) between Japan and the United States, with its emphasis on issues such as Japan's spending on infrastructure, its distribution system, and its antitrust policy.

- Regional arrangements such as the single-market initiative in
  Europe, with its social dimension and increased harmonization
  and mutual recognition of national standards.

- Multilateral agreements, such as the Uruguay Round, with its
  detailed rules on intellectual property rights, and the Basel
  Accord on capital standards for banks.

It is also emerging that the post-Uruguay Round agenda could include
issues such as competition policy, labor standards, and the environment.

Reasons for Change

Technological convergence, lower trade barriers, and the increased out-ward orientation of developing countries have all contributed to this trend. The postwar period has been marked by a convergence of income levels among developed countries. This reflects the convergence in tech-nological capabilities, capital per worker, education levels, and man-agerial practices. As national differences narrow, transportation and communications costs decline, and the mobility of capital and technology increases, locational decisions become increasingly sensitive to relatively small differences in domestic policies and practices. Paradoxically, therefore, the more similar countries are, the more significant their remaining differences become in determining trade and investment flows. This naturally creates pressures for harmonization of domestic rules and policies and increases calls for "a level playing field."

The most dynamic developing countries have promoted manufactured exports. Those able to offer export platforms have been particularly suc-cessful in attracting foreign direct investment. This gives rise to pres-sures for deeper integration from three sources. First, the developing country governments seek to secure access to foreign markets and signal their commitment to liberal policies by joining international arrange-ments that constrain domestic policies. Second, firms that plan to source in one country and sell in others seek secure operating rules, intellectual property rights, and technical standards and regulations that are interna-tionally compatible. Third, workers and environmentalists in developed countries who fear that competitive pressures will force a weakening of environmental and labor standards seek to raise these standards in devel-oping countries.

Probable Consequences

Deeper integration offers both opportunities for and threats to global prosperity. The promise stems from increasing the scale and scope of global competition by removing the obstacles presented by divergent national practices. For many nations, it also provides opportunities to import new and superior institutional arrangements. The danger, how-ever, lies in the erosion of the creative strengths of local diversity. Carried too far, the pressures for convergence could unduly restrict policies that reflect different local conditions and preferences. Deeper integration can also become a pretext for new forms of imperialism, in which some nations try to impose their standards and rules on others. These pressures are particularly problematic for developing countries, which legitimately fear the imposition of standards and norms that are inappropriate to their level of economic development. These pressures could also unleash local backlashes that ultimately lead to global fragmentation.

Proposed Actions

The challenge for policy makers lies in achieving the appropriate balance between international harmonization and local autonomy—in creating a global community in which nations are both open and diverse. In some cases, where the issues are truly international, as for example the global environment, there is no substitute for global action. In other cases, where they are purely domestic, there is no need for action.

Nonetheless, the scope and need for the joint exercise of sovereignty is growing. "Cosovereignty" can and should come in a wide variety of permutations. It is certainly not necessary to have identical national regulations. Combinations of minimum standards and mutual recognition are often more appropriate. Nor is it necessary for the same group of nations to be party to agreements of all types. Nonetheless, sorting out these cases and determining appropriate governance mechanisms will increasingly occupy the agenda of the international community.

A World of Clubs

The pressing issue areas include high-tech industrial policies, competition policies, product standards, labor market policies, financial regulation, corporate governance, environmental and natural resources, taxation, monetary arrangements, and stabilization policies. In principle, each of these issue areas could be dealt with separately in a multilateral arrangement (e.g., the Montreal Protocol on reducing chlorofluorocarbons) or issues could be grouped together in a single overarching international organization (e.g., the World Trade Organization). Alternatively, they could be dealt with plurilaterally (e.g., the Basel Accord on international capital standards between developed country banking authorities) or grouped together in overarching regional arrangements (e.g., the European Union).

A combination of these approaches should be followed. Promoting such arrangements would produce an interlocking system of organizations, some aimed at specific functional goals, some organized along regional lines, and some dealing with groups of issues of common international concern. This would create a "world of clubs"—a collection of voluntary associations, operating perhaps under the aegis of an expanded and strengthened WTO or UN.

In each club:

- Trust would be achieved by agreement on minimum standards, institution building, and cooperation.
- Goals would be to preserve autonomy, ensure diversity, and minimize the scope for political capture of the clubs. Beyond adherence to minimum standards, club members would grant one another mutual recognition—meeting the norms or regulatory standards of one club member would suffice for participation in others.
- A community would be achieved through equal treatment. Club members, particularly from developing countries, might be given longer transitional periods to meet obligations. In addition, clubs might develop redistributive mechanisms that would provide technical and financial assistance to developing countries desirous of meeting high norms. However, beyond such periods there should be no special and preferential treatment.
- Openness would be achieved through an emphasis on transparency. All clubs would include arrangements to improve transparency through such mechanisms as international information sharing, frequent exchanges between officials, and open systems for determining and enforcing rules.

-12-
Peace and Prosperity Require International Cooperation
Gert Haller

Description of Change

With the dramatic increase in the flow of capital, goods, and services, with the growing integration of developing countries into the world economy, and with the collapse of communism, the world has grown together, mutual dependence has increased, and the potential for economic spillover effects between countries has risen.

Most of these changes have been continuous, and Western societies have generally adapted well to these changes. The collapse of communism, of the Soviet Union, and of the economic and political institutions in the East (e.g., COMECON, the Warsaw Pact), however, have had profound and disruptive effects on many economies. Literally overnight, traditional markets disappeared with disruptive effects on external trade, and because of substantial cuts in military expenditures, part of the capital stock in both East and West became obsolete.

As ideological barriers have been overcome, economic issues are taking precedent over security needs. Therefore, economic cooperation will increasingly dominate traditional security arrangements.

Reasons for Change

The success of the Western world's model of a free society, free trade, and free exchange of ideas, information, and technologies has had two important effects. First, through a rapid increase in the international division of labor, the openness of the industrial countries' economies has risen substantially. Second, people in the Third and Second worlds demanded changes in their political and economic systems to gain the freedom and the standard of living experienced in the West.

Developing countries have learned from the erroneous development strategies pursued in parts of the developing world in the 1960s and 1970s. Beginning in Southeast Asia and spreading to Latin America and other parts of Asia, countries have realized that to generate growth inward-looking strategies must be replaced by outward-oriented strategies, economies should be deregulated, and the role of governments curtailed. Macroeconomic stability with low inflation and sound fiscal policies has become the key policy objective of many governments. Consequently, a greater number of developing countries have become part of an increasingly integrated and complex world economy.

Through the collapse of communism, another large part of the world has been brought into the global market economy. These countries want to integrate into the world economy as quickly as possible in order to catch up with the much higher standard of living in industrial countries.

Probable Consequences

Worldwide integration and interdependence will continue and may well intensify—given the now almost universal access to information and the trend of decreasing share of transportation cost in the price of tradables. The world economy is becoming an integrated system.

A widening of international exchange of capital, goods, and services and a deepening in the international division of labor offer the opportunity to raise the welfare of all participating countries. However, it also implies a much higher degree of mutual dependence. Consequently, the need for and the task of economic cooperation will increase if unproductive conflicts are to be contained. For example, compliance with the principle of free trade will be required, even if this implies, as must be expected, a reallocation of shares in world trade and thus job losses in the traditional sectors of mature economies.

Proposed Actions

In defining the scope of necessary international cooperation, there is a need to distinguish between problems that can primarily be solved at home and problems that—because of their magnitude and/or possible spillovers—have to be addressed in a cooperative manner at the multilateral level. Undeniably, there is some scope for macroeconomic coordination. Nonetheless macroeconomic policy issues must, in the first instance, be addressed at home. These include sound fiscal policies, anti-inflationary, medium-term oriented monetary policy, and the growth necessary to create employment. Each country must formulate its own macroeconomic strategy based on these principles, taking account of its own specific economic, social, and political situation. By pursuing an economic policy strategy that is best suited to a country's needs, but based on common market-based principles, the world economy as a whole will also benefit.

Of course, when economic policies are formulated, possible repercussions on partner countries have to be taken into account, but this should not mean that the blame is placed on another country when a nation is unable to solve its problems.

On the other hand, there are issues which, by their very nature, cannot be tackled successfully by individual countries. Preserving and strengthening the international trade system is a prime example of the need for close cooperation among countries. The successful conclusion of the Uruguay Round and the establishment of the WTO has put international cooperation in the area of trade on a new and broader footing. However, preserving and further strengthening the open trade system is a continuous and politically often difficult task that requires ongoing support by all countries.

Assisting the former centrally planned economies in their transformation is a further challenge for the international community and cannot be tackled successfully by only a few countries. The benefits of integrating these countries into the world economy as well as the potential risks if the transformation process fails are so great that everybody must be prepared to help. Other examples of issues that can only be addressed successfully at the international level are the supervision of financial markets, environmental issues, population growth, and migration.

Against this background, the different fora for international cooperation have become increasingly important. Each one has to pay due regard to its own mandate and responsibility. The G-7 nations have to play a particularly important role in the economic field. The leading nations must accept a special responsibility for the economic system and the world economy, particularly in light of their economic weight and the fact that they share common economic and political values. Moreover, complex economic issues often are not suitable for protracted political debates among too many players; they require swift decisions.

As the process of global economic integration continues, the international financial and economic institutions, in particular the International Monetary Fund, the World Bank, the regional development banks, and the WTO, will have to adapt to this process as well—as they have done successfully over the past fifty years since their establishment. The successful management of the international debt problem has demonstrated the ability of international financial institutions (IFIs) to respond efficiently and flexibly to new challenges. It is now important to maintain and, if and where necessary, to strengthen these institutions.

Finally, regional economic arrangements, such as the European Union and NAFTA, can play an important role as promoters of free markets and free exchange of ideas, goods, capital, and services. More than anything else, this will help to maintain basic Western values and to achieve a peaceful and prosperous world.

Chapter 7
Integrating Asia

Introduction
George V. Vassiliou

The rapid development of Asia and the Pacific Rim countries, where more than one half of the world's population lives, has given a new dimension to competition. At the same time, it has created huge new opportunities. Asia is in a state of frenzied change. Driven by economic growth at a pace unknown in history, the Asian people moved from subsistence standards of living to mass consumerism—all, in some cases, within a single generation. The international community needs to digest the implications of such rapid development. As Carl Hahn points out very succinctly, there will be almost one billion new consumers with incomes comparable to Western standards in this new dynamic Asia.

The challenge of integrating Asia into the world economy carries with it inadequately acknowledged economic, political, and cultural complexities. At best, the West's understanding of Asia is incomplete, and the danger exists for a reversion to traditional notions of once-subjugated civilizations. The rise of Asia also presents a historic opportunity. Recognition of Asia's transformation as a momentous and exemplary historical event casts this change in a constructive light, and the West might draw powerful lessons from once-subjugated societies. Viewed as a victory of social order and economic development, the rise of Asia will benefit all humanity. The roles of prudent macroeconomic policies, investment in human capital, and a minimal social welfare state are available to all and may have meaning for developing and developed countries alike.

"Asia has come of age and now treats itself to dreams of world preeminence," says Michael Vlahos. Together with the emergence of the new tigers, there has been the rise of a sense of "regional consciousness," asserts Noordin Sopiee, and he concludes by underlining the need to see East Asia not as a threat, but as an opportunity. This is especially pertinent, since, as James Lilley demonstrates, Asian societies are rapidly changing, shedding authoritarianism and strengthening democratic institutions.

"In the latter half of the twentieth century, Asia, particularly East Asia, has made great progress economically, and this has created a renewed confidence among Asians," says Masayoshi Morita. "This renewed confidence could be a good foundation on which the Asians would make further endeavors to contribute to the betterment of the international community, integrating their renewed energies into the various forms in the international system." Despite the talk about a clash of civilizations, Morita believes that East Asia is meeting West every day. This process needs to be strengthened and improved through greater cooperation in international organizations, openness and mutual interaction of regional institutions, multicultural education and research, and joint developments in science and technology.

Mohammad Sadli also argues in favor of a new East-West relationship. Asia is the new challenge to the West; it has geographical connotations and straddles Samuel P. Huntington's seven or eight major civilizations. Both differences of values and commercial conflict exist today. These have to be addressed through cooperation and recognition of the new importance of Asia. APEC can play a very useful role in this connection.

Within this new Asia, one cannot underestimate the huge importance of China, particularly of the greater Chinese area, which is obviously becoming the fourth locomotive force for global economic growth.

"China would probably not have emerged at such a pace," points out Victor Fung of the Hong Kong Trade Development Council, "if it had not been for U.S. trade policy in the Pacific, which has tackled rising trade deficits with export dynamos like Japan, South Korea, Taiwan, and Singapore by persuading these countries to adopt a policy of currency appreciation."

The economic development of China will also change the methods of doing business with the country. The disappearance of the large centrally controlled state corporations will create both difficulties and new opportunities. It could also lead to greater corruption and confusion; unclear regulations and circumstances may impose serious environmental risks. For this reason, it is imperative that China be integrated as rapidly as possible into the world economy through membership in GATT, by encouraging full Chinese participation in regional forums, and by providing investment infrastructure and environmental projects.

-1-
Asia: The New Center of the World Economy
Carl H. Hahn

Description of Change

Without doubt, one of the most far-reaching changes in the world economy is the development of Asia, a continent that, as a result of its headlong pace of progress, is rapidly catching up in industrial terms with the traditional industrialized nations. In many ways, it is already a full-fledged protagonist on the world market.

In many Asian countries, both the gross national product and per capita income are doubling in real terms every eight to ten years. Since 1978 this has also applied to China, the future economic epicenter not only of this region, but probably of the world. Asia has a current population of three billion people, of which one billion will in the foreseeable future be consumers by Western standards. The rapidly accelerating process of industrialization in Asia, combined with the enormous economic and demographic potentials of the region, will give rise to a new dimension not only of competition but also of opportunity.

Reasons for Change

The establishment of market economic structures is without doubt an important reason for the dynamism and the economic success of the young industrialized nations of Asia. For these nations, what Western civilization has spent the last hundred years creating—namely the preconditions for the industrialization of the rest of the world—is available right from the start. To this must be added a high level of training and education, a willingness to perform, creativity, and discipline.

In addition, savings rates of between 35 and 50 percent of GNP make it possible to finance investments; this helps create jobs at a speed in line with prevailing growth rates. The know-how and growing capital input from foreign investors, which is a result of the increasing economic attractiveness of the region, give an additional boost to this process. For example, American investors today can achieve twice the yield in Asia that they can at home. It is a similar story for Japanese investments in the region, when compared with those in Europe or the United States.

Probable Consequences

Asia's rapidly emerging potential will radically alter the relative position of the hitherto dominant OECD countries in the world economy in both economic and political terms. Whereas the Japanese have already aligned their policy and corporate strategies to the newly emerging global constellations, trade within Asia has now taken on a greater significance for Japanese industry than that with North America or Europe; the United States has also taken important steps in this direction, as the Seattle conference showed at the end of 1993. Europe, in particular, seems likely to be marginalized by the developments in Asia. The role played by Europe in Asia today is far too small to enable it to profit from the growth in prosperity in this part of the world.

At a time when capital and know-how are moving at nothing short of the speed of light, the segmentation of production permits the exploitation of all conceivable location advantages throughout the world, and a worldwide harmonization of the price/benefit ratios of industrial products has been introduced. Europe, mainly because of its inability to adapt swiftly enough, is running the risk of falling further behind in terms of competitiveness. This will have predictable results not only for employment, but also for Europe's economic and political influence in the world.

Europeans must realize that the world is moving toward a new bipolar structure. North America, strengthened by NAFTA, will continue to be one center, but the other will be Asia, with China as the inevitable central power. Europe must align itself to this new situation both politically and in terms of management strategy, so as not to run the risk of being elbowed from the center to the periphery of the industrialized world.

Proposed Actions

To assure the future of Europe as an industrial center, it must urgently find new structures for its relationship with the Asian world. Only by grasping the opportunities for growth to be found there will Europe return to the competitive growth rates necessary to keep up with the speed of progress in the global economy, to confront unemployment with any hope of success, and to avoid destabilization.

From a political and entrepreneurial point of view, Europe has a clearly defined set of priorities. In these changed circumstances, Europe must abandon its philosophy of demands and expectations, and return to a philosophy of performance and innovation built on the firm basis of appropriate fiscal, economic, and educational policies that are supported by the parties and have a vision extending beyond the frontiers of the old continent. Only a targeted integration into the world economy, characterized by the sharing of tasks and on the broad basis of a single European market, will bring the European countries the possibility of a future influential participation in the world economy and a political voice.

-2-
The East
Asian Revolution

Noordin Sopiee

Description of Change

Forty years ago, East Asia was regarded in the bleakest of terms. It was generally seen, and rightly so, as a region of political turbulence, economic backwardness, and social and cultural decay. China, the mother of all dominoes, had fallen. It seemed that a row of dominoes would follow. Today, this region of dominoes is a region of dynamos, of economic miracles. What is less recognized is the political progress that has been made, and the cultural and psychological transformation that has taken place.

A renaissance, centered on East Asia, could well be in the making. After 500 years of eclipse and decay—and often humiliation and submission—the world could well see a repeat of history—an era in which Asia will once again be a rich cradle of human welfare and civilization. No longer on the periphery, Asia will be very much at the heart of global decision making and history.

Whether all this will come to pass depends, of course, on whether the great East Asian revolution will persist well into the future. The already historic rise of East Asia has certainly been the result of the massive political, economic, and psychological revolution of the past generation and a half.

Reasons for Change

The political revolution that has occurred in East Asia has three critical dimensions: a peace revolution, a democracy revolution, and a human rights revolution.

Since World War II, East Asia has been the most violent and turbulent region of the world. There was civil war or large-scale domestic violence in every country or territory with the exception of four islands or groups of islands: Singapore, Hong Kong, Taiwan, and Japan. There was the Korean War, the Vietnam War, and a number of other lesser known international conflicts. Today, the strategic environment is better than at any time in the last 150 years. There is real concern only in the Korean Peninsula. East Asia is more "at peace" than Europe.

The winds of democracy have also swept far and wide; they will remain unstoppable if the region continues its economic development.

Any fair accounting of comprehensive human rights must also conclude that despite obscenities and transgressions that cannot be overlooked or tolerated, never before in the field of human affairs has so much been done for so many people in so short a time. Interestingly, life expectancy is higher today in Shanghai than in New York City.

From today's perspective, it is astounding to realize that at one point or another in the postwar period every East Asian economy, including Japan, was regarded very much in the way the world now sees Bangladesh—as countries with no hope for the future. This is a measure of the dynamism revolution that has been made by the peoples of East Asia.

East Asia also used to count for very little in the world economy. Its revolution in economic importance, however, will result in a larger GNP in the year 2000 than in North America or Western Europe. In purchasing power parity terms, the countries of the proposed East Asia Economic Caucus (EAEC) already have a GNP substantially exceeding the GNP of NAFTA and the EEA.

Further, the East Asian economic integration revolution has seen a level of GNP-weighted trade integration equal to that achieved in the European Union—without any treaty or institutional or formal intergovernmental cooperation. The integration revolution has been completely market driven, open to the full participation of all, with no rules of discrimination whatsoever against those outside the regional economy.

Three elements of the psychological/cultural revolution might also be mentioned. There has been a dramatic and sustained rise in self-confidence, self-assertion, and regional consciousness. Asia is rediscovering Asia and its intrinsic worth. These changes are fundamental.

Probable Consequences

General MacArthur in 1951 likened Europe and the United States to a 45-year-old man and Japan to a 12-year-old boy. The people of not only Japan, but of the rest of East Asia, have become adults and can no longer be treated as children. They, on their part, have to assume the full responsibilities of adults. Everyone has to "grow up."

East Asia will organize and seek greater empowerment. It must be expected to wield more clout—to have a bigger say in world events. The psychological adjustment for the region and the world will be a big one.

Proposed Actions

East Asia has to do a better job of explaining itself to others. There is a real danger of the rise of a new sense of "yellow peril" despite the fact that East Asians come in many colors. At the same time, other nations have to be more open minded and less arrogant; they should view East Asia not as a threat but as an awesome opportunity. While the region has to accept a greater share of responsibility in the world community, the West has to accept the greater democratization of international decision making. The successful "integration" of a new East Asia promises much. Equally clearly, failure threatens a great deal.

-3-
The Resurgence
of Asian Confidence

Masayoshi Morita

Description of Change

Asia once had prosperous civilizations in Ancient East Asia, South Asia, and West Asia. With the beginning of the modern age in the sixteenth century, however, Asia became a symbol of stagnation and poverty. Now, in the latter half of the twentieth century, Asia, particularly East Asia, has made great economic progress. This has created among Asians a renewed confidence—confidence on which they could build a solid foundation for further contributions to the betterment of the international community. They could thus integrate their renewed energies into the international system.

Reasons for Change

Although this confidence among Asians is based on domestic accomplishments, it has also been nurtured by a favorable international environment, which includes the post-World War II institutional frameworks of GATT, the IMF, IBRD, and the vast networks of the United Nations.

The work ethic, family values, and team work are all Asian cultural traits and traditions; these community values played significant roles in Asian economic and social progress, as did the Western values of individualism, free and fair competition, and rational approach. This positive intermingling of Asian and Western values must be further promoted through economic competition and cultural exchange.

Probable Consequences

Samuel P. Huntington argues that, with the end of the ideological Cold War, the world will be dominated by a "clash of civilizations." Rudyard Kipling once said that "East is East; West is West." Now, East Asia is meeting West every day and is gaining a new civilizational confidence, not through conflict or clash, but through "peaceful competition and enlightenment" in minds and hearts as well as in markets and economies.

In the real world, however, we have witnessed many regional military conflicts since the end of the Cold War. The disappearance of the Soviet communist ideology has increasingly brought forth the traditional types of political struggles, which often develop into military conflicts within national borders. The existing UN organizations and sovereign states are not well equipped to cope with these conflicts.

In the past several centuries, there have been many wars, conflicts, and clashes. However, our experiences in World War I and World War II have taught us how to better manage our destinies on this resource-precious and increasingly information-oriented world.

Proposed Actions

This peaceful competition, however, could become disruptive indeed if the actors involved refuse the mutually interactive process of rational discourse and human compassion. Arnold Toynbee described mutually interactive relations among civilizations as conflictive or responsible. We must strengthen the positive, responsive system among the civilizations—that is, between Asia and the West in our case. In this way, we could improve the global capacity of human managerial realms.

This could be done by improving and strengthening the:

1. Functions of international organizations, such as GATT (and its WTO), the IMF, IBRD, OECD, and the United Nations. It is particularly important to strengthen the foundations of the WTO, as well as the strategic and operational capabilities of the UN. The nations in the Asian region, with their dynamic growing economies, are in a good position to promote the causes of free trade and economic systems, avoiding the trend toward protectionism.

2. "Openness" and mutual interactions of such regional institutions as AFTA, APEC, NAFTA, and the EU. Although these regional organizations are intended to strengthen such free trade credos as GATT, they might first act as protectors of regional interests and then later in global interests. The Asian nations should keep APEC as a truly open forum for the universal interests of all GATT/WTO members. The Pacific region must be maintained as a peaceful, free, and democratic bastion for the world.

3. Multicultural education and research in basic and higher institutions in Asia and the West to meet the growing needs of such multicultural challenges, as well as to preserve the common cultural assets of the world for humanity. A number of excellent institutions, including the East-West Center in

Hawaii, are already engaged in multicultural research. Many universities also support educational and research programs and projects on various cultures in the world. The nations in the Asian Pacific region must make significant financial and institutional contributions to the promotion of multicultural studies. The Western nations could also increase the capacity and capability of their research institutions by promoting joint multicultural studies with their counterparts in the Asian Pacific region.

4. Joint developments of science and technology in Asia and the West. As a result of joint ventures, licensings, and direct investments, technological exchange between Asia and the West has grown. In the past, the flow was predominantly from the West to Asia. Nowadays, however, the flow of technological trade is more balanced.

5. Civilizational studies through the establishment of the Institute for Civilizational Research under the auspices of the UN. The institute would engage in in-depth studies of major civilizations and their interactions. It would also propose, from time to time, policy options for the management of difficult international and intranational issues originating in differences in civilizational values and perspectives. The Institute for Civilizational Research will have its own research staff, will be affiliated with major research universities in each identified main civilizational region, and will have on-going research programs and projects conducted by multicivilizational research teams. Additionally, the Institute will carry out the special research projects commissioned by the UN General Assembly or Security Council, as occasions arise.

-4-
Democratization in Asia
James Lilley

Description of Change

In the early twentieth century, Japan was under a strong and aggressive dictatorship that seized Korea and Taiwan as its colonies. Since its defeat in World War II, Japan has become, under American protection and guidance, a pluralistic democracy. Taiwan and Korea, freed from Japan after World War II, were ruled by their own strong authoritarian leaders for several decades. By the end of the 1980s, however, both had shed authoritarianism and also become prosperous pluralistic democracies.

Reasons for Change

Japanese, Korean, and Taiwanese societies were all based on Confucianism; they were also heavily influenced by Buddhism. These principles, however, did not fully answer the social, political, and economic demands of modernization. Communism also failed to do so, despite early attempts to expand by use of force and indigenous revolutions. Behind the protective shield of U.S. power, these countries responded to democratic principles and free market concepts, but added their own Asian characteristics.

Reviewing the process of their economic and political development, one can see clearly several common elements and one common trend. The process started with basic economic development. In all three cases, the economy was strongly oriented toward foreign trade, relying heavily on imported raw materials and large quantities of exported manufactures. A second stage stressed foreign investment in labor-intensive industry; a third technology transfer as well as capital-intensive and technology-intensive industry; and finally the exportation of advanced industrial products. At the same time, per capital GNP grew rapidly, people's living standards improved, and educational levels rose. All of these paved the way for society, with enlightened leadership and U.S. support, to move toward political pluralism.

During this process, in all three countries, government leadership played a major role in economic development. Economic decision making was largely centralized and the executive branch of government dominated. However, the government encouraged private enterprise, which made the economy more dependent on market forces. Once the economy was sufficiently successful and was basically market oriented and modernized, institutions became necessary to protect the mobility and freedom of entrepreneurial initiative. Economic development then merged with constitutional reform, and the evolution toward a pluralistic form of democratic government emerged.

But the democratic process remains fragile in each of these countries, in part because of its newness and their inexperience in utilizing the consensual methods that are central to democracy. Along the road of political evolution, their economies must stay competitive to sustain a material base for democracy.

Probable Consequences

Authoritarian models could remain strong in Asia—some are based on communism (for example, North Korea, China, and Vietnam); others are based on a combination of democracy and Asian nationalistic institutions (for example, Indonesia, Singapore, and Malaysia). Asia is developing inclusive regional organizations, such as APEC and ASEAN, and strong interregional economic ties, such as those between South China, Hong Kong, and Taiwan. There remain, unfortunately, powerful military forces in the area that could destabilize the region if not kept in check.

Nevertheless, several trends do favor the continuation of democracy in Japan, South Korea, and Taiwan. All are increasingly wealthy, with relative equality in per capita GNP. In each, society has been democratized, with a strong, educated middle class. Each society understands that there is a compatibility between democracy and important elements of traditional Confucian and Buddhist beliefs. Each has had bitter experience with communism or authoritarianism and therefore has embraced democracy as an attractive alternative. And each still looks to the United States as an example of a working and still successful democracy.

Asia's future stability is enhanced by its strong economic growth, its interdependence, and a current balance of military power that rules out large-scale military aggression. All these factors augur well for the future of Asia. In the short term, however, flash points such as the Korean Peninsula, South China Sea, and Taiwan Strait must be defused.

Proposed Actions

Regional collective responsibility must be strengthened to deal with such problems as the Spratly Islands in the South China Sea. These islands are claimed by several Asian countries and have already caused military confrontation among the claimants. The Law of the Sea, the ASEAN postministerial conference that now includes China, Russia, and Vietnam, and the continuing presence of U.S. naval power (possibly in the future under UN peace-keeping authority) should all contribute to continuing stability. A renunciation of the use of force by all claimants under UN auspices would also be a key to a peaceful solution.

All countries in North Asia, as well as the United States and the IAEA (and possibly the UNSC) are involved in resolving the North Korean nuclear weapons problem. The UN has played a key role on the Korean Peninsula since 1950, when it stopped North Korean aggression. This close cooperation must be maintained and strengthened if peace and stability are to be achieved.

In the economic field, APEC, PEBC, PECC, ASEAN, the UN, and GATT will all be important in dealing with such diverse problems as fair market access, protection of intellectual property rights, stability of competing economies, and secure and dependable lines of transportation and communication.

Until such time as strongly regional security organizations exist with sufficient force, bilateral security treaties and arrangements should be kept active and strong, especially in view of the presence of over-militarized countries in the area.

The issue of human rights should be handled through existing private nongovernmental international organizations and with international support. It should not be allowed to become a cause for unilateral intervention by one government into the internal affairs of other societies. Take the human rights situation in China as an example. In 1990, pressure was effective because it was not coming just from the United States—it was multilateral. The United States should also support democracy among the Chinese where it already exists, particularly in Taiwan and Hong Kong. These Chinese forces will change China more effectively and rapidly than any number of ultimatums or threats by foreign countries against the central government in Beijing. The evolution of genuine democracy in China will come from within, just as we have seen it develop in Taiwan, Korea, and Japan. Foreign pressure historically often has resulted in catastrophe and tragic consequences.

-5-
Asia Has Come of Age
Michael Vlahos

Description of Change

For more than a century, the European world saw Asia alternately as playground, battleground, or fertile ground for its own agendas and interests. All that changed after 1980. The East Asian Tigers, the Japanese economic superstate, and the transformation of China forever changed the terms of Asia's relationship with the West. Asia has come of age and now treats itself to dreams of world preeminence.

These dreams, however, are couched in vague, rosy, economic terms, where the image of a cooperative Asia is held up as the world's peaceful center of growth and development. This is not to be.

Asia is experiencing the tectonic stresses of revolution. The world economic revolution is swirling throughout the Pacific rim, including North America, and this revolution is putting immense pressure on Asian societies. It is a force that far outstrips the tension Europe will feel in its own, painful restructuring.

Reasons for Change

The power of change comes from great pools of skilled labor surging on-line throughout Asia: hundreds of millions of people in China, India, and the ASEAN states; hundreds of millions that will be as capable as any in the G-7 nations. But they are still low-wage labor pools. As their ability to generate demand grows, so will their political voice, and they will rebel much as the working peoples of Europe rebelled against their economic servitude in the nineteenth century.

They will rebel against the same intolerable income inequalities, the same kind of lagging social infrastructure (which, in plain English, means they will refuse to live in human cesspools), and the same kind of lordly rule over their lives that Asian elites today share in spirit with Prussian Junkers and British Beer Barons from another century.

Chinese communism will die, and so also the enlightened authoritarian stand-ins of the kind Singapore takes such pride in. But what new visions of society will the mass polities of Asia pursue?

Probable Consequences

The great Asian social upheavals early in the next century will include Japan. Japan's change may be triggered by dramatic shifts elsewhere in Asia, and especially by Korea, whose society will be turned upside down as it is reunified.

China could keep its trajectory to become the predominant Asian state. Or, it might devolve into the old Germany of Asia, in the sense that the rest of Europe viewed Germany before 1871: the rich, unfocused, and fragmented center of Europe; a culture without a state; a people without a connection. Either way, what happens in China redefines relations throughout Asia.

Tomorrow's Asia is full of big, rich states. They have money, they have agendas, they have needs. And because the stresses of growth and political turmoil are pulsing in all of them, their relations with each other are inherently unstable. Japan, Korea, and China will each have powerful military forces, nothing like the backward or vestigial militaries they maintained in the postwar period. Even the smaller states will sport highly advanced capabilities, with the technical and managerial expertise to use them.

And the United States no longer stands astride East Asia; it observes.

But big states and big military forces are less important than what people in Asian societies believe in. The series of political revolutions in Asia we can expect in the next century will be fueled by passionate ideas. We can expect visions of life and society that will give triumphal political movements in Asia a world significance. And we can expect that the most successful of these movements may offer a vision that Americans find competitive rather than complementary. And it may be a very compelling vision, if it is able to tackle the physical problems of meteoric growth, while also providing for the spiritual needs of millions of people.

-6-
A New East-West Relationship
Mohammad Sadli

Description of Change

East-West relations not so long ago had the connotation of a sharp
ideological divide: that is, between the countries and governments based
on Marxist models and the Western democracies. That conflict is over,
but a new East-West dichotomy is emerging, which is related to the
centuries-old geographical and cultural division. In most of modern history the East, or Asia, was inferior, at least in the power relationship.
Now, Asia has acquired new economic strength and its economic growth
is far surpassing that of the European and American continents.

Most of the Asian continent is still developing economically and perhaps also politically. Japan, however, is a mature economy and very
much an OECD country. But not so long ago—that is, at the end of
World War II—it regarded itself as developing, or redeveloping. In its
present sentiments, it is ambiguous as to whether it is "East" or "West"
and ambivalent vis-à-vis some of the values espoused by the Cartesian
West. The new East-West relation has something of a North-South
syndrome, but with the South, because of economic success, becoming
more and more self-confident and searching back for its own identity.

On the other hand, the global community should not forget that one
continent, Africa, is still mired in poverty and stagnation, running the
grave risk of becoming "marginalized" and forgotten by the world.
Africa is still the typical South, a slow moving underdeveloped region
that requires the constant attention and aid of the industrialized world.
Africa is definitely not part of the "East," although the World Bank
(together with the IMF and Japan) is trying to "re-create the Asian
miracle" in this continent.

Reasons for Change

There are probably cultural reasons for the modern Eastern syndrome.
Asians appear to work harder and longer. Because education is spreading
rapidly throughout Asian societies, their capacity to absorb Western science and technology is giving their economies additional strength. Al-

though Japan is beginning to slow down in its economic growth, becoming a mature economy just as Western Europe and North America, the process of catching up is faster in East Asia than elsewhere in the world.

Samuel P. Huntington of Harvard University talks about a coming "clash of civilizations." He may be right, but his idea of civilizations is based both on the major religions as well as on geographic areas or continents. Asia, as the new challenge to the West, has geographic connotations and straddles Huntington's seven or eight major civilizations: Western, Confucian, Japanese, Islamic, Hindu, Slavic-Orthodox, Latin American, and possibly African. Asia is only partially Islam, and Islam is a minority. If China is included, Confucianism is the majority religion and civilization; Hindu and Buddhism are other major religions. At the present juncture, if one speaks of dynamic Asia, East Asia (including Southeast Asia) is meant. Whether South Asia will join East Asia in the economic renaissance is still to be seen, but it is a distinct possibility in the coming decades. The East Asian fever is spreading because of the force of success and emulation.

Probable Consequences

Skirmishes of an economic confrontation, which are already visible, are having political impact on relations between the "West" at one hand and Japan, China, and some of the industrializing economies of East Asia on the other hand. The West is bashing the East and demands that the latter play by the rules of the former. Such rules are part of its culture or civilization, although these are time-bound values. The industrial and political culture of the West is now much different from that of a century or so ago. But the developing East and the South are pushed to make the jump in time and become instantly modern.

Asia is starting to talk back, strengthened by a new self-confidence. Asia wants to reassert itself based on "Asian values," which, although unclear and not even similar in all countries, nevertheless are perceived as "different from those of the West." One example is the concept of the role of government in a developing economy; another is the way of the "golden mean."

There is the beginning of a movement of a new Asia, an Asian renaissance, that is not concerned with the delineations of Asia. It probably has the character of an underdog movement of an emerging force against a perceived establishment.

As Asian (economic) strength accumulates, trade frictions must be properly contained or they may escalate into political and strategic tensions. A growing Asia will for a long time need European and American markets. Hence everybody has an interest in keeping the global (economic and political) system open and freely interacting.

Proposed Actions

There will be no quick fix since the problem is multidimensional and has taken time to emerge and be recognized.

At the global intergovernmental level, the restructuring of the United Nations system, the Bretton Woods System, GATT, and the regional systems should be consummated. The new importance of Asia should be recognized and accommodated.

The UN Security Council should be expanded to include more Asian members and thereby dilute the veto powers of the major Western countries. The interest of the developing countries should be given greater attention. In addition, an organization such as UNCTAD, in its advocacy role for the development of the Third World, should receive support rather than find itself with less influence and mistrusted as a rabble-rouser, as occurred in the 1970s.

The developing countries should espouse a cooperative stance vis-à-vis the industrial countries and suppress confrontational inclinations. In the West, for example, particularly the United States, hard bargaining and adversary relationships is used to arrive at a social contract between employer and labor. In international relations, however, a similar relationship is not accepted by the North as a productive diplomatic stance.

The new GATT aims to underpin more equitable and nondiscriminating rules of international behavior in conducting trade in goods and services. It is said that the new GATT could, or should, make regional preferential arrangements redundant. One should support this proposition, but the large powers should abide by the new international rules and subject themselves more effectively to international discipline.

The new GATT rules are still a product of Western supremacy, and the rest of the world has to go along. This rest of the world will accept the rules if there is proof that all contracting parties will abide by them. The globalization of rules and concomitant civilization, will be a long-term process, but it should be transparent and predictable according to accepted rules of the game.

International cooperation at a regional level can be an effective instrument for the diffusion of East-West tensions and conflicts. For instance, in the Asia-Pacific area, the APEC (Asia Pacific Economic Cooperation) framework could function as such an instrument. It is an inter-governmental forum in which the new East-West clashes of interests, such as those between the United States and Japan, or with China, can be discussed in a more multilateral setting, where the harshness of the bilateral conflict can be ameliorated. If within the APEC framework ministers, and even heads of government, meet regularly, they can avoid having tensions reach a boiling point. The merit of this regional cooperation is that it could accommodate East-West, West-West, and North-South differences in interests, perceptions, and sentiments through constructive dialogues and by trying to better understand and appreciate each other.

Apart from intergovernmental frameworks, nongovernmental and private sector cooperation could also ameliorate tensions and help work out mutually beneficial arrangements. A potentially contentious nonzero game conflict can be transformed into a benign nonzero sum game. International organizations in the private (business) sector do play an important role. The APEC mechanism has incorporated the Pacific Economic Cooperation Council (PECC) (a tripartite forum of academics, businesspeople, and government people in their private capacities) and two private business fora (a government-appointed Business Forum and a Business Network as a private sector initiative). The Davos annual conferences of the World Economic Forum (WEF) is another very popular forum at a global level. The more recent annual "Europe/East Asia Summits," an initiative launched by the World Economic Forum, is trying to replicate the Davos experience in an Asian setting.

At present, international diplomacy does not constitute affairs of the state only. Moreover, foreign ministers are not the prima donnas of the stage. Economic and finance ministers are also involved in reshaping international relations, sometimes going against the grain of the traditional sentiments of foreign ministers by preferring slow and incremental movements from a status quo position. Frequent or regular summits are another instrument used to compensate for entrenched institutional inflexibilities.

Private business should come out more strongly in favor of globalization and internationalization and tune in to the new trend in international relations in which nongovernmental organizations have a recognized role to play.

-7-
The Implications of
China's Emergence

Victor K. Fung

Description of Change

Economists are beginning to talk of the "greater Chinese area" as a force for global economic growth, particularly as the mainland Chinese economy engages more fully in international trade and investment—not just on an export platform, but as a significant consumer market.

Economic growth in China, which has averaged 10 percent per year for the past two decades, has contributed strongly to the resilience of the economies of the Asia-Pacific region. This during a period regarded by many in Europe and the United States as the severest recession since the 1940s. Tens of thousands of Asian companies have established export platforms on the Chinese mainland, taking advantage of low-wage costs, comparatively skilled and flexible labor, and low land costs. This has enabled them to remain competitive in spite of rising costs in their home markets, and perhaps even more significantly, has contributed to closer economic integration across the region.

A sea change is occurring as rising income levels inside China have spawned an increasingly significant domestic consumer market. This, combined with an insatiable need for equipment to upgrade factories and to rebuild the country's dilapidated infrastructure, has created large trade deficits that are more likely to grow than shrink in the years ahead.

In parallel with this development, large mainland Chinese corporations are in the process of being privatized, being floated on stock exchanges inside China, in Hong Kong, and in ADR form in the United States. This means that China's emerging enterprises will not simply be the principal target for foreign investment flows during the decade ahead, but will also become a significant source of FDI both inside and outside China—further adding to the economic integration of the region.

Reasons for Change

A steady relaxation of central Communist party control over the economy since 1978, coupled with a set of highly pragmatic economic policies, laid the foundations for China's emergence.

Also significant was the leadership's success in persuading the 45-million strong diasporic Chinese community to invest in their homeland. Few developing countries have matched China's success in reharnessing "flight capital" to stimulate the domestic economy. China has been doubly lucky in that such a large proportion of overseas Chinese are entrepreneurs who still have powerful emotional ties to their home country, and that Hong Kong, the principal conduit for overseas Chinese investment into the mainland, is separate from, but physically part of, the mainland. This enabled Western and overseas Chinese business-people alike to retain close control over their plants established across Hong Kong's border, while at the same time offering these business-people the security of a stable, well-administered territory in which to live and work.

China would probably not have emerged at such a pace if it had not been for U.S. trade policy in the Pacific. This policy tackled rising trade deficits with such export dynamos as Japan, South Korea, Taiwan, and Singapore by persuading these countries to adopt a policy of currency appreciation. This raised domestic manufacturing costs, but instead of correcting trade imbalances, it prompted manufacturers to seek new and cheaper export platforms to serve the U.S. market. Without this U.S. trade policy pressure, neither China nor other developing economies in Southeast Asia could have expected such strong investment inflows and such substantial transfers of technology.

Probable Consequences

There are a wide range of economic, political, and social consequences. The reintegration of an economy the size of China's into the mainstream has profound ramifications that are likely to change the balance of global economic and political power in a variety of ways. It is uncertain how the foreign policies of China's leadership will evolve as its political and economic importance grows—particularly in light of the many decades during which it has been subjected to indignities and humiliations at the hands of industrialized powers, such as the United States, Japan, and Britain.

On a practical level, China's increased involvement in international commerce is likely to create mounting trade tensions. China's trade surplus with the United States, for example, has already triggered contention. Putting aside the political motivations behind such pressures, China's companies must be certain to abide carefully by international trade and investment rules in order to avoid conflict linked with issues such as patent and copyright protection, subsidies, alleged dumping, rules of origin, and opening contracts to international competition. Its government will be under pressure to open its markets to international competition in services, particularly such financial services as banking and insurance.

China's hectic growth, which is forecast to continue virtually unabated throughout the 1990s, is certain to create bottlenecks and a wide range of pressures in its domestic economy. Inflation is already recognized as a serious problem. The uneven pace of growth across such a large country has triggered concern over potential tensions and rivalries between different regions. There will be shortages of labor, in particular of skilled labor. Competition for limited resources—whether physical or financial—will be acute. This has global implications, since rising domestic demand for a range of raw materials that China has traditionally exported is likely to reduce supplies available for sale in the international market. Similarly, China's rising need for imported natural resources may put additional pressure on the world market prices for those goods.

There is likely to be immense and growing pressure on the country's infrastructure. Power will remain in short supply; road and rail transport inadequate; and ports hard pressed to cope with the increasing volume of through traffic. Building materials of all kinds will also be in short supply as national and regional authorities try to keep pace with these pressures.

As large government-controlled corporations are floated and privatized, and the role of the country's private and collective enterprises grows in importance, so the methods of doing business in China will change dramatically. It is likely to become more bewildering. Ventures will no longer be channeled through large, centrally controlled ministries and state corporations; the rules for doing business may vary from province to province; and unclear circumstances could foster confusion and corruption.

It is impossible to be sanguine about the potential environmental risks linked with China's emergence as an industrial power and as a middle-income consuming nation. Many of the factories hectically set up there during the past decade have been constructed with scant regard for the environment. Nor is a government hard-pressed to meet even basic industrial and human needs able to budget for the environmental protections that Western nations regard as essential. It is hard to estimate the impact on the environment of industrialization occurring at the pace, and on the scale, being witnessed in China—except to say it will be colossal. The capacity of the country's infrastructure to deal with sewage and other wastes is already severely stretched; how it will cope through a decade of nine percent annual growth will be hard to predict.

Proposed Actions

Among the proposed actions are the following:

- Chinese membership in GATT. It is imperative that China resume full membership in GATT as soon as possible in order to reduce the dangers of serious trade conflict. At the same time, China will need to recognize that the scale of its potential impact on the international economy is such that other countries may require it to meet stricter qualification standards than they would apply to smaller countries.

- Encouraging full Chinese participation in regional forums. China must be encouraged to play a role in the region that is commensurate with its economic and political importance. To allay fears of smaller nations—and to allay China's own difficulties in dealing with powers like Japan and the United States—this should be particularly encouraged in multilateral fora like GATT, APEC, and PECC.

- High priority help to facilitate investment in infrastructure, capital market formation, transformation of unprofitable state factories, liberalization of the economy, and the creation of an effective legal system. Particular help should be available to China in these sensitive areas. The faster the central government can staunch the hemorrhaging of funds into unprofitable state factories, the faster it can channel urgently needed funds into improved education, infrastructure spending, and protecting the environment.

- Special environmental protection. China's problems are likely to be unique, given the size of its population. A special program should be set up to work with Chinese officials in identifying key problems, setting priorities for tackling them, and raising the necessary funds.

- Encourage use of Hong Kong as a conduit. Hong Kong is uniquely placed to play a key role in China's reintegration into the global economy. It is already China's principal capital market and place of training for the country's financial and business sector. Hong Kong's excellent infrastructure should be maintained and enhanced to ameliorate, where appropriate, China's infrastructure problems. This is particularly the case with its port, its telecommunications infrastructure, and its deep-rooted services sector providing expertise for China in legal and accounting services, business arbitration, and so on.

Chapter 8
Creating Sufficient Employment

Introduction
George V. Vassiliou

The creation of adequate employment and the combating of unemployment is by far the most important challenge facing political and business leaders today. The shattering of the assumptions that growth automatically creates employment and that unemployment is a provisional and transient phenomenon in the developed world is possibly the greatest change and, at the same time, the greatest challenge people have to face. Without exaggeration, we can claim that the political stability and cohesion of our societies will depend on the degree to which we are able to rise to this challenge and find ways to restore the balance between population growth and work opportunities. Because people today derive disproportionate value from their work, their inability to find employment represents an attack on one of the most imperative of human activities. High rates of unemployment spell bloated fiscal deficits and the attendant threats to macroeconomic stability; they also carry a separate political threat to the viability of national policies. Disenchantment and the fragmentation of societies brought on by rising unemployment was a chief cause of the rise of fascism in Europe in the 1930s, and its ramifications should not be underestimated.

All of the contributors deal with the unemployment problem as it appears in the developed world. They are probably justified in doing so. It is the citizens of the industrialized world who have come to accept the basic assumptions that growth creates unemployment and that every citizen is entitled to the right to work. People in the developing countries accepted the fact that employment in the modern sector—that is, industry, services, and government—was the exception rather than the rule and that the majority of the population was simply scraping a living from the land and occasional outside work. The structural and particularly permanent unemployment now faced by the OECD countries is a completely new phenomenon.

Horst Siebert draws attention to a fundamental change. The developed world has moved from a period of shortage of labor and abundance of capital to a new period of shortage of capital and an ample supply of labor. The shortage of capital is the result of the huge demand for capital in Central and Eastern Europe, which are the new emerging markets for infrastructural projects and reequipping industrial enterprises. The developed world also has sustainable development policies and gives greater attention to the protection of the environment; these are creating additional requests for capital.

As a result of the revolution in technology and telecommunications, the emerging markets can combine high technology, high productivity, and high quality with low labor costs. This development creates pressures on the existing enterprises in the industrialized world, leads to a substantial migration of capital to low-cost countries, and has obliged firms in all industrialized countries to shed large numbers of workers as they restructure in order to increase their competitiveness.

The increase in unemployment and the new phenomenon of structural long-term unemployment is creating a new situation, writes Eberhard von Koerber. The traditional solidarity of working people is disappearing, and there are obvious signs of a lack of solidarity between the unemployed and the employed. This gives rise to the danger of social upheavals and civil disorder.

The new realities are there for all to see, and no contributor doubts the validity or the gravity of the new assumptions. The key question is what can be done, if anything at all. It is obvious from the various contributions that no single or simple formula exists. There are no fast solutions, no short cuts.

Several contributors, among them von Koerber, Hugo Vandamme, and André de Clercq, point to the need to drastically rethink the educational system in an effort to improve standards, give more emphasis to technological and scientific education, develop and enhance the apprenticeship system, and ensure education and training for life. Siebert emphasizes the need for leaner government. He compares the share of government in GDP in Germany, which has increased to 52 percent, to that of Japan and the United States, where it is only 35 percent.

Michael Hammer and Tom Sommerlatte argue in favor of encouraging the creation of small businesses, innovation, and risk taking. Characteristically, Hammer states that existing enterprises will shed jobs much faster than new ones will create them and, in his opinion, we can create new employment only through the encouragement of innovation and new business formation. At the same time, however, we must take into account that the policy of massive layoffs, which has been typical business behavior in times of difficulty, is less and less easy to implement. The reaction of organized labor all around the world and the difficulties in finding reemployment increases the social cost of layoffs. Recent examples of reactions in France, Spain, and Italy clearly indicate that there is a limit to how many layoffs and how much unemployment public opinion in the developed countries is willing to accept.

This is why some people wonder whether the traditional approach can solve the problem. Niels Petersen, the Minister of Foreign Affairs of Denmark, suggests that a new approach to work has to be developed. In its traditional sense, he says, working is not a blessing. By definition people only do it for money. What matters is income and social participation. Western societies will need to find new means and ways to equally distribute both. Short-time working, work sharing, and longer holidays are all important elements in this process, but more important will be the cultural change, whereby our living conditions and social prestige will be much less associated with our work and profession.

-1-
The Increased Labor Supply in the World Economy

Horst Siebert

Description of Change

With the integration of China into the international economy, the world labor supply will effectively increase by approximately one-fifth. In Eastern Europe, there is an additional supply of qualified labor ready to enter the international markets with the commodities it produces. Wage differentials are in the ratio of 1 to 10 between Poland, the Czech Republic, Hungary, and Western Europe, and much larger ratios prevail with respect to the other Eastern European countries. We have no historical experience on the adjustment process with wage differentials of this size, especially in countries in such geographical proximity.

There is not only an increase in the supply of labor, there is also an excessive demand for capital in the world economy; the capital stock of postsocialist countries, including China, now has to be built up. Especially in Eastern Europe, existing capital is obsolete—that is, it is not geared to the current price vector. The relative factor endowment of the world economy has changed; there is a larger relative supply of labor. In a transitional period, relative factor prices must follow. The margin for wage increases has thus been newly defined.

Reasons for Change

The reason for change is obvious. Postcommunist countries in transition are giving up their seclusion from the international division of labor; they are now entering the world economy.

Probable Consequences

The impact of this change can move through three channels: trade flows, capital flows, or migrations of people. If the new countries meet open markets for their products, they can improve their economic lot and have an opportunity to attract capital. Preconditions include the undertaking of credible reforms and the prevelance of institutional stability. If exports do not develop and foreign capital is not attracted, the probability increases that people will migrate. If people are to remain in place, they must have positive expectations for development at home. In short, the option value of staying at home must be positive and not negligible.

In a Heckscher-Ohlin context, the labor-rich countries will specialize on labor-intensive and, in the case of Eastern Europe, human capital-intensive activities. In these areas, the industrial countries will experience a decline in production. In a Helpman-Krugman world, however, there is an increased potential for intra-industry trade if the new countries represent additional demand for the products of the industrial countries. Thus, the change is an opportunity for the world economy, because there are new markets, new possibilities for investment, and a new frontier, but severe structural adjustments in the economies of the industrial countries and in their labor markets will be necesary.

Proposed Actions

Areas that require attention if these problems are to be resolved are given below.

- Industrial countries should open up their markets so that the new labor-rich countries can participate in the international division of labor. In the long run, the labor-rich countries will represent new markets for the industrial countries.
- Industrial countries should intensify the structural adjustment of their economies, refraining from conservation policies for ailing industries.
- Labor of the industrial countries will have to undertake intensified efforts to create new and better human capital when its industry-specific human capital has become obsolete because of structural change.
- Evaluate how the relatively rigid Western European labor markets will adjust to the relative change in factor endowments of the world economy. A case in point is Germany, where unemployment has risen in the last 25 years. It has now reached 6 million persons, including those who are in government employment projects. The population must change its aspiration level of high wages; it has to realize that the status of a high-wage country does not fall like manna from heaven.
- Besides a complete reorientation of the population, changes in the institutions of the labor market and a new wage policy are necessary.

- Each country has a ladder with higher and lower rungs of labor productivity. Western Europe has not succeeded in creating jobs on the lower rungs of the productivity ladder.
- The welfare system represents a cornerstone for the structuring of wages that influences the supply and behavior of labor, wage negotiations, and eventually the demand for labor.
- Wages need to be further differentiated according to conditions in a business and its specific regions, as well as the qualifications of the people.
- Economic growth alone will not solve the labor market problems, because the employment factor of economic growth in Western Europe is low.
- Governments compete in their institutional arrangements, in their tax systems, in their infrastructures. The West European countries must modernize their institutional settings. Again, in the case of Germany, the share of government in GDP has risen from 45 to 52 percent. This indicates a loss in efficiency and a reduced potential for economic growth because the expenditure has to be financed by additional taxes or additional credit. Credits are the taxes of the future and they limit the maneuvering space of the government. Relative to other industrial countries, such as Japan and the United States, where the share of government expenditure in GDP is 35 percent, the German economic system has to become leaner. The same holds true for other European countries.

-2-
The End of Industrial Era Employment
Michael Hammer

Description of Change

For the last hundred years, employment in developed economies has been based on the principles of specialization of labor and hierarchical control. Large numbers of people were employed to perform narrow task-based jobs under the watchful eye of managers. This model is now coming to an end, as organizations use reengineering to reinvent how they operate. As a result:

1. Organizations will have far fewer jobs to fill. Through innovations in technology and work design, organizations are routinely achieving productivity improvements from 30 to 80 percent. This means that many jobs will be eliminated and many more will not be created.

2. The jobs that remain will be much bigger jobs. Process-oriented and customer-focused, these jobs will encompass a variety of tasks and demand a range of skills, the ability to make decisions, and a capacity for hard work, flexibility, teamwork, and constant learning.

3. Managerial jobs will virtually disappear. The traditional 1:7 managerial ratio is giving way to one that ranges from 1:20 to 1:50, as workers evolve into self-managing professionals.

Reasons for Change

Industrial-era jobs inevitably spawn bureaucracies, and organizations can no longer afford the penalties of bureaucracy, which include fragmentation of responsibility, poor quality and customer service, inflexibility, slow cycle times, and high overhead costs.

Reengineering, a radical reconsideration of how work is performed, eliminates handoffs, complexity, and nonvalue-adding administration. It also leaves in its aftermath jobs that are broad, substantive, and empowered.

Probable Consequences

Among the consequences:

- Existing enterprises will shed jobs much faster than new ones will create them. The result is likely to be an increase in the structural unemployment rate in industrialized countries.
- There will be a shortage of jobs for the least-educated and capable segments of society (such as the American underclass), which will exacerbate social polarization and unrest.
- Many new jobs will go begging, as people educated and socialized in traditional societies will be unable to fill them.
- Governments will find themselves impotent to create jobs through monetary policy, since stimulated demand will not necessarily translate into increased employment.
- To stem inexorable job losses, governments may respond by enacting restrictions on job movement. These efforts will be in vain and even counterproductive, with negative effects on GDP.
- The work environment will be characterized by increased ambiguity, responsibility, and stress, as well as by unrelenting hard work, as "easy work" is automated or eliminated.

Proposed Actions

To resolve these problems, the following actions should be considered:

- Governments must aggressively pursue policies that encourage innovation and new business formation, the only real sources for new employment.
- A coordinating mechanism similar to GATT may have to be established to negotiate and enforce open employment laws.
- Opinion leaders, within and without government, will need to promote a value system that stresses the importance of personal responsibility, the nobility of hard work, and the virtue of self-denial on behalf of the customers.
- Impediments to effective educational systems, such as self-serving bureaucracies, will have to be confronted and destroyed if a country's work force is to be internationally competitive.

-3-
Increased Growth Rates and Long-Term Structural Unemployment

Niels Helveg Petersen

Description of Change

During the recession of the 1980s, Western governments concentrated on increasing growth rates and improving labor market policies in their efforts to combat soaring unemployment rates. Unemployment was treated as a fluctuation. No adequate explanations for the misplaced stagflation were offered except through references to the inability of Western European governments to coordinate an inflationary and growth-oriented international economic policy.

Economic growth is on the rise again, but even Westerners now realize that this growth may only marginally influence unemployment figures. There has been a dramatic change in the structure of the world economy. World economic leaders must face the fact that inflationary policies and other traditional growth strategies alone will not eradicate unemployment.

For other reasons too (among them, ecological and demographic reasons), growth is no longer regarded as the panacea for the diverse problems facing Western societies in the next 25 years. The concept of sustainability has become the word of the day and is more often than not confronting traditional growth ideologies of yesterday. Ironically, these new values for world development may hold within themselves new hope for the old order.

Reasons for Change

The growth in unemployment figures in the late 1970s and early 1980s was generally ascribed to an economic recession of a fluctuational nature in the wake of the two oil crises. The stagflation that followed was explained by the inadequacies of the world financial markets as well as structural inflexibilities in Western economies and labor markets. In short, these were temporary problems that would wither away if trade remained free and the world economy was allowed to adapt to the new conditions and regain its comfortable post-World War II growth rates.

Growing competition from Third World countries in labor-intensive industries obviously had an important effect, but this could be overcome, it was said, when the industrialized countries, in a new global division of labor, benefited from booming exports in informatics and sophisticated technology. The exorbitant balance-of-payments surpluses of the newly industrialized countries were clearly a temporary phenomenon that market forces and consumerism would soon equalize.

Some economists thought that a coordinated inflationary boost of a new-Keynesian type, that is, European or world scale, would speed up the process. Others developed theories of natural unemployment rates and believed the market should be left to do the job itself. None of them, however, imagined that open Western-type economies would experience sustained unemployment rates of 10 to 20 percent for more than a decade.

In the late 1980s and early 1990s, the composition of unemployment changed significantly, as did explanations for its occurrence. Unemployment no longer affects mainly unskilled blue-collar workers. Other layers of society, such as employees of the financial sector and university graduates, are now experiencing growing unemployment. Some question whether economic growth influences unemployment rates at all. Denmark's GDP, for example, grew by 66 percent from 1970 to 1992, while employment rose by only 12 percent—an indeed disquietingly weak correlation. As most Western societies now experience moderate growth rates again, unemployment figures are only marginally affected.

What is more, developments in the industrialized and Third World countries are parallel, not complementary. Automation and computerization in both may now be acknowledged as important structural explanations of growing unemployment; processes that will accelerate rather than slow down in the next century.

As a consequence, some economists talk about the "jobless growth" that characterizes modern economies as they deny any correlation between unemployment figures and overall economic growth. Politicians should stop thinking about the latter, they argue, and concentrate on remaking societies to avoid marginalization of an ever-growing army of unemployed.

Disregarding economic growth as an important tool for combating unemployment is taking the point too far. In real politics, economic growth is still an indispensable, if not sufficient, prerequisite for the development of efficient employment policies. And, after all, Western economies have only just emerged from the recession of the 1980s. It is only natural that the expected effect on unemployment figures should lag somewhat behind.

Probable Consequences

However, regarding the "jobless growth," economists do indeed have a point. It is plausible that modern societies, even with satisfactory growth rates, will have to live with very high unemployment rates for the forseeable future. And public opinion is beginning to realize exactly that.

If mass unemployment gradually is perceived as a permanent feature of Western societies, it will affect their social psychology dramatically. The achievements of Westen societies in social welfare, egalitarian income distribution, and individual opportunities, which were made at a high cost during the last fifty years, may be in jeopardy. The present social welfare systems are created for another society and are unlikely to function indefinitely if present unemployment levels become permanent.

The socially and morally unacceptable division of Western societies into a 75 percent group of well-off workaholics and a 25 percent group of marginalized poor people with few prospects for improving their personal welfare would create new cleavages, frustrations, and thus social unrest. Even if such societies proved economically viable, politically they would be volatile.

Unemployment will undoubtedly be the principal economic, social, and political problem of the beginning of the twenty-first century. And new thinking is very much called for to deal with it. If, however, it is accompanied by some degree of economic growth, the problem will certainly not be insurmountable. It becomes more a question of social psychology than of hard economic facts.

Proposed Actions

In the short term, some fiscal measures may do much. Taxing consumption of natural resources and pollution through levies rather than taxing labor through income taxes is one important step along a road on which the present Danish government embarked with its latest tax reform.

However, in the long term, a change in values is needed.

In its traditional sense, work is not a blessing. By definition, people only do it for money. What matters is income and social participation. Western societies will need to find new means and ways to equally distribute both.

Short-time working, worksharing, more time off from work, and flexible working hours are all important elements in this process. As are publicly paid educational leaves, training, and parental leaves.

More important than these specific measures, however, is the cultural change that will lessen the connection between our living conditions and social prestige on the one hand and our work and profession on the other. An increasingly greater part of modern life will be spent outside the work sphere in its traditional sense. Long midlife leaves, permanent (lifelong) education, and cultural (unpaid) work will be important features in the next century. Increased growth rates alone will not eradicate long-term structural unemployment. Societies will have to change. And these changes need not be unpleasant.

-4-
The Lack of Solidarity Between the Employed and Unemployed

Eberhard von Koerber

Description of Change

The number of long-term unemployed in the industrialized nations increases with every recession. The creation of new jobs that comes with each recovery is no longer sufficient to bring unemployment back to or below the levels obtained before the latest trough in the business cycle. Although the actual amount of work in postindustrial societies increases in parallel with overall economic growth, the work involved is becoming less and less affordable, and therefore does not show up in the job figures.

The social systems of the industrialized nations are not prepared to cope with this trend, and the consequence is an employment policy that seeks to satisfy the spiraling expectations of a shrinking number of job-holders. Instead, we should redefine our ideas about work, its organization, and its distribution, and thus significantly reduce the number of jobless people. Humanity is becoming aware of a growing lack of solidarity between the employed and the unemployed.

Reasons for Change

The increasing level of structural unemployment in the indusrialized nations must be ascribed to a whole series of factors, which have progressively come to the fore during the past ten years. Sustained periods of growth, increasing affluence, shorter working hours, and inordinate expansion of the social security networks have weakened the innovative and creative capacities so urgently needed. But instead of focusing societies' energies on progressive new innovations, thereby achieving new levels of competitiveness, these states often prefer to preserve their old industries and obsolescent structures by means of protectionism or permanent subsidies. And all the time global competition is becoming fiercer.

Growth in the OECD countries has slowed down independently of the recession, as more and more competitors are moving into the growth markets of Europe and Asia. Companies are under increasing pressure to reduce costs and cut prices, sometimes by as much as 50 percent. Although the international division of labor, sourcing in soft-currency nations, and repeated rationalization programs have enabled many firms to cope with this pressure, it is inevitably at the cost of jobs.

The creation of new jobs is further hampered by the current lack of innovation and creativity. Unemployment figures of more than 10 percent have now become the harsh reality in many of the OECD countries. Even in Japan, where jobless rates of only about 2 percent had been the norm for decades, employment is now shrinking. But our societies are slow to react to this structural transformation. Strategies like deregulating the labor markets or formulating new concepts for working hours and the division of labor, are not being tackled decisively. All the while, the rift between jobholders and the jobless is widening.

Probable Consequences

The lack of solidarity between the unemployed and the employed will lead to social upheavals in the industrialized nations, with a real possibility of civil disorder in some cases. The issue of competitiveness will change from a question of competing industrial locations to a question of competing systems and cultures. Those systems and cultures that lack a broadly based social consensus will focus increasingly on the social compatibility of their benefits for private individuals, rather than on new achievement. In the end, they will simply not be able to compete. But without the ability to compete, the industrialized nations can no longer perform their locomotive function for the global economy.

Proposed Actions

People in the industrialized nations have to redefine their role in the world's economy and concentrate on sophisticated, high-utility technology. This, in turn, necessitates a technology offensive and educational reform.

Technology Offensive

All of the relevant groups in society must contribute to improving both the acceptance of technology and technical creativity. Even the service sector cannot succeed without an industrial base on which to build. So it is up to the European governments to pursue technology friendly policies and to encourage the acceptance of advanced technology. Above all, research and development resources have to be used more efficiently.

Educational Reform

We must give more people the know-how they need to perform in increasingly complex economic structures and increasingly demanding production processes.

-5-
Permanent Education: A Must for Survival

Hugo Vandamme
André de Clercq

Description of Change

Unemployment, especially in the Western hemisphere, is now extremely high. Global recession is often mentioned as the main reason for this problem. On the other hand, quite often the right skills are missing, especially in the field of technological innovation, in which the West is systematically overrun by the Far East. The West needs to fundamentally rethink its schooling system and training culture.

Reasons for Change

Barely two centuries ago, nobody "went to school." Youngsters were educated by their parents and their immediate environment. At that time, the volume of know-how and experience that one generation transferred to the next was rather limited. In time, the brighter people became convinced that the growth of knowledge required a more structured system of learning. To avoid the possibility of a civilization split into educated and noneducated people, formal schooling was established.

For two centuries this system educated individuals for life. Although this system is still acceptable for comparatively unchanging patterns and areas of learning, it does not apply to the exploding domains of science and engineering. In these areas, education must be an ongoing process.

Even if a student were capable of assimilating current technological know-how, the extent and speed of new technological developments would quickly outdate much of that knowledge. There is only one way to remain successful—continue to learn. This is not only true for individuals, but also for companies, a regions, and civilizations. Two hundred years ago, "schooling for life" began; today survival requires that we begin a policy of lifelong education.

Lifelong education should no longer be considered an exceptional scenario. Success in the twenty-first century will require formal and permanent educational systems. Because of newly emerging tools, such as computers and video technology, the entire school system will probably need to be reorganized.

Probable Consequences

A reconsideration of the schooling system is not a trivial task. Who is taking the initiative? What curricula are important? What background is needed for teachers? So many questions remain unsolved.

Without specifically answering these questions, it is clear that the industrial environment has an important role to play. Since industrial innovation caused the explosion in know-how, the business world and existing educational organizations are best placed to guide this educational revolution.

Industry can indeed play a role in different areas of education. It can, for example, assist in preparing new curriculae. The result would be an improved match between what is being taught and the know-how necessary for success in the industrial environment.

In addition, industry can play an even more important role in the preparation of curriculae for lifelong training programs. Without this kind of guidance, programs for lifelong training may become less, instead of more, relevant for industry.

Proposed Actions

Without elaborating on all of the above in detail, the following two developments should be considered.

First of all, Western society needs "realization power." Book knowledge, without practical application and creativity, is of minimal help. Young engineers, especially in Europe, must be explicity and repetitively asked to "invent." Although this is not standard educational practice today, it will offer the best evidence that students have really assimilated the "know-how." This important step, which needs to be added to the current training chain, can also be part of lifelong training programs.

A second element that is often underestimated as a learning tool is the "understanding why things don't work" culture. Failure analysis is the most important on the job training tool for creative engineers. It is an attitude, a reflex, that can be taught. It is the ultimate proof that a student has mastered a situation and has the knowledge to avoid or correct later problems. In the long run, it is the only way to teach the "first time right" approach.

The above considerations should be superposed on our different schooling systems. Technology is changing so fast, that we must change the way we acquire and implement practical knowledge. In the future, survival will depend on a societal and individual policy of lifelong learning.

-6-
The Reduced Acceptability
of Layoffs

Tom Sommerlatte

Description of Change

It is becoming less and less acceptable for enterprises in financial difficulty to lay off people or to close down. In the past, a basic assumption was that if a company, for whatever reason, went bankrupt, it would close down and its employees would eventually find new jobs in better performing companies. As opportunities for new business and employment diminish and as entire regions lose their established economic basis without being able to build a new one, we may have to transform our old assumption into a more appropriate one.

Enterprises need help to adjust to the changing competitive and technological environments and to maintain employment, even if the investment in change exceeds the risk level that private investors are prepared to take.

Reasons for Change

In a stable-state environment, short- and medium-term profit performance can be used as a yardstick for optimizing investment. The natural processes of economic pruning are acceptable—in fact, desirable—for steering resources to better-performing enterprises. In a highly dynamic environment undergoing profound restructuring, seizing new economic potentials requires a different approach. There is a danger that traditional approaches to dealing with risk lead to the destruction of potentials.

Turnaround and redirection are often better routes to a satisfactory return on investment then letting the number of investment opportunities shrink and contributing to an environment of social unrest.

Business is currently caught in a vicious circle: In order to stay competitive, companies have to layoff people. At a level of 10 percent unemployment or more, many national economies have not only created a tremendous financial burden but, more importantly, are destroying an increasing part of their internal customer base.

There are also entire regions outside the Triad that require substantial investment to activate their economic potential. To achieve this, they need to tap the Triad markets and their purchasing potential. If the latter is negatively affected through growing unemployment, then there will be a deadlock preventing the non-Triad regions from developing.

Probable Consequences

As the number of companies in difficulty or closing down increases and unemployment goes up, massive economic potential is destroyed.

The taxes imposed on the remaining companies and their employees (which together often reach the same order of magnitude as labor costs) are to an ever-greater percentage used to pay unemployment premiums to the people laid off. These reduce spending and therefore trigger a shrinkage of the market. This, in turn, leads to more unemployment.

In addition, one of the main assets of going concerns is an established organization of employees with complementary skills who are used to working together. This asset is lost once the organization folds and the employees join the ranks of the unemployed. To create new, functioning organizations is, even when the people needed are available, a costly and time-consuming undertaking.

In the overall environment of high-tax loads, reduced buying potential, and growing social tensions, the drive to invest in innovation and to take business risks is sharply constrained. Therefore, the necessary revectoring and restructuring of national economies and of the world economy are slowed down, if not inhibited.

Proposed Actions

We need a better balance between business risk and business opportunity. This requires action from investors and governments. Investors have to more thoroughly consider shorter-term versus longer-term risks and opportunities. Often it can be shown that the longer-term risk of avoiding the shorter-term risk is higher and that judging risks on a one-by-one basis can lead to a much higher risk of political and economic instability.

Even in difficult situations, as currently exist in the automotive or the IT industries, investors and the companies concerned need to commit more strongly to revectoring existing operations and to recognizing their inherent value, which can be exploited by reengineering, innovation, change of culture, and alliances.

Governments need to create higher incentives for risk taking and for going after new business opportunities, even under difficult conditions. The community has to share the business risks by reducing the tax burden on the return on risky investment.

The rewards for the national economies have to be seen to come from more entrepreneurial investment in new busines opportunities with a longer-term perspective and from the resulting economic growth, rather than from immediate skimming through high taxes.

Chapter 9
Ensuring National Policy-Making in a Global World

Introduction

George V. Vassiliou

National policy-making in our global village is becoming more and more difficult. As Robert Solomon shows, the world economy has substantially transformed itself since 1980. The new environment of global trade and competition on a world scale, of the liberalization of capital markets, and of the massive daily movement of funds that amount to fifty times the value of world trade, make the formulation of effective national policies a virtually impossible task.

In the new circumstances, governments, according to Fritz Scharpf of the Max Planck Institute, are obliged to give up the prevailing notion of controlling the economic environment and are trying to develop strategies simply to cope with it.

In these circumstances, it is not surprising that long-term policy has given way to short-term considerations. This trend to short-termism—of fire extinguishing—instead of creating conditions to avoid the fires in a metaphorical sense, makes it even more difficult to develop, formulate, and implement the necessary long-term policies. This difficulty is compounded by the fact that the disenchantment and dissatisfaction of citizens leads to a voters' revolt and their readiness to switch votes from traditional parties. Thus, political leaders are obliged to electioneer on a more or less continuous basis. The contributors describe the new changed environment—the difficulties—but do not offer overall solutions. Rather, they concentrate on addressing specific policy issues.

Roger Altman, the former Deputy Secretary of the Treasury, underlines the fact that the inflationary era has ended in the United States. To dampen the prospects of future inflation, the Federal Reserve raises interest rates to slow down growth. In this new era, Altman hopes that savings will again become more attractive. Investors will become more confident if they know that inflation will not accelerate.

Kenneth Clarke, the Chancellor of the Exchequer of Great Britain, points out that despite the globalization of the world economy, domestic policies still count. Globalization has limited the room that governments have to maneuver with respect to macroeconomic policies. However, government actions at the national level can still have a dramatic impact on economic performance. He does not emphasize manipulating demand, but rather creating the right kind of environment for business. Robert Solomon sees the government's role mainly as maintaining macro-economic stability and fulfilling effectively its responsibilities for other services, such as education, health, and security.

Jean-François Lepetit underscores the limitations of monetary policy. As fiscal policy has reached its limits, monetary policy is the only weapon left to stimulate growth. However, Lepetit warns that monetary policy should not be entrusted with the resolution of structural problems. The solution to the unemployment problem requires modification of the labor market. Central banks, while continuing to monitor inflation, should pay even greater attention to the inflation of asset values, which is a more significant problem than inflation in the prices of goods.

Hans-Peter Froehlich and Guillermo de la Dehesa deal with the problems created by the increasing liberalization in the movement of funds. Froehlich establishes that in the new conditions exchange rate volatility has become a normal fact of life; governments can do nothing about it. Overall, he considers the vast increase in international currency transactions a welcome development because it instills discipline, encourages monetary stability, and discourages profligate spending.

De la Dehesa looks at the effects that liberalization of capital movements will have on tax rates. In the medium- to long-term, competition may lead to an unwarranted reduction of profits and taxes; he recommends cooperation between states to establish a minimum floor rate similar to the agreement on VAT in the European union.

Scharpf warns that the welfare state is itself in jeopardy and suggests that the welfare states subsidize incomes from low-wage employment rather than to provide replacement incomes to those who are unemployed full time. This would expand employment in less productive jobs in the domestic economy and facilitate the expansion of a low-wage sector without creating a subproletarian population of working poor.

Frank Trümper stresses increasing efficiency in the "production of collective goods," that is, education, traffic, health, and environment. Until now, there has been no competition in these areas and costs have increased disproportionately at the expense of other goods. The problem of productivity within a country and society has to be addressed for the entire range of products. He therefore recommends greater competition and transparency to increase the efficiency of the public sector.

Governments in developing countries, Luis Rubio states, need to compete not only in the provision of incentives, but also in securing the proper functioning of the legal system and the ability to settle disputes and protect property rights in the event of conflict. The rule of law, states Rubio, is rapidly becoming the crucial ingredient in the success of the developing process.

Ho Khai Leong of Singapore deals with the potential for expanding the scope of privatization, which would have a positive effect on overall economic development. But privatization can only work when there are adequate market mechanisms. Therefore he recommends assistance to developing countries to create the necessary infrastructure. International organizations should not emphasize providing funds for specific projects and development administration, but rather financial assistance for the development of capital markets and financial institutions and for the improved functioning of market mechanisms.

-1-
The Transformation of
the World Economy
Since 1980

Robert Solomon

Description of Change

Many of the countries in the three categories of the world economy—industrial nations, countries in transition from central planning, and developing nations—have undergone profound changes in the past fifteen years. The common thread has been a shift away from government involvement in economic processes and a greater reliance on market forces.

Among industrial countries, both Reaganomics and Thatcherism had these effects with mixed results on the United States and the United Kingdom. Ronald Regan reformed the tax system, reducing marginal income tax rates, and increased defense spending. He also pursued deregulation, which had begun under the Carter presidency. Margaret Thatcher left her successor with problems, but also with an economy more privatized and less "overmanned," in which the power of trade unions to push up wages and prices is much weaker. François Mitterrand, after being elected on a socialist platform, shifted macroeconomic policies toward economic austerity, brought down inflation, and created a strong franc. The transformation in Germany has been less one of policy change than of the effects of unification. Japan undertook some deregulation, became a major exporter of capital, permitted a bubble economy to develop in the latter part of the 1980s, and is now mired in its worse recession since World War II.

The countries of Eastern Europe have moved, with varying degrees of success, toward democracy and free markets, as they struggle to throw off the remnants of central planning and to deal with state-owned enterprises that are, in many cases, "loss-making." Russia, after the temporizing economic reform policies created by Mikhail Gorbachev, began a process of reform, including privatization, under Boris Yeltsin.

This paper is based on *The Transformation of the World Economy, 1980-93*. London and New York: St. Martin's Press, (forthcoming).

But, hyperinflation hindered reform and contributed to the disenchantment of the voting public. As a result, the elections of December 1993 left a legacy of great uncertainty regarding Russia's economic and political future.

China, under Deng Xiaoping, has experienced significant economic reforms in both agriculture and industry. Although there has been no formal privatization of state-owned enterprises, much of China's ouput—in fact, well over half—is now produced by entities such as town and village enterprises, newly created private firms, joint ventures with foreign companies, and foreign-owned businesses that operate according to market principles.

Numerous developing countries have turned away from policies of import substitution and government controls toward freer markets in domestic and international transactions. This is evident in many nations, including Indonesia, Malaysia, Thailand, India, Egypt, Mexico, and Argentina. The reforms include deregulation of industry, privatization, and lower barriers to imports of goods, services, and foreign capital.

Reasons for Change

The motivations for these changes vary from one country or category of country to another. Reagan and Thatcher were responding to a decade of popular discontent with the economic performance of their economies in which stagflation—an unhappy combination of inflation and economic stagnation—prevailed. Mitterrand had the same initial motivation, but a large balance-of-payments deficit and a weakening franc led to the shift of policies toward "rigeur."

In Eastern Europe and Russia, dissatisfaction with economic performance was widespread, as centralized planning proved incapable of improving living standards in a world of rapidly advancing technology. In China, the reforms appear to have been more spontaneous, often based on local initiatives that spread from one region to another and were tolerated by the central government in Beijing.

Developing countries were also dissatisfied with the status quo. Many, especially those in Latin America, were burdened with heavy debts that built up in the 1970s and early 1980s. After 1982, their per capita incomes declined. Moreover, the successful economic performance of the "newly industrialized countries" (NICs) of Asia (Hong Kong, Korea, Singapore, and Taiwan) began to be emulated elsewhere.

More generally, the revolutions in telecommunications and computer technology had much to do with the economic transformations under review. The spread of television (including many satellite dishes in China, for example) encouraged rising expectations, both economic and political, as people could see how much better others were living under systems with greater freedom. Television played an important role in the spread of revolution across Eastern Europe in 1989. The computer not only helps to disseminate new information around the world instantaneously, but it facilitates the international mobility of capital, as funds move more readily from country to country in response to actual or expected changes in interest rates, securities prices, or exchange rates.

Another reason for the changes is the chance emergence of new leaders at a time when they can have an impact. Lech Walesa in Poland, Mikhail Gorbachev in the former Soviet Union, Margaret Thatcher in Great Britain, Deng Xiaoping in China, Vaclav Klaus in the Czech Republic, and Miguel de la Madrid in Mexico are examples of leaders who started a process of transformation when economic and political conditions were ripe. Under different leaders, the opportunities might not have been seized upon.

Probable Consequences

Reagan's economic policies, influenced by the so-called supply siders, who claimed that reductions in marginal tax rates would increase incentives to work, to save, and to invest, did not produce the promised results, but saddled the country with too large a budget deficit and national debt. On the other hand, Reagan succeeded in altering the terms of the economic debate, as reflected in the relatively probusiness policies of the Clinton administration. Thatcher also altered the terms of economic debate, as may be seen in the change in the Labour Party as exemplified by the views of its late leader John Smith. In France, today, presided over by a socialist president, economic policies are hardly distinguishable from those in the "Anglo-Saxon" countries, and Mitterrand no longer uses the word "socialism."

Countries, especially in the industrial world, have become increasingly interdependent, as trade has grown much faster than GDP and capital has become much more mobile. This makes them more susceptible to each others' economic developments and policies and strengthens the case for the coordination of economic policies, a process that has been pursued from time to time among members of the G-7.

In Eastern Europe and Russia, the process of evolution from centrally planned to market economies is taking time and often results in unemployment and inflation. After drastic declines in output, which was exaggerated in the official statistics because they often fail to measure the growing output of newly established nonstate enterprises, a number of the economies of Eastern Europe appear to be on the way up again. Dissatisfactions, however, do exist, as shown in election results in a number of countries. Thus the political and economic outcome remains uncertain, more in some countries—for example, Russia—than in others. Although state-owned enterprises in China, as in Eastern Europe and Russia, need time to be restructured or dissolved, the economy has a very high growth rate, Many regions, especially those along the east cost, are flourishing. Rising living standards are evident, although not all regions are sharing equally.

The improved economic conditions of many developing countries was demonstrated during the industrial country recession of the early 1990s. During that recession, the developing world as a whole acted as a locomotive, supporting economic activity in Europe, Japan, and North America. Instead of being dragged down by that recession, developing countries as a group maintained output growth of 5.5 percent per year from 1991 to 1993. At the same time, GDP growth in the industrial countries was only 1.1 percent per year. Part of the explanation is that the developing countries attracted large amounts of capital. Beyond that, many of them are experiencing accelerations in productivity growth under their new policies. There are sad exceptions to these generalizations, especially among the countries of sub-Saharan Africa.

Proposed Actions

As a general rule, governments are not very effective entrepreneurs; state-owned enterprises have not done well in most countries where they exist. Thus, there is a world trend toward privatization, which began on a large scale in the United Kingdom under Thatcher. Ironically, one of the incentives for governments is that privatization brings revenue to treasuries. Whatever the incentive, the result is favorable.

Governments have also been less than successful as controllers of market activity both in domestic and international transactions. Here too governments have been letting market forces take over.

Nevertheless, governments still have important economic functions. They are responsible for maintaining macroeconomic stability through effective fiscal and monetary policies. They also provide services that the market cannot be expected to supply, such as national defense and sidewalks, and services that markets would make available only on an inequitable basis, such as education. Finally, governments have a vital regulatory function, including protection of health, the environment, and the safety of citizens. The shift away from public involvement in economies, which was at the heart of the economic philosophy of Thatcher and Reagan and which characterizes much of what has happened in economic policy since 1980, still leaves important roles for governments in the economies of all countries.

-2-
Globalization: Domestic Economic Policies Still Count

Kenneth Clarke

Description of Change

As the postwar era has unfolded, there has been a gradual change in perceptions of the effectiveness of domestic economic policies. It is now increasingly argued that the globalization of the world economy means that economic policies have to be coordinated at the international level in order to have any significant impact.

Reasons for Change

The world economy is becoming more and more integrated because of its increasing openness to international trade and to international capital flows.

Economic progress in the last three or four decades owes a great deal to the impetus of international trade. Successive rounds of trade liberalization have seen world exports rise from $60 billion in 1950 to $3.5 trillion in 1992. Trade flows have grown much more quickly than output. Since 1960, for example, the volume of OECD trade has expanded sevenfold, while OECD output has only trebled.

But the pace of growth in world trade, although rapid, has been far exceeded by the growth of world capital flows. Financial liberalization in domestic markets, the removal of cross-border controls, and technological advances have all brought enormous changes to the world's capital markets during the past two or three decades. International financial transaction have also expanded dramatically.

On foreign exchange markets, for example, the volume of transactions is now estimated at $880 billion a day. Gross transactions in bonds and equities between the United States and foreign residents, barely 3 percent of U.S. GNP in 1970, had expanded to about 100 percent of U.S. GNP in 1990. In the United Kingdom in 1990 similar transactions exceeded GNP by a staggering sevenfold.

Probable Consequences

The increasing openness of the world economy to trade and capital flows is very much to be welcomed. As openness increases, so too does competition. And competition is the spur to greater efficiency, encouraging innovation and reducing costs, to the benefit of both consumers and producers. Openness is thus a vital element in maximizing the opportunities for growth and improving the allocation of the world's resources.

But the obvious consequence is that governments have lost some faith in the effectiveness of domestic economic policies. Increased world trade means that output in one country is now more dependent on demand in others. World bond markets are now more integrated. Exchange rates are more responsive to portfolio investment flows than they were in the 1960s and 1970s. So the ability of countries to pursue an independent monetary policy by setting and manipulating interest and exchange rates has been reduced. Governments and monetary authorities now have to be much more aware of what the markets will make of their actions, a discipline that reinforces the need for economic policies to be credible.

One way in which countries have responded to these developments has been to look to cooperate and coordinate their economic policies with other countries. The G-7 countries, for example, regularly meet to discuss recent developments and policy issues. And the United Kingdom is exchanging views and working with other countries in a number of other fora: the IMF and the OECD, for example, and of course, the European Community. Occasionally, there has been a role for coordinated action; the Plaza agreement in 1985, for example, succeeded in realigning exchange rates that had moved far out of line with fundamental economic factors.

Nevertheless, economic performance still varies greatly among countries and regions. The way the current economic cycles in the industrial nations have become desynchronized is evidence of that. And productivity levels, and hence living standards, are by no means equalized, even across countries at similar stages of economic development.

Proposed Actions

It is certainly true that globalization has encroached on the room governments have to maneuver with respect to macroeconomic policies. But government actions at the national level can still have a dramatic and decisive impact on economic performance by establishing the right environment for the rest of the economy. That environment has two main ingredients. First, a stable macroeconomic background against which businesses and individuals can confidently plan for the future. Second, supply-side policies that encourage and establish flexible and responsive markets.

Volatile inflation, unsustainable public finances, and sharp fluctuations in economic activity are all undesirable. Monetary and fiscal policies thus need to be set in a medium-term framework to secure two key objectives: permanently low inflation and sound public finances. Policies that keep inflation down and stabilize public finances will contribute to a climate of domestic confidence, establish international credibility, and help to create the right conditions for sustainable growth.

Although these are objectives to be pursued at the national level, they are common to nearly all industrial countries. They underpinned the Economic Declaration from the Tokyo G-7 Economic Summit in 1993. And price stability and sound public finances are central to the EC's broad guidelines for economic policy adopted by ECOFIN last December.

But economic growth is generated by businesses and their employees, not by governments. So governments have the further responsibility of ensuring that markets work properly and that the regulatory and tax burdens on enterprise are kept to an absolute minimum. In this context, the key role for international cooperation is to agree on the ground rules for free trade, so that microeconomic policy can focus on encouraging greater economic prosperity rather than being diverted into protectionist cul-de-sacs.

There is a whole range of areas where governments can make a difference through supply-side policies. Some of the more important include:

- Pursuing measures that increase the flexibility and efficiency of product markets. For example, a central part of the United Kingdom's efforts to make product markets more responsive to the needs and preferences of consumers has been its privatization program. Through it, nearly one million jobs have been transferred from the public to the private sector, and competition has been introduced into a number of industries that were previously public sector monopolies. Even where the public sector continues to finance the purchase of services, competitive discipline and responsiveness can still be introduced by creating internal markets and subcontracting.

- Undertaking similar reforms in labor markets to make them work better, achieving a better balance between the interests of people with jobs and unemployed people who want jobs. For instance, by abolishing or reforming unnecessary regulations that add to employers' costs or deter job creation; by allowing wages and working conditions to be determined flexibly in response to pressures in the local labor market; and by rationalizing tax benefit systems to minimize disincentives to work.

- Ensuring that business is conducted in competitive and open markets. Financial liberalization in the 1980s, for example, gave an enormous boost to the United Kingdom's financial sector, which expanded rapidly, generating vast numbers of new products and services.

- Establishing supervisory institutions. Where government has a continuing role in the oversight of an industry, to prevent the abuse of monopoly power, for example, or to ensure adequate protection of financially unsophisticated investors, the supervisory institutions must have a clear focus and a light touch.

Constructing the right kind of environment in which businesses can thrive is the key to long-term economic prosperity. The sound macroeconomic framework and supply-side initiatives required will be as much tasks for domestic economic policies in the future as they were in the past.

Monetary Policy Cannot Do Everything

Jean-François Lepetit

Description of Change

In most countries, fiscal policy has reached its limits because public debt ratios are at critical levels. This means that monetary policy is the only weapon left for stimulating growth. However, the conduct of monetary policy, which at one time was aimed at controlling inflation, today—because of the breaking down of domestic and external compartmental barriers—affects all the financial markets, to the point of being capable of destabilizing them.

Reasons for Change

Generally speaking, economies have moved toward a more efficient organization of their markets, with the aim of obtaining stronger growth through a reduction in the cost of borrowing. Financial investments are increasingly well managed, while a growing number of economic agents now have access to, and so can switch between, different sources of finance. Economic policies have encouraged this tendency by improving the remuneration on current savings and creating incentives for long-term savings. The excellent performance of the markets in recent years has rewarded agents for this more efficient management of their lending capacity. Collective asset management and the surging derivatives markets have made it possible to achieve greater performance without too great an increase in risk.

Probable Consequences

The stance taken over monetary policy has consequences for all the financial markets. In particular, too lax a policy leads to overpricing of bonds and equities. In a world in which the accumulated overindebtedness of the 1980s has so far been only marginally absorbed by the recession and with inflation no longer present to slash the amounts owed, there is a great risk that the monetary policies applied by the over-indebted countries will be too lax. The risk is all the greater because of the high level of unemployment, which is being attributed to slow growth—growth which it hoped to stimulate by cutting interest rates.

Proposed Actions

The role of the central banks, which are steering policy by reference to inflation in the prices of goods, should be expanded. Central banks will have to pay greater attention to the inflation of asset values, which could take over from inflation in the prices of goods as the dominant problem.

-4-
The End of the Inflationary Era

Roger C. Altman

Description of Change

For the past thirty years, investors in industrial economies have feared inflation. In the United States in the 1970s, inflation ran between five and ten percent. Twice—in 1975 and 1980— it threatened to break out into high, double-digit ranges. In the 1960s, defense spending during the Vietnam War created demand pressures. As a result, the Johnson Administration and the Federal Reserve erred by keeping the economy closer to full employment than was sustainable, and inflation crept up. In the 1970s, the authorities attempted to control inflation and deal with large oil price rises provoked by OPEC without sending the economy into a severe recession. In response, annual inflation rates swung from near 5 to near 10 percent and back again several times.

Reasons for Change

Only at the end of the 1970s did Federal Reserve chair Paul Volcker rededicate monetary policy to restraining inflation. By 1983, the inflation rate was 4 percent; it has remained in the 2.5 to 4.5 range since. The "Volcker disinflation" was an impressive achievement. Because it occurred at a time of high inflation, the Volcker tightening had to be severe. The cost was unavoidably high: roughly 20 million additional workers lost their jobs for some period of time.

Under Volcker until 1987, and since 1987 under Alan Greenspan, the Federal Reserve has vigilantly kept watch against rising inflation. The Federal Reserve Board and several of its international counterparts recognize that any repetition of the inflationary surge of the late 1960s and early 1970s would only set the stage for another deep and costly recession.

As a result of the inflationary experience of the 1970s, central banks have strengthened their independence and renewed their commitment to what Greenspan has called "effective price stability": keeping inflation sufficiently low so that it does not become an important factor in economic decisions. That is why financial commentators now write of "preemptive strikes." Today, the Federal Reserve raises interest rates to slow down growth, not because inflation has risen but to dampen the prospects of any future rise.

Probable Consequences

The fact that we now live in a different era from that of the 1960s and 1970s, an era in which there is no tolerance for rising inflation, has a number of implications:

- For the first time in a generation, it is possible to save with security. For a generation, equity investors faced the risk of inflation-induced recessions, and fixed-income investors faced the risk that inflation would corrode the real value of principal. Now, investors can proceed with the confidence that inflation should not accelerate.
- As financial markets worldwide realize that independent central banks committed to low inflation are a very effective guarantor of effective price-level stability, saving will become more attractive and could serve to keep long-term interest rates low.
- Since World War II, there has been little danger of a true depression. The 1980 to 1982 recession was the worst of the post-World War II recessions, and it was less than one-twentieth—one-fifth as deep and one-quarter as long—as the Great Depression. Improvements in monetary powers and a variety of safety nets put a floor under the economy, limiting how far down it can fall in recession.
- As we proceed through the current era of low inflation, however, we must not forget that deflationary pressures are not inconceivable. A downward spiral of falling prices, foreclosed loans, bankruptcies, falling production, and renewed falls in the overall price level were impossible in the old era of moderate inflation. In an era of low inflation, such a scenario is unlikely but not impossible. So we must make sure that government management of the financial system is prepared for such a contingency.

Overall, an era of low inflation is a blessing. With proper macroeconomic management, effective price stability gives renewed confidence to savers and investors. We may well see a generation-long investment boom. Moreover, in an era of low inflation, individuals have an easier time planning for retirement, for their children's educations, for home buying, and other events in their life cycles. It should provide a firm foundation and also produce an era of renewed economic growth.

-5-
Foreign Exchanges: Markets Versus Policy

Hans-Peter Froehlich

Description of Change

One of the most outstanding recent developments in the world economy is the shift in balance between global economic forces and national economic policy. Nowhere is this more apparent than in international capital markets. The invisible hand of thousands of anonymous market participants can easily thwart the actions of national governments. Their impact is felt primarily through exchange rate changes.

Reasons for Change

Some key statistics may illustrate the point. Daily turnover in global currency markers is estimated to be more than $1,000 billion. This implies transactions in the foreign exchange market are more than 50 times the value of global GDP. At the same time today's figure is equivalent to a tenfold increase over the last decade. The growth dynamics has been due to a number of factors: a worldwide wave of deregulation and liberalization in national financial markets; the development of new financial instruments and trading techniques; and a general trend toward international portfolio diversification.

Probable Consequences

Against this backdrop, it is no surprise that exchange rate volatility has become a normal fact of life. Currency markets after all are highly speculative in the sense that expectations matter as much as, or even more than, economic fundamentals. Random fluctuations of 2 to 3 percent in either direction within just a few hours are commonplace. More importantly, exchange rates often move in one direction for protracted periods of time, with little apparent justification from underlying economic data. Currency misalignments of this kind come at a high cost:

- On a microeconomic level, they change the competitive position of firms. Currency devaluation brings windfall profits to exporting companies. By contrast, currency appreciation implies declining profit margins and/or shrinking market shares for domestic firms. Appreciation in fact can easily wipe out any productivity increases or cost reductions individual firms may have worked long and hard to achieve.

- On a macroeconomic level, exchange market developments have a direct impact on the performance of national economies. The changing competitive position of firms translates into variations of net exports, which in turn affect aggregate economic growth. Currency changes at the same time have price level effects. Depreciation tends to feed inflation, while appreciation exerts downward pressure on prices.

- Through their effects on variables such as jobs and prices, which are of vital interest to policy-makers, currency changes are a likely source of international trade frictions. Exchange market disruptions thus may even put in jeopardy the proper functioning of the world trading order.

Proposed Actions

Two decades or so ago, when national economies were much less inter-related and hence less vulnerable to external shocks, a policy of "benign neglect" vis-à-vis the exchange rate may have been a viable policy option. Today, this is no longer true. Numerous governments over the past twenty years have felt with pain the adverse impact of exchange rate changes on domestic economic developments. Therefore, the desire to eliminate exchange rate volatility is almost ubiquitous. In the final analysis, there are only two ways to do so:

- Create a global currency. By abolishing all national currencies and establishing a common currency for worldwide use instead, exchange rate changes could be eliminated by definition.
- Commit to an exchange rate target. Currency volatility may alternatively be eliminated by a firm government policy to keep the exchange rate stable relative to an anchor currency.

Leaving all technical aspects and practical difficulties aside, these options confront policy-makers with an awkward choice. To get rid of the exchange rate problem, they have to give up national sovereignty with respect to the conduct of economic policy. This is the essence of what economists call the "incompatible trio" of economic policy: the fact that governments cannot simultaneously achieve freedom of cross-border capital movements, exchange rate stability, and national autonomy in the conduct of monetary policy.

Faced with this dilemma, most small countries tend to willingly renounce policy autonomy. Their high degree of dependence on external economic relations makes exchange rate stability an overriding objective. National sovereignty in the conduct of economic policy, by contrast, ranks considerably lower on their list of policy priorities. Being small countries, they are fully aware that their domestic room for maneuver is very limited anyway.

Bigger countries with more powerful economies find it much harder to give up control over key economic variables. At the same time, they are not prepared to live with the consequences their actions may produce in the foreign exchange markets. That inconsistency is reflected in a policy of muddling through: shifting policy priorities lead to sporadic, and sometimes inconsistent, stabilization efforts in the form of exchange market intervention. Any international initiatives under such labels as "policy coordination" or "target zones," so far have failed to define more coherent and transparent rules for currency stabilization among the big economies. This is unlikely to change in the future as long as the national commitment to external monetary stability remains half-hearted.

The member states of the European Union have adopted a specific approach to reconcile exchange rate stability and policy autonomy. In comparison with the outside world—most notably the U.S. dollar—they accept currency volatility. Among themselves, they have established a zone of regional exchange rate stability by fixing bilateral parities within the European Monetary System (EMS) that eventually is supposed to be replaced by a common European currency.

Even on the regional level, the underlying conflict between exchange rate stability and policy autonomy is manifest. In the past, a number of EMS countries found it impossible to stick to the official parities in the face of heavy exchange market speculation. In purely technical terms, they could well have coped with speculative pressure by raising short-term interest rates, thus making speculation unattractive for market participants. Some countries actually tried but only for very short periods. The level of interest rates required to bring speculation to a halt soon was deemed unacceptably high. The governments concerned invariably chose to give up their exchange rate commitment rather than to subordinate domestic policies to what they call the whims of the market.

While it is understandable that politicians display little sympathy for the "gnomes of Zurich," it would be mistaken to view international capital movements primarily as a disruptive force. Investors seek to optimize the return and risk characteristics of their portfolios. If they consider country A less safe a place to put their money than country B, they will shift their funds accordingly. This activity serves a useful social function. It makes sure countries have to compete with each other on the grounds of monetary stability and financial attractiveness.

Currency devaluation, in particular, has to be interpreted as a negative verdict on the respective country's policy stance. Its government would be well advised to heed that information—that is, to adopt more stability oriented policies. In this way, the international financial markets are able to instill discipline into otherwise profligate or short-sighted governments. As a matter of fact, there was virtually no major instance of stability oriented policy reform in recent years that was not prompted by prior currency devaluation and/or loss of international reserves.

Any administrative restrictions on international capital flows, which some observers advocate as a means to achieve currency stability without loss of control over domestic policy, would hamper that disciplinary mechanism. On a more individual level, it would prevent the respective country's citizens to transfer their wealth abroad. This is an essential element of personal freedom. Seen from this perspective, the vast increase in international currency transactions in the last two decades is a wholly welcome development, even if that makes the job of national politicians more difficult.

-6-
The Conflict Between Globalization and Subsidiarity

Guillermo de la Dehesa

Description of Change

The trend toward globalization (that is, the integration of markets and the free movement of goods, services, capital, and people among nations) of the world economy is growing faster since the collapse of communism, the opening to world markets of large regions that had followed, for many years, protectionist policies (Latin America, India, China, and so on), the completion of the Uruguay Round of GATT, and finally, the new impulse to regional integration. Not only is world trade in merchandise growing faster than world production, but more significantly there is increasing international mobility among the factors of production, mainly capital, technology, and highly qualified labor.

At the same time that economic globalization and centralization are increasing, there is a growing trend to apply the principle of subsidiarity (that is, decentralization) in politics. On the one hand, there is a fear of a large bureaucracy in Brussels and the excessive growth of bureaucracies all over Europe. On the other hand, the increasing overlap of competencies and institutions in national administrations has pressed some European member countries to introduce the principle of subsidiarity in the Maastricht Treaty. This establishes that the community will intervene only if the member states are not able to reach community objectives.

The subsidiarity principle is, without doubt, an accepted instrument for the avoidance of overlapping and excessive centralization, but if taken too far it can conflict with the globalization of the economy. At the same time as the economy is becoming global, nation-states are trying to avoid any loss of sovereignty. Thus, they try to impede both political centralization to supranational governments and, in some instances, political decentralization to regional governments.

Reasons for Change

Globalization is both the result of the political conviction by governments that protectionist policies do not bring growth in the long run, but rather stagnation, and that some problems, such as the environment, drugs, and terrorism, have only global solutions. Globalization is also the result of technical progress, mainly in the transport and communications industries, and the process of regional integration.

Probable Consequences

The trend toward globalization of the factors of production will eventually conflict with the trend toward political subsidiarity. For instance, although capital movements are already totally free within the European Union and are becoming freer all around the world, taxes on capital remain the responsibility of national authorities. The freedom of capital movements will gradually bring a convergence of rates of return on capital, first in Europe and later in the OECD area. But as investors are concerned mainly with the after tax return, the different national tax rates on capital will be a key factor by allowing investors to allocate capital. This fact will enhance tax competition among countries to attract capital. Unless there is a global decision to coordinate the taxes on capital, there will be a progressive reduction of individual country tax rates. Very soon thereafter, investment capital will not be taxed at all or will be subjected to very low tax rates. Since this would result in lower revenues for most countries, other sources of income will have to be more highly taxed. At one time, those sources might have included individuals and businesses, but present reality shows that highly qualified people and large corporations also have a high degree of international mobility. Therefore, in the end, many countries will have to increase taxes on the less mobile factors of production (for example, land, small- and medium-sized companies, local savings, and less-qualified labor) to cope with the loss of tax base.

This will mean, finally, that most governments will be unable make redistribution wealth among citizens and will be unable to maintain their present welfare states. As a matter of fact, they may end up doing the reverse, that is, redistributing wealth from poor to rich.

Proposed Actions

There are many more examples of the conflict between economic globalization and subsidiarity within the nation-states. I am not advocating a global government or strong supranational governments in the regional integration areas like the European Union. It is essential, however, that a totally global market have rules that are either global or are coordinated by the participating nation-states.

Tax competition may help to reduce the excessive size of governments, but in the regions where capital movements are already totally free, such as the European Union, the member countries should try to establish a common floor rate on capital. This would prevent capital from escaping taxation as a result of tax competition and would thereby avoid a negative redistribution of wealth. Something similar has been done in the European Union with VAT, where, with some exceptions, a 15 percent floor rate was agreed on.

I am not advocating so much coordination that the game of compara tive advantages in international trade is impeded. I am not, for instance, in favor of applying in full the "Social Chapter" introduced in the Maastricht Treaty. The coordination of some basic labor conditions, such as safety and health, is a positive measure, but the harmonization of working hours, minimum wages, and unemployment benefits, for example, will affect the interplay of the comparative advantages of member countries at the expense of countries that work longer hours and have lower wages only because they have lower productivity. That will produce a serious recession in those countries similar to the one that German reunification produced in Eastern Germany.

-7-
Death of the
Welfare State?

Fritz Scharpf

Description of Change

The benign postwar environment for highly industrialized countries, where the national economy could for practical purposes be treated as a closed system under the control of the national government, is over. And so are the luxuries it permitted in terms of the European welfare state. For the first time, industrialized economies are confronted with the possibility that world markets may be captured by high-quality industrial goods (and services) produced by very low cost in what used to be Third or Second World countries.

The question for these First World economies is not primarily how to avoid the welfare losses following the massive changes in the world economy—they are more or less inevitable. The question is how to allocate these losses in ways that will least disrupt the social fabric of affected countries or the viability of their democratic political systems.

Reasons for Change

The welfare state is, of course, part of the problem. Welfare costs are foremost among the cost burdens of First World economies and rising mass unemployment overtaxes the capacity of existing systems of financing welfare expenditures. By providing income support for the unemployed and raising the reservation wage of job seekers, the welfare state is itself a cause of minimum wage unemployment. As a consequence, economic pressures and political demands to cut welfare are mounting everywhere.

They are particularly acute in countries where welfare expenditures are primarily financed through payroll taxes or insurance contributions that directly add to the costs of production; countries where the welfare state is mainly supported from general tax revenues have a choice of allocating the cost in ways which reduce the competitive disadvantages of their internationally exposed industries. The least burdensome source of welfare finance (apart from protectionist tariffs) would, of course, be a form of consumption taxes, but this would be very difficult to enact.

Yet, it would have the great advantage of reframing political disputes over the future of the welfare state in terms that replace the rhetoric of class conflict with a more realistic focus on the trade-off between public welfare consumption and the private consumption of goods and services.

Probable Consequences

Regardless of the form of finance, however, the question remains how welfare states will cope with the causes and consequences of income losses and persistent mass unemployment. If nothing is done, capital owners, but also employees in highly productive jobs (in management, marketing, research and development, design, communications, and the media, for example) will gain from the race to increase competitiveness. Meanwhile, employees in skilled white and blue collar jobs of average productivity will see their real incomes reduced and their jobs endangered. Low-skill jobs will either disappear or pay wages below the poverty level, unemployment will continue to rise, and governments will continue to cut unemployment and welfare benefits in order to reduce tax and welfare burdens on firms. The result will be a dramatic increase in inequality with implications of social unrest and political radicalism reminiscent of the last years of Weimar Germany.

Compared with these grim prospects, it might seem socially more attractive to spread the consequences of reduced competitiveness more evenly by a policy of gradual devaluation, even if it has inflationary consequences. But, of course, gradual devaluation and inflation will be anticipated by capital markets, interest rates will rise or capital will flee, real investment will decline, productivity will fall further behind, and competitiveness will suffer even more. The result could well be a downward spiral in which impoverishment will accelerate. Similar consequences might follow the adoption of protectionist strategies which, however, would require explicit political decisions on specific measures differing in their impact on individual sectors of the economy. But such measures would raise the level of international conflict and might, as they did in the 1930s, destroy the positive welfare effects of an integrated world economy.

Of course, protectionism might take on a different, and more attractive, identity if it were practiced not within nation-states, but within the large economic regions of the world—Europe, the Americas, and Asia. In order to be acceptable, however, each of these regions would need to include its advanced as well as its backward and newly industrializing countries. For Europe, for instance, this would not only imply the inclusion of Central and Eastern Europe, but also of the Near East and of Africa—a burden that may be too large to bear. At the same time, regionalism would prevent, or at least inhibit, the access of European industries to the growing American and Asian export markets. Given the present degree of integration of the world economy, the loss may already be greater than the benefits of keeping American, Japanese, Korean, and Indian competitors away from European markets. In any case, the completion of the last GATT round must also be read as a commitment against regional protectionism.

Proposed Actions

So what can be done? The foremost precondition of any effective solution is the explicit acknowledgment of the globalization of capital markets and production, and the abdication of all illusions of continuing control at the national or even at the regional (European) level. In place of the old notions of controlling the economic environment through the instruments of national monetary policy, fiscal policy, and regulation, governments need to develop strategies for coping with an uncontrolled, and basically uncontrollable, environment, where interest rates and exchange rates may fluctuate chaotically, where seemingly secure markets may be invaded by high-quality competitors from low-cost locations, where production processes and products may become obsolete through technological and organizational innovations introduced elsewhere, and where conditions generally will be too unstable to permit long-range planning.

Under such conditions, coping implies exploiting temporary opportunities and niches in the environment, evading head-on confrontation with overwhelming forces, and immunizing one's own system as best as possible against external shocks. This change of perspective from control to coping has important general policy implications that cannot be explored here. While the effectiveness of control is likely to increase with the size and the resource base of the political unit, successful coping depends much more on the fit between political strategies and given conditions. If environmental conditions fluctuate in time, there is a premium on flexibility and speed of adjustment; if problems and capabilities vary in space, coping may benefit more from economies of small scale than from economies of large scale. Under such conditions, small countries (and subnational governments in large countries) may be more successful than large nation-states, and the EU may have to be redesigned with a view to facilitating and enhancing the coping capabilities of its national and subnational units, rather than constraining them through excesses of centralization, harmonization, and standardization.

The same logic applies to the welfare state. Here, too, the question must be how its goals may be reached without undercutting the coping capabilities of national and regional economies under conditions of global competition. Shifting all or part of the burden from payroll taxes to consumption taxes (including taxes on the consumption of energy) will certainly help. But without effective solutions for the problems of rising mass unemployment, the welfare state itself will either become an intolerable burden on the economy or lose its viability.

Employment in the internationally exposed sectors of the economy cannot be the solution. if competitiveness is to be maintained or regained, these will be the sectors where labor productivity is bound to increase more rapidly than output. Thus, full employment strategies must focus on segments of the economy where local and regional demand is met by local and regional producers. Among these segments are the construction and maintenance of housing stock, retailing and servicing of industrial products, some branches of agriculture and food processing, environmental protection, the media, education and training, child care, health care, and care for the aged, household services, and the like. These fields are often neglected in the discussion of employment strategies, but it is here, rather than in the internationally exposed industrial and service sector, that additional jobs are likely to be found.

In many of these areas, however, labor productivity is low and cannot be raised very much through the introduction of modern technology. Thus, if wages (and payroll taxes) should be close to those paid in the highly productive sectors, these jobs will be driven from the private market and may, at best, survive in the public sector. If, on the other hand, wages were paid at a level corresponding to the productivity of these jobs so that private employers could still expect to make a profit, working incomes are likely to fall below the poverty level. In the United States, this is true of a large percentage of the new jobs created in the domestic service sectors. Thus, the much admired American employment miracle has been accompanied by a rapid increase in the number of working poor.

In European welfare states, where social incomes at or above the poverty level are still assured, an American-style low-wage sector could not develop in the past, and would, even now, be politically and socially unacceptable. As a consequence, however, the share of persons who are permanently excluded from contributing to the process of wealth creation and from participating in socially recognized forms of employment, is considerably larger in Europe than it is in the United States. From a social and political point of view, this is unfortunate. Even if replacement incomes for the unemployed were to be maintained above the poverty line, they are not enough to stabilize personal self-respect, to assure social integration, and to prevent political alienation.

From this perspective, it would be better all around if European welfare states could be reconstructed so as to subsidize incomes from low-wage employment, rather than to provide replacement incomes to those people who are unemployed full time. This suggests solutions that apply the logic of a negative income tax which, however, should not include the option, much discussed in the 1980s, of a basic income or citizen's wage paid to all, regardless of their need and their participation in the labor market. The scheme should not replace existing programs of income support for persons who are unable to work for reasons of health, disability, or family responsibilities, and it should probably not interfere with insurance-based (and time-limited) unemployment benefits either.

With these provisos, a practicable scheme could define a lower and an upper limit of eligible (hourly) wages at the bottom end of the present labor market. Within this range, an income subsidy would be paid that would increase take-home pay at the lower end to a level above the poverty line and which would only gradually decrease as wages increase toward the upper limit of subsidization. The rate of decrease would have to be set in such a way that employees would always have a strong interest to seek higher-paying jobs. In other words, the subsidy scheme would need to avoid the Speenhamland trap, which also characterizes present-day social welfare regulations that impose a confiscatory tax on any additional income from work.

If such a scheme were in place, wages at the lower end of the labor market could be determined by the market or by collective bargaining with regard to the actual productivity of the various kinds of jobs. Under such conditions, it would be profitable for private employers to invest in additional employment opportunities in service sectors where market demand depends crucially on price. At the same time, the scheme would assure incomes above the poverty level for those who accept these new jobs. In other words, European welfare states could benefit from the expansion of an American-style low-wage employment sector without having to accept the spread of American-style poverty and social degradation. Since, under the conditions of European welfare states, every additional job will reduce present expenditures for unemployment relief and welfare payments, the net fiscal costs of such a scheme would be quite low even though it would, of course, also have to apply to workers who are presently employed at low-wage levels. In Germany, for instance, the subsidy would begin to pay for itself if 500,000 new jobs could be created.

The conclusions are clear. What matters is the ability of national governments to cope successfully with the vagaries and challenges of an inherently turbulent and increasingly inclement global economic environment. This places a premium on relatively decentralized capacities for political action, and on strategies that support, rather than impede, the efforts of internationally exposed industrial and service sectors to reduce production costs and to increase productivity and innovation. The implication is that mass unemployment cannot be solved in these exposed sectors. If it is to be solved at all, there is a need to expand employment in less productive jobs in the domestic economy. At present, European welfare states impede, rather than facilitate, the utilization of such employment opportunities. It seems worthwhile, therefore, to explore options of reconstructing the welfare state in ways that would facilitate the expansion of a low-wage sector without creating a subproletarian population of the working poor.

-8-
Making the State
Efficient and Consumption
Levels Sustainable
Frank Trümper

Description of Change

Competitive market economies have proved to be very successful in continuously enhancing the production of tradable goods and services. Where markets and competition are missing, as in the public sector, performance is far from satisfactory. Because of the rapid acceleration of economic and social change, the lack of efficiency, productivity, and flexibility of public services (administration, education, jurisdiction, traffic, health, information, environment, and so on) becomes a real impediment to progress.

Market economies have also been impressively inventive with regard to the designing and marketing of ever-new products for individual consumption. In the future, however, global welfare as well as individual living standards will depend much more on intelligent systems and services to be used collectively ("collective goods"), rather than on further increases of strictly individual consumption.

Reasons for Change

Until very recently, ever-growing state budgets compensated for the inefficiency of the public sector. Today, tightening budgets render this policy increasingly impossible. At the same time, governments of both developed and underdeveloped countries are confronted with not less, but more and more complex tasks. Hence, efficiency and effectiveness of the public sector, its responsiveness and accountability as well as its ability to adapt to changes and to constantly improve its performance and quality of services, will become decisive to the welfare of individuals, countries, and the world as a whole.

In the advanced industrialized countries, individual living standards have reached such a high level that any substantial increase of individual consumption is at least partly offset by negative external effects affecting all. Traffic congestion and garbage disposal are obvious examples. Thus, even from the individuals' point of view, joint efforts to limit these external effects might be more advantageous than simply increasing personal consumption. This implies concerted action and a greater sense of responsibility on the part of the state or the public sector in general.

For many disadvantaged regions of the world, hopes for substantial growth of private sector activity and/or withdrawal of governments from economic activity are very low. Yet, when national governments, administrations, and international institutions continue to play a major economic role, including the direct and continuous provision of basic goods and services, efficiency and effectiveness of the public services directly determine people's welfare.

But even in the advanced societies, privatization is no solution. From the process of political decision making itself to numerous new problems and challenges (migration, pollution, health, crime, and so on), a plethora of tasks remains that for reasons of democratic control or effectiveness can only be solved on a collective level. Although state budgets have to be reduced, one may expect that a substantial proportion of GNP will continue to be allocated and/or spent by the state.

For ecological reasons, the current level, mix, and quality of individual consumption within the advanced industrialized countries will not be sustainable worldwide. On a global level, living standards can only be equalized, without being minimized, if intelligent "collective" goods and services are substituted for the consumption of "individual" goods. These need not be provided by the state itself. In any case, the inducement and regulation of collective goods will require some kind of government involvement. The innovativeness and effectiveness of governmental behavior will thus be central to the success of these processes.

Because of the rapid integration of global markets, countries and regions are competing for investment (i.e., employment). Public sector performance thus turns into a hard economic factor. Besides, it is also of pivotal importance to political stability, especially in young or fragile democracies where the credibility of newly established democratic institutions often hinges on measurable performance gains.

But even in advanced economies and old democracies, people become increasingly disconcerted by state action—or rather inertia. Here, too, because of the great discrepancy in productivity between the private and the public sectors, any serious effort to raise the efficiency of the public sector will have a much higher marginal effect on welfare in general, as well as on individual living standards (better service, less taxes, and higher personal budgets) than a similar effort in the private sector.

Probable Consequences

When modern-type administrations were "invented," reliability, equality, order, and freedom from arbitrary intervention were great achievements.

Yet, today's public sector has to cope with the new challenges of a rapidly changing environment. This places a premium on flexibility, decentralization, and organizational inventiveness. The state, however, has not yet developed mechanisms or incentive systems similar to those forces that continuously induce change and progress within the market. Administrations have no reason to drop the inefficient production of unwanted, obsolete "services" and to adapt its intelligence and resources to new tasks. Nor is there any incentive to pursue serious organizational reforms. Bureaucracies tend to grow, not to change. Thus, there is a real danger that governments and administrations might be paralyzed by self-complacency and privilege.

In the face of increasing global competition, as well as the spread of the negative external effects of economic growth and inequality, states as well as individuals might also develop an "isolationist" or protectionist attitude. On a personal level, this implies exponentially growing expenditures for the protection of ever-diminishing marginal gains. The same could hold true for countries or regions. Instead of concentrating all efforts on adaptation to new global challenges, societies could turn inward and forsake any real chance to cope.

Proposed Actions

The operation and management of the public sector must be principally changed. In the public sector, effectiveness equals efficiency plus political accountability. Thus, enhancing the effectiveness of public sector activity means getting down to where decisions have to be taken and where the action takes place. Here, the following should be observed.

First and foremost, the public sector has to change its self-perception. Although in the past it was governing, administrating, preserving a predefined order, in the future it will be expected to deliver good service, that is, value added for scarce tax resources. This means developing a real service mentality.

Among citizens, politicians, and administrators, not only funds, but goals, of public administration and service agencies—that is, the amount and quality of concrete goods and services—have to be specified and agreed on. Although the general definition of public policies falls clearly in the realm of councils and parliaments, administrators and their staffs should have the freedom to decide operational aspects. What successfully works in business should thus also be introduced in the public sector: a clear-cut separation of strategic and operational management.

This will involve a much higher degree of delegation of responsibilities from politicians to the public sector and, within it, to the lowest possible level, including every staff member and citizen. The possibility and efficiency of decentralization, however, depends on effective political and societal control. Yet, very few cities or countries have developed effective controlling systems that match those of the public sector's performance (be it schools, hospitals, general administration, institutions, or others). Yet, although performance indicators of a public institution naturally involve much more than purely quantitative or financial data, a number of compelling examples exist where appropriate qualitative indicators were successfully developed and introduced for almost all public sector activities.

Measuring real performance—and real costs—leads to transparency, which again is conditional to democratic choice and political competition. Only if citizens assess performance and costs by meaningful data, can they also be confronted with clear-cut alternative political options (within limited budgets) and be more closely involved in the decision-making process itself. Only if governments and the public sector as a whole work efficiently, can flexible and satisfactory sustainable provisions of public and/or "collective" goods and services become real alternatives to the many wasteful—and often purely substitutional—forms of individual consumption.

-9-
The Expanding Scope of Privatization in Development

Ho Khai Leong

Description of Change

The scope of privatization throughout the world in general, and in Southeast Asia and East Asia in particular, has been expanding rapidly. Even countries in the socialist quarters, such as China and Vietnam, have adopted privatization policies. This further strengthened the movement. Indeed, the diminishing importance of ideology is a compelling reason for the change, together with the rapid technological changes witnessed in today's world. The rapid changes in technology and the greater need to reap benefits from the available technology have compelled many countries to reconsider and reassess the management of the developmental process. The privatization process—that is, the substitution of market systems of allocation for nonmarket systems—has come to define the trend of economic development in the developing states since the late 1980s.

The concept of privatization covers a wide range of policies. It is loosely defined as the transfer of assets or service functions from public to private ownership or control. It also means contracting with or selling to private parties the functions or firms previously controlled by governments. The appeal of privatization rests on the belief that the private sector can more efficiently and effectively deliver goods and services to the people. Indeed, privatization became a catch phrase in the 1980s, especially when the British government under Margaret Thatcher inaugurated the practice. If the 1960s and 1970s can be labeled as the decades of public enterprise, merger, and acquisition, then without doubt the 1990s will be known as the decade of privatization and market economy.

Reasons for Change

Most developing countries in the postindependence period saw the number of state-owned enterprises grow rapidly. The state and the public sector have come to dominate the country's economic, political, and social development. This state domination has been found acceptable since many of the newly established governments were used to the emphasis on socialist principles. In addition, state participation in the economy was regarded as necessary and critical in initiating and sustaining economic development in countries with a lackluster private sector. The desire for a more equitable distribution of resources further justified the establishment of state-owned enterprises.

Although the public sector has succeeded in many areas, its performance was considered gravely unsatisfactory. Most state enterprises have the following common weaknesses: unclear objectives, bureaucratic meddling, red tape, insufficient capitalization, and excessive control. In many developing countries, government patience with inefficiency and ineffectiveness worn thin in the 1980s. Various ways had been examined to remedy the problem. Privatization is one such solution.

The rush to privatization is thus a reaction to the problems experienced by the public sector. There seems to be a widespread sense of frustration and disillusionment with the results and performance of the public enterprise sector. The public enterprise sector, as an instrument for growth and development, has certainly reached a crisis point. Among its problems are exaggerated expectations, faulty implementation of policies, corruption, and mismanagement.

This is now an antipublic sector ethos prevalent in many countries. This is partly ideological and partly practical. The ideological question has raised the fundamental question about the political philosophy of governing. What it means in economic terms is that the state now has to make room for a more assertive private sector in decision making. Politically, it means a greater likelihood of a more diffuse governmental structure, decentralization of authority, and greater autonomy for local governments.

It is believed that privatization can resolve some of these problem by transferring some governmental responsibilities to the private sector. By doing so, it is hoped that economic performance will improve.

Probable Consequences

In developing countries, the process of privatization has already begun. Some of the consequences may be:

- An increasing degree of interdependence of the developing states with the global economy which, over the years, has made national competitiveness a prerequisite for sustained economic growth.
- The rapid changes in technology will tend to make bureaucratic control and direct government intervention obsolete. Governments will have to adjust accordingly and do away with un-

necessary supervision and control to ensure a greater degree of interdependence and flexibility.
- A gradually strengthened private sector, both in terms of management and financial resources.

Proposed Actions

Empirical evidence suggests that privatization is an appropriate policy only where market mechanisms are already in place and working well. In most developing countries, privatization policy faces an uphill battle precisely because they lack facilities and resources. Therefore, for privatization to succeed, it must go hand in hand with assistance in developing capital markets, provisions of credit facilities, and most importantly of all, reform of macroeconomic policies.

The attitude and policies of the international community will have to change accordingly. In the 1960s and 1970s, a strong emphasis was placed on the concept of development administration—that is, the development of administration and the administration of development. Privatization would probably mean a complete reversal of this concept of administered growth. International organizations, such as the World Bank and the IMF, would have to reorient their objectives in granting financial assistance to the developing world.

At the same time, the political consequences of privatization cannot be ignored by the international community. In the foreseeable future, a greater degree of local autonomy, a stronger civic society, and a more participatory citizenry will emerge. In order to cope with these political changes, the emphasis on politics, democratic principles, and human rights by the developed states when dealing with the developing states should be on the agenda.

-10-
The Rule of Law
and Development
Luis Rubio

Description of Change

What makes some countries succeed while others fail? This question has been posed by many economists, thinkers, and philosophers all over the world for more than two centuries. There is no lack of theories and explanations. The fact is, however, that not all nations reach similar performance levels. Despite the variety of views and ideas about what generates wealth, few of these theories deal with the rule of law.

Lately, many countries have been reforming their economies, closely imitating many of the macroeconomic policies that characterize the successful economies of the world. Will they make it? Will they succeed in developing their economies? There is strong evidence that market mechanisms and the right macroeconomic framework are necessary, but not sufficient, conditions for success. In fact, it appears that the rule of law is as important, if not more, than the macroeconomic framework that so many governments are striving to straighten. In Hong Kong, for instance, there is an ongoing debate: What are the critical factors that make it work and that China will have to respect for Hong Kong to remain an economic jewel? According to one view, much more than democracy or macroeconomics is necessary; three things are crucial for Hong Kong to function: "the rule of law, the free flow of information (principally a free press), and the free flow of capital."[1] None of these has much to do with the economy itself.

The rule of law, protection of property rights, the enforcement of contracts, and strong institutional structures have become the crucial ingredients for economic growth and will increasingly be more critical. In fact, the ongoing attempts by many underdeveloped countries to reduce inflation and introduce market mechanisms in the hope of revitalizing their economies may well prove to be flawed in the absence of a strong institutional and legal framework. There are good reasons for this. People enter into business transactions if, and only if, they can trust

---

[1]*The Economist,* quoting a former head of the Hong Kong Stock Exchange, December 18, 1993, p. 38.

the legal system to enforce, at minimal cost, property rights and contracts. In the absence of such basic structures, market mechanisms cannot function and, thus, become irrelevant. The challenge for many developing nations is precisely that of creating the conditions where market mechanisms can work.

Reasons for Change

The idea that development requires much more than good government policies is not new. The rapidly changing structure of the world economy, however, has made this issue one of primary concern for developing nations. Until recently, each nation functioned on the basis of its own particular type of institutions. Some of these resulted from a long maturation process; others were adapted from third countries that were deemed to have been successful. Culture, history, and experience determined how each nation fared along the way. Some nations have been, historically, exceptionally successful in creating the conditions for people to produce wealth; others have not. Some have been less successful than others and yet remained viable. What each nation did or did not do mattered to its people only. The specific type of legal and institutional system that characterized each nation made it possible for some to be more successful than others.

The rapid globalization of the world economy, however, has changed all that. Today, no individual nation, with the possible exception of extraordinarily big economies like the United States, can isolate itself from the rest of the world. In that context, the ability of one nation to succeed depends not only on its own internal structures and policies, but on how these compare with those of other nations. Domestic institutions and policies determined the success of nations such as Britain, France, and the United States, while they condemned nations such as Mexico, Algeria, or Brazil to economic failure. In the era of globalization, these differences matter much more. In the past, one nation succeeded more than another and that was that. In today's world, where everything is interconnected, the success of one nation depends on its ability to attract capital flows and to foster an environment where the economy can prosper. That requires institutions and laws that are at least as dependable as those of the successful nations.

Thus, the globalization of the world economy is rapidly and neatly dividing all nations into two groups: those that have solid, credible, and respected legal and judicial institutions that guarantee low transaction costs and stable flows of capital and technology and those that have remained with costly, inefficient, or inoperative legal systems that are politicized, that do not serve their purpose of settling disputes, and that do not assign unequivocal property rights so that property holders can multiply and markets can begin to work and develop.

Probable Consequences

The globalization of the world economy has altered the way the world works. In the past, each national government could impose its own ways within its borders. Some governments created a solid foundation for development, while others created inappropriate institutions or none at all. Insofar as economic growth was possible (or at least conceivable) within a nation, even in relative isolation, its legal system, property rights, and institutional structure were secondary issues; these affected each nation internally but had little impact elsewhere. Today, trade is the key to development; it is no longer an option.

As the world economy has become completely integrated, nations can no longer remain in relative isolation, for that means economic stagnation and decline. Industrial production is no longer limited to the borders of one nation; the typical manufacturing process consists of several plants, each located in a different nation—close to its market, to its raw materials, to critical distribution points, and so on—and where what is produced in one place is critical for the success of all the others. The idea that one product is to be built in one single place has largely evaporated; most products today are multinational and, thus, the ability of a nation to develop has a lot to do with the ability of its industry to successfully integrate itself into these chains of production and capital flows. For that, it needs to have institutions that can guarantee the interests of investors as well as their rights. Contracts have to be enforceable and rights practiced. Without that, nobody would be willing to participate in the process.

Investors, consumers, businesspeople, developers, and financial analysts now compare the relative strengths of each nation before committing any investment to it. One key factor in these comparisons is the strength of the legal system and the ability to settle a dispute and to protect a property right in case of conflict. Conflicts are naturally bound to appear in the course of business relationships. Will the interests of the parties be protected? Will there be a proper court system to settle a dispute? In the absence of the rule of law, no nation can succeed.

From this perspective, the legal system and property rights are today much more important than macroeconomic management of an economy. Clearly, the overall management of an economy does matter. It does make a difference for workers and investors, producers and consumers, whether prices are basically stable or whether they increase at 45 percent per month. Similarly, it does matter whether there are discriminatory policies and whether markets are competitive. Yet, these necessary conditions are not sufficient. The rule of law is rapidly becoming the critical ingredient in the success of a developing process.

Contrary to more basic factors of economic strength, such as macroeconomic stabilty and the quality of education, however, the adequacy of institutions, laws, judicial procedures, and property rights is much more difficult to define. Furthermore, culture and tradition are critical in the respectability and enforcement that have to be associated with such factors. While a proper legal structure is a prerequisite for economic success, having it does not guarantee that success will be forthcoming. What is certain is that those nations that have succeeded in attaining rapid rates of growth for a long period of time, such as many of the Southeast Asian nations, are also those that have created solid legal structures and property rights, making their investors and savers capable and willing to take risks.

The critical ingredients that determine the existence of the rule of law are the existence of laws that clearly define and protect property rights; clearly established limits to government action, including its discretionary power; the availability of a court system to settle disputes; and the ability of individuals to enforce laws and court decisions.

Proposed Actions

The rapidly growing global economy is ultimately the cause of these new pressures to change. In this context, by deciding where to invest, whom to trade with and how, the international community is forcing all nations to come to grips with the demands of the international economy, but out of self-interest. The question is whether those governments that succeed in reforming their economies, bringing down inflation, privatizing government-owned corporations, and introducing wide deregulation will also realize the critical role played by the rule of law, property rights, and the institutions that make these work. From the evidence of the last decade of efforts to reform economies East and West, South and North, it seems clear that only a few economies will understand this lesson.

Building legal and institutional structures that can guarantee the property rights and protect them before the law is likely to become one of the single most important factors in determining the economic success of developing nations. As markets become possible and begin to prosper, so too will the people of each of those nations. Nations that fail to set up appropriate legal structures will neither create markets nor prosper.

The Need to Overcome Short-Term Problem Solving

George V. Vassiliou

Description of Change

The faster the technological development in recent years, the greater the switch of emphasis of world leaders and policy-makers from medium- and long-term planning to immediate problem solving and fire extinguishing. The conflict between the short-term nature of policy-making in most developed countries and the need for long-term planning to cater to and harness the social, political, and economic consequences of the technological revolution is greater than ever.

Reasons for Change

The decline in the rate of economic growth in the developed countries, the huge fluctuations caused by the liberalization of international capital movements, growing unemployment coupled with the crisis of the welfare state, increasing budget deficits, and the feeling of security that resulted from the "victory" of capitalism over communism have created a new political climate. The emphasis is no longer on the long-term, but on the problems of today or tomorrow. The increase in the strength of the various producer and consumer lobbies also contributes to this change of focus. Furthermore, the internationalization of politics—the proliferation of multilateral organizations—creates tremendous pressures on the agendas of world leaders, who now spend more time traveling than deliberating and addressing problems. The problems are compounded by the need for continuous electioneering. Local, regional, and national elections quickly follow one another, leaving practically no time for governments to focus on longer-term policy issues.

Probable Consequences

Without long-term policy thinking and programming, the world appears to be moving ungoverned like a huge tanker with no clearly set direction. Technological changes, demographic movements, and the globalization of the world economy have led to changes that should have been addressed at an earlier stage. As a result, social tensions increased and difficulties were compounded. An example of this is the growth of unemployment, which did not attract enough attention until it was virtually too late to address it effectively.

Proposed Actions

The diagnosis of this problem is relatively easy. The solution is much more difficult. There are no magic cures, no short cuts. The first and very important step, however, is to recognize the existence of the problem. A major public relations and educational exercise should focus the electorate's attention on longer-term issues. For this purpose, medium- and long-term planning should be given special status and not be limited to a support function of treasuries. We should also encourage the creation of special long-term planning units in existing institutes, and the establishment of an international institute under the United Nations, whose sole task would be to study the effects of technological, demographic, and other changes that will take place in the next ten, twenty, thirty, or fifty years.

Furthermore, serious consideration should be given to the need to reduce the number of electoral campaigns, to combine, for example, local with regional elections, and to coordinate, to the extent possible, elections in major countries. Also, as an institution, the G-7 needs to change both in structure and objectives and to give more emphasis to addressing problems with a medium- and long-term perspective. It should be less of a media event and more of an opportunity for world leaders to understand each other better and, in an information environment, ponder on the major challenges humanity faces on the eve of the twenty-first century.

Chapter 10
Reengineering the Corporation

Introduction

George V. Vassiliou

Reengineering is a new slogan for the corporate world. Under the pressure of increasing competition from the newly industrializing countries, corporate leaders in the world realize that they have to adapt to the new conditions of global competition or perish. In the new environment, the old models of industrial organization are no longer relevant and, as Michael Hammer, the father of the reengineering concept, points out, the new models focus on processes rather than tasks, emphasize decentralized decision making, and encourage innovation and risk taking. Reengineering, therefore, is no longer an option, but a necessity, writes Hammer. Governments must adopt policies in areas ranging from labor legislation to taxation that encourage, rather than impede, reengineering. Leaders will have to educate their populations to accept that this painful transition is inevitable and that attempting to avoid it will have even more negative consequences than embracing it.

Following up on this pattern, J. E. Andriessen points out that big is no longer beautiful. As the traditional advantages of large-scale production have disappeared, "being big is no longer necessarily an advantage." New technology enables small companies to produce sophisticated products at costs competitive with those of big businesses. Accordingly, job growth in the future will come from companies that are flexible and act small. This is why governments have to encourage flexibility and decrease regulation.

Daniel Roos takes this argument a step further. "Mass production is no longer compatible with today's market realities," he says. "Companies that practice lean production principles have changed the dynamics of international competition by establishing new standards in manufacturing systems and new levels of best practice. . . . Mass production is a static system designed to achieve a fixed performance level where an acceptable level of defects is tolerated. With lean production, the emphasis is on perfect first time quality and continuous improvement. The system is dynamic—it is constantly changing and improving. Good enough is not good enough." Roos is convinced that the future belongs to the lean enterprises, and that we have just witnessed the beginning of the lean revolution. Therefore, companies must introduce different performance measures and compensation systems that motivate individuals.

Gary Moreau focuses attention on the importance of time. Traditionally, productivity meant producing more output with less input. Today, this concept has to be redefined; it now means producing more output with less input, but producing it more quickly. Speed and on-time delivery are the keys to success. This leads to new organizational structures, new forms of supervision and compensation, and new criteria for advancement. According to Moreau, this approach "puts a premium on worker and management education and training" and requires governments to "promote the free flow of information through standardization of electronic communication formats and the support of communication system projects."

In this new environment, customer satisfaction is even more important than before. In fact, according to Gunter Pauli, clients expect to be spoiled nowadays, not just satisfied. Companies will have to focus more on fully satisfying a client and securing a large base of clients, rather than thinking in abstract terms of market shares. Furthermore, companies need to convince consumers that they are committed to society and the environment. When goods are priced the same and are of the same quality, many consumers base their purchasing decisions on moral and environmental issues.

The concluding contribution to this chapter is by Robert Palmer, the president of three major multinationals—Digital, Siemens, and ABB. Palmer writes, "What made many companies—especially large companies—successful has led to a hierarchy and structure and information systems that support the hierarchy and structure." The information systems, not only people, resist the change that we all must experience as we reengineer our companies.

Heinrich von Pierer says that for Europe to remain competitive, both politicians and management have a job to do. To outsiders, the European community may appear to be unified, but in reality the European market is far from homogeneous. Aggressive national interest still prevails in both human and research policies in many states, and there remains a general reluctance to formulate political objectives on a European level. However, Europe's businesses need the economies of scale provided by the single market. Management needs to reduce management costs, accelerate innovation, and win new markets, not only by exporting, but by building up local content.

Percy Barnevik points out that big corporations must use their size advantage to standardize and integrate. At the same time, however, they need to decentralize, reduce management levels, and delegate more responsibility to the labor force. His concluding remarks provide a good overall summary: "If companies are to survive, they must see change as a normal activity. It has been said that when you are through changing, you are through."

-1-
A Shift in Global Economic Leadership
Michael Hammer

Description of Change

Economic leadership is moving away from the industrialized world, such as the G-7 countries, to a set of relatively newly industrializing countries whose corporations are aggressively adopting new models of organization. These models focus on processes rather than on tasks; emphasize decentralized decision making; and encourage innovation and risk taking. Adopting these models enables companies to respond more quickly to changing technologies and market conditions and to offer superior products and services at lower costs.

Many of the leading industrialized countries are experiencing great difficulty in converting to these new models (generally referred to as "reengineering"). Decentralization of authority and flexibility are anathema to the German managerial culture, for example, with its emphasis on hierarchy, control, and planning. Many German workers are also uncomfortable with the autonomy and responsibility that a relatively "manager-free" environment implies. Moreover, the restrictive labor laws of many European countries impede the ability of companies to reconfigure. Japan is also at something of a disadvantage. Japan is more comfortable with gradual improvement of existing models than with a radical shift to a new way of doing business and with improvement and consensus rather than innovation and contention.

On the other hand, a group of countries that came late to the first Industrial Revolution are leading the second one. Enterprises in Korea, Venezuela, Singapore, and Mexico are often farther along in this transition than their European counterparts. They are leapfrogging the rich nations into their new industrial structures.

Reasons for Change

Traditional modes of operation are entirely inadequate in a global marketplace characterized by intense competition, sophisticated customers, restless capital, and constant change. In response, the reengineering movement had developed a new approach to operations and organization. But enterprises with a successful history of operating in traditional ways find it more difficult to change than those who are unencumbered by such baggage.

Probable Consequences

The specter of protectionism and trade wars is never far off; the opposition in the United States to NAFTA was essentially a response to the phenomenon we are describing. Capital markets and other financial institutions may have difficulty redeploying resources to these new centers. The rise of additional new and strong competitors to the industrialized countries will further increase the unemployment rate in Europe and North America, which could destabilize their governments, encourage extremist elements, and give rise to adventurous foreign policies.

Proposed Actions

The industrialized world must embrace reengineering or suffer the consequences. Governments must adopt policies in areas from labor legislation to taxation that encourage rather than impede reengineering. Leaders will have to educate their populaces that this painful transition is inevitable and that attempting to avoid it will have even worse consequences than embracing it. International organizations will need to create venues for adjusting the world order to the aftermath of the Industrial era.

-2-
Firms That Behave
Like Dinosaurs
Will Die Out
J.E. Andriessen

Description of Change

During most of the postwar period, big was beautiful. Big companies boomed, profiting from economies of scale. Inevitably this was somewhat to the detriment of small companies. Between 1958 and 1979, the share of small companies in total business receipts decreased from 52 percent to 29 percent. Now, however, the fast-changing market makes life more difficult for big companies, which are trying to copy the flexibility of small companies.

Being big is no longer necessarily an advantage. The traditional advantages of large-scale production have disappeared. In many industries (except, for example, cars and chemicals), economies of scale have become meaningless. New technology enables small companies to produce sophisticated products at costs competitive with those of big businesses. In addition, telecommunications also enable small companies to operate internationally.

Many big companies have been slow to adapt. If we consider employment figures, for example, job growth these past years has been in small companies rather than in big ones. Small and mid-size companies were responsible for all of the 5.8 million new jobs in the United States in the period from 1987 to 1992. In the same period, large companies (with more than 500 employees) lost 2.3 million jobs.

Reasons for Change

The disappearance of the advantages of large-scale production is one of the main reasons why big is no longer better. Another reason is the fast development of consumer tastes. Companies have to adapt quickly to new demand. They have to be flexible and consumer oriented. Here also, being small is an advantage; it is easier to stay in touch with customers and adapt to new demand. For big companies, with large bureaucracies and many decision makers, it is difficult to remain flexible. Now, big companies are reforming their organizations in an effort to emulate small companies. Vertically integrated and hierarchically organized firms are being decentralized and split up into independent business units.

Probable Consequences

Companies that are unable to adapt to the changing situation will die out, just like dinosaurs did. Only if companies are as flexible as chameleons will they survive. The future is for innovative companies that are responsive to consumers' wishes and able to supply their needs. This challenge to stay flexible will probably be greater for big companies than for small ones.

Proposed Actions

Job growth will come mainly from flexible companies that act small. To facilitate flexible entrepreneurship, governments should liberalize regulation. Regulation prevents flexible business operations and often proves to be a relatively heavy burden on small companies. Also regulation prevents new companies from entering a market. Increased competition in the home market is another, almost obligatory, line of action in a global economy. More competition forces companies to look closely at customer's needs. To increase domestic competition antitrust laws should be strengthened.

To enhance international competition, trade barriers should be further abolished. Lifting trade barriers will stimulate international trade and is inevitable in a globalizing world economy.

-3-
The Transition to Lean Processes at the Firm Level

Daniel Roos

Description of Change

Corporations around the world are undergoing a transformation from mass production to a new lean production logic. Mass production is no longer compatible with today's market realities:

- Large-scale manufacturing of a limited number of mass-produced products has been replaced by smaller-scale lean production of many different products to satisfy a diverse range of market niches and changing consumer demand.
- Corporate success is based not only on price performance emphasized in mass production, but also on achieving best practice in other performance measures emphasized in lean production, such as quality, time to market, and sustainability.
- Companies require quick responses to economic, political, and technological change and uncertainty. Mass production lacks the flexibility and adaptability of lean production to respond quickly.

Reasons for Change

Companies that practice lean production principles have changed the dynamics of international competition by establishing new standards in manufacturing systems and new levels of best practice. They can assemble products of superior quality more productively, assembly lines have greater flexibility to shift between different models, the product development time is shorter and more efficient, the replacement cycle is quicker,

---

The ideas in this article are further developed in James P. Womack, Daniel Jones, and Daniel Roos, *The Machine That Changed the World*. New York: Rawson Associates, 1990.

and the scale of production is smaller, thereby allowing for greater product variety. Taken together, these performance characteristics constitute a significant competitive advantage.

Mass production is a static system designed to achieve a fixed performance level where an acceptable level of defects is tolerated. With lean production, the emphasis is on perfect first-time quality and continuous improvement. The system is dynamic—it is constantly changing and improving. Good enough is not good enough. Workers are always encouraged to do better.

With lean production, waste of all kinds is removed from the system. Mass production buffers of spare parts are replaced by a just-in-time inventory system. People who do not add value to the product, such as supervisory and overhead personnel, are minimized. Responsibility is passed as far down in the value chain as possible. Workers organized in teams are empowered to actively participate in the production process. A worker in a lean system is responsible for three functions—to perform the task, to inspect the task to ensure it is of acceptable quality, and to recommend improvements. Lean production requires trained workers who understand the production process.

Mass production companies focus on individuals organized around narrow functional specialties, whereas lean companies focus on teams organized around products and processes. Lean companies can eliminate unnecessary overhead, conflicts, and time delays resulting from the coordination, interfacing, and integration of functional specialists necessary in mass production firms.

Structural differences exist in the relationship of mass and lean companies to their suppliers. With mass production, supplier and assembler relationships are short term, power based, market driven, and adversarial, with a focus on cost as the primary criteria for supplier selection. In contrast, lean production incorporates long-term relationships with far fewer suppliers utilizing tier structured arrangements. Assemblers and suppliers join together through a group structure to form an association of independent, but closely linked, companies that function as an extended corporation.

Probable Consequences

To be world class competitors, companies that are structured around mass production principles must make the transition to a more efficient, lean production framework. There are three critical steps in the transition: recognition of the need to change, an assessment of what change is needed, and implementation of change. Top management must also recognize the need for change to reshape the corporate mind set and initiate structural transformation. Fundamental change is extremely difficult for organizations to accomplish. In some companies, there is an intellectual acceptance of lean production, but an inability to institutionalize it. Lean production can be most threatening to middle management, since it results in a reduction of overhead and supervisory personnel. Middle management will not support change unless they are convinced that top management is totally committed.

Lean production implies more than downsizing. Not only are fewer resources utilized, but they are used differently. The entire organization is structured under a different set of operating and management principles. Lean production extends far beyond the factory floor. It is based on a different philosophy with different objectives resulting in different approaches to organizing human resources and work processes.

Benchmarking metrics provide a mechanisms for companies to understand how much improvement is required to achieve world-class, best-practice standards by comparing their performances with other organizations and tracking their own performances over time. A CEO of a major auto manufacturer emphasized the importance of benchmarking data. "For the last five years, I have been telling my middle managers that we have a huge productivity problem, but the middle managers denied any problem existed. Now, based on benchmarking data, I have the proof to show that we have a big problem." As a result of benchmarking that organization understood, for the first time, how it performed relative to the competition.

Working with a lean company can help an organization understand the different principles involved in a lean facility. For example, NUMMI, a joint venture between Toyota and General Motors, transformed a GM plant in Fremont, California, utilizing unionized former GM workers. As a result of Toyota management and lean production principles, the plant moved from bottom of the productivity and quality ladder of all GM plants in the United States to the top.

A major challenge is how companies can leverage experience gained through a functional equivalent such as NUMMI to develop a diffusion strategy of lean principles throughout the entire organization. This is not easy to accomplish. A senior GM executive with extensive technical understanding commented, "I visited NUMMI six times, but it was not until the sixth visit that I finally understood what was different. I was looking for the wrong thing." Transferring the production philosophy of NUMMI to plant supervisors who have operated under a different manufacturing environment for many years is a complicated process that requires sufficient time and a diffusion strategy. It cannot be achieved simply through plant visits.

Proposed Actions

The transition to lean production requires restructuring operations; the reorganization of human resources and work processes. Companies must introduce different performance measures and compensation systems that motivate and reward individuals in a manner consistent with lean production principles. Some changes are relatively easy to accomplish, such as implementing just-in-time inventory and changing the layout on the factory floor. Other changes are more complicated because they require individuals to change their behavior.

Let me provide a few examples. A CEO can encourage new cooperative relationships with suppliers, but if plant performance is evaluated on short-term cost criteria, it is difficult to develop mutually supportive long-term assembler/supplier relationships. Conventional accounting systems consider inventory an asset, while lean production considers inventory a liability. Companies need activity-based accounting systems that provide management with realistic performance assessments. Are companies restructuring operations to remove nonvalue added functions, providing workers with broader responsibilities and educational programs to prepare them for a different lean production environment? If a company believes in teams, does its compensation system reward workers for team participation as well as individual excellence? If a company wants to empower workers and pass responsibility down the value chain, are the workers given the necessary authority to match their responsibility?

Each of these changes profoundly affects an organization. In combination, they constitute a fundamental change. Unless an organization is willing to undergo that change, the transition to lean production will be difficult or impossible to achieve. It is not easy to transform bureaucracies, but it is feasible. Alfred Sloan demonstrated that many years ago at GM.

We have just begun to witness the beginning of the lean revolution and development of global lean enterprises. Lean companies will work together in global network relationships reflecting core competencies and complementary strategic objectives. Participating organizations can gain access to complementary rapidly changing technologies, share the risks, and escalating product development costs, and have access to worldwide production and distribution facilities. These networked relationships require a new balance between competition and cooperation, where companies work together on projects of mutual economic gain and/or social benefit and compete in the marketplace on other projects.

Lean production is about building such relationships between individuals and organizations. These relationships can exist at many levels, individuals working together as members of a team, labor and management working together to achieve common objectives, companies working together because of mutual dependencies, and industry and government working together to foster economic development in a socially responsible manner.

-4-
Time Is No
Longer Just Money

Gary L. Moreau

Description of Change

Productivity has historically been defined as a two-dimensional relationship of input and output, both narrowly calculated to include direct
costs only. Time was the common unit of measure. Increasingly, however, productivity is viewed on a much broader basis, encompassing the
entire business process and including all direct and indirect costs and
assets employed. And measurement has been turned on its head, with
time as the all-inclusive standard. Now productivity improvement must
be defined as doing more with less, more quickly.

This perspective was first suggested by just-in-time (JIT) production
techniques that seek to eliminate disruptions to the production process.
These techniques significantly compress production lead times and reduce production run quantities, thus enhancing item scheduling flexibility and reducing finished and work-in-process inventories. While wor-
thy ends in themselves, these results also represent a means to an end.
Inventory and its counterpart, lead time, mask inefficiency and waste in
the production process. By removing the mask, the true cause and cost
of rework, nonstandard processing, and process interruption are starkly
visible and can be addressed.

This perspective has now been broadly expanded to encompass all aspects of the business process—the complete cycle of defining and satisfying customer needs. Flexibility and responsiveness are now primary
business objectives, both as ends in themselves and as a means to an
end. Those things that inhibit responsiveness and create delay, such as
bureaucracy, and those things that represent delay, such as backlog, are
the things that consume a business' resources and restrict its income.

Future business success will depend on meeting, or exceeding,
heightened customer expectations and minimizing the human and financial assets employed to achieve this goal. Time is the one common
denominator of all of these diverse variables. By focusing on time in
every aspect of business, from the boardroom to the factory floor, from
the selling of the product or service to the procurement of the raw
material, true productivity improvement can be realized. This can be

thought of as improving the flow of the business, flow property denoting movement over time, a fluid rather than static concept.

Reasons for Change

Item scheduling flexibility has become increasingly important to manufacturers, as product lines have proliferated in response to the fragmentation of many markets. Product and market niches have increased in number due to varied competitive and market forces, causing manufacturers to frequently cope with declining unit volumes and enhanced logistical challenges. Conflicting with this need has been the fact that many advances in automation and production technology have put a premium on item unit volume and further restricted item flexibility.

Additionally, because of past success in increasing productivity as historically defined, in part resulting from those same advances in automation and production technology, the cost profile of most companies has changed dramatically. Direct labor and direct overhead costs frequently represent a relatively small portion of total business cost today, reducing the incremental return from further improvements in these areas.

At the same time, advances in information technology and information systems have given companies more plentiful and accurate information with which to analyze and understand the needs of their customers and the fundamental components of their business, to understand what really happens in the office and on the shop floor and how the company's financial resources are really generated and spent. Many have used this information to establish new sources of value added and competitive advantage in customer service through responsiveness to customer desires, reliability, timely delivery, and quick and efficient problem resolution.

The global competitive bar has been raised substantially through heightened global competition reinforced by economic weakness in most of the developed countries. The global consumer has also helped to raise the competitive bar. Having been shown that product quality and service need not come at a price, they have raised their expectations and standards of performance and accountability.

Probable Consequences

Removing the backwaters and eddies from the entire business process means everything from significantly shortened product development lead-time, production lead-time, and delivery lead-time to reducing the time it takes to define and satisfy a customer desire—even how long it takes to answer the phone. Defined in this way, productivity improvement is more of a human resource process than an engineering process. Employees, typically working as teams, properly motivated, trained, and empowered, are the key to success. This puts a premium on the organization's soft skills and assets, compared to its technology and physical plant, although these are not unimportant. This, in turn, dramatically enhances worker challenge and satisfaction. The opportunity for every worker to control his or her activities and eliminate mind-numbing routine is greatly increased. They can impact the organization and the product in dramatic ways, improving job satisfaction and reward.

One of the most visible signs of this change will be the elimination of much of the current division of labor that exists in most large organizations. Responsibilities will tend to be defined more around the customer or process than the function. This promotes understanding of the entire process, increases awareness of cause and effect, and eliminates the transit time and queuing inherent in a highly divisionalized labor stream, where a worker performs only one specialized function in the process and passes the work along to the next department or specialist. Properly trained and empowered, these broadly acting workers will enhance customer responsiveness while giving a personal face to the traditionally impersonal organization.

These workers will not, however, fit into traditional organization structures. New forms of supervision and performance evaluation will have to be developed. Even new forms of compensation and new criteria for advancement must be considered. Organizations will tend to be flatter, less hierarchical, less formal, and organized more around customers or processes than functions.

Proposed Actions

This approach puts a premium on worker and management education and training. Workers must be able to apply the tools of analysis and communicate effectively. Managers must develop their interpersonal skills, their ability to listen, and their leadership skills to nurture and sustain this more complex, although rewarding, environment. All workers, particularly senior executives, must be cross-trained in all business disciplines in order to bring a total business process perspective to problem solving and reengineering, mirroring the change occurring in the organization's structure and alignment.

Consequently, educational institutions must restructure their curriculae, deemphasizing facts and results and emphasizing the processes of analysis and learning. These abilities must be coupled with enhanced communication skills. And since existing workers must be reeducated, educational institutions must support and partner with the business community to retrain and enlighten existing organizations.

Engineering schools must integrate more material on manufacturing, process, and logistics management. Most importantly, engineering students must be taught how their responsibilities fit within the whole. On a macro level, they must adopt the perspective of the production process as part of a larger, continuous business process and thus receive some training in other business disciplines. On a micro level, they must learn to overcome the tendency to view production processes as discrete operations, to see the objective of technology advancement as improvement in the flow of the entire process, not the instantaneous throughput of the isolated machine or process.

Business schools must likewise promote broad cross-training in all business disciplines. They must particularly expand training in organizational behavior and management. There must be a shift from the hard and superficial disciplines of finance, accounting, and marketing, to strategic reengineering and human resource management as it relates to organizational structure and employee development.

Government must encourage and support the business community in this dramatic transformation. Tax and regulatory codes should not discourage new approaches to the workplace. New job structures and new forms of compensation and benefits should be given wide latitude in the search for innovative ways to motivate and reward employees. The regulatory environment should likewise be supportive, not destructive or encumbering. Specifically, regulations should not discourage cooperation between business entities and should encourage the joint development and sharing of ideas and training.

But most importantly, the common thread in all of this change and advancement is information and its communication. Government must promote the free flow of information through standardization of electronic communication formats and the support of communication systems projects. These networks are the infrastructure of the transformation to worker enrichment and productivity enhancement.

-5-
How to Compete in the Twenty-First Century

Gunter Pauli

Description of Change

Traditional economic theory prescribes that the competitive edge of a company depends on the efficient combination of capital, raw materials, and labor. Over the past decades, economists have expanded this to include the importance of technology and information.

Companies in crisis often wonder how to improve their competitive edge. This was relevant in the 1960s; it is relevant today; it will be relevant in the twenty-first century. Whereas the questions remain the same, the answers will change. This article will outline which were the determining factors needed to outcompete others on the market and which additional elements will be required in the next century. It can be considered a major change in the basic assumptions for humanity in the twenty-first century.

Reasons for Change

In the 1960s when a corporation felt the pinch from its competitors and looked for a solution, the president was told to stop trying to just sell products and to develop a marketing strategy. The need to listen to the clients' wishes and preferences was the first sign that the market was characterized by oversupply. If a company could not adapt to the customer, it would be replaced by a company that could. It was the era of Philip Kotler and the 4Ps. There is no company today that questions the importance of marketing.

When, in the early 1970s, the first oil crisis devastated industry, the key question was how to regain a competitive edge, particularly at a time when increased energy costs affected the pricing and high inflation undermined customer confidence. At the time, the answer was productivity. Those who could produce more with the same level of input in terms of raw materials, capital, and labor would win on the market. It was the first time that Japanese industry was called on to serve as an example. Indeed, they overcame the first oil crisis faster than anyone else, integrating more robots and information technology and catapulting their production industries to the forefront of worldwide competition. It was considered the driving force behind their successful strategy to conquer markets.

In the late 1970s, the second oil crisis hit the West. Again, industries that were losing market shares searched for a renaissance of their business. Quality was identified as the cutting-edge factor. It was the time of quality control circles and total quality management. Indeed, bad quality was considered a cost and the elimination of mistakes was expected to lead to a better cost structure and higher customer loyalty. No one could escape the investments needed to convert their production system into a zero defects unit.

In the early 1980s, Western industry again faced decreasing market shares. After investing massively and successfully in quality and productivity programs, it became obvious that more was needed for long-term success in the world competitive game. The concept of just-in-time (JIT) was advanced as the next step to success. The Japanese were supposed to have implemented the *kan-ban* system and the West was advised to learn from the Land of the Rising Sun once more.

In spite of all the trade missions, books, and educational programs on marketing, productivity, quality, and just-in-time, the quest for competitiveness never ends. Service became the next panacea for success. Japanese industry outsources some 16 percent of all business services. European companies typically only subcontract 4 percent to third professional parties. It became clear that up to 75 percent of the value added created by industry were services to production. The swatch was a prime example. The high labor costs did not matter anymore; the design factor and the communication skills represent the real service to the customer.

Probable Consequences

It is necessary to produce goods with the right quality at the right price, but the customer, operating in a market characterized by oversupply with equivalent products, will look for the supplier with the best service.

Today, companies are expected to excel simultaneously in all five elements: marketing, productivity, quality, just-in-time, and services. Performance in each of these areas is a precondition for entry into the market. If a business integrates all these elements, then it will have a right to be on the market. If a company wishes to outperform average businesses, if it is out to gain market share, more will be needed.

Over the past five years, consumers have enjoyed low levels of inflation. Today, the continuous drive toward better perceived value for less money is even more difficult to achieve. Business cannot hide increased value in price hikes, or hide the higher costs behind inflation. Today, more is needed to perform well and a lot more is required from business if it is to gain. The question is what is needed?

At present few economists agree on any one factor. Market analyses in Europe, Japan, and the United States have shown, however, that ethical standards, a moral commitment, and a high environmental performance will be an integral part of corporate strategy. More important, it will become one way to outperform other businesses and to reestablish that unique selling position so badly needed in the competitive game.

Today, more than 40 percent of consumers in the United States indicate that when the same price and quality level is being offered, ethical issues will determine their choice. Of course, there is a very broad variety of themes that companies can address. Several though have succeeded in setting the agenda. And, what is most interesting, the consumer is increasingly well informed and capable of seeing through issue marketing strategies that are not based on a genuine commitment.

This does not mean that companies today are not ethical or moral, but they will have to be thoroughly committed to improving society; they cannot merely playing a role in an effort to create profits for shareholders. The company of the twenty-first century will have to assume different responsibilities than would be expected today. The companies that see this will be the winners in the future. Those who neglect it will be the dinosaurs of tomorrow. It is dramatic to note that not even ten percent of the population believes company statements on environmental issues. In a recent survey in Europe, environmental volunteer organizations were identified as the most credible source of information.

At the time when companies have to reengineer their operations, it is timely to take the next leap forward and retool the company, integrating the most rigid moral and ethical standards. In addition, the company is a most efficiently organized structure, the only one in society to create value added. At a time when governments and cultural organizations are searching for a more efficient mode of operation, business practice is welcome indeed. And, if a combination is made with all six factors, it will be a formidable force indeed. The competitive edge will have been transformed into a sustainable advantage.

The Successful Business in the Twenty-First Century

Input Factors	Management System	Values
labor	marketing	ethical
raw materials	productivity	moral
capital	quality	environmental
technology	just-in-time	
information	services	

-6-
The Need for
Innovative Strategies

Heinrich von Pierer

Description of Change

The old saying goes that if the gods want to destroy you, they will bless you with forty years of success.

Classic industrial nations in the triad of Western Europe, North America, and Japan have enjoyed great success in the last forty years, with practically no high-tech competition from outside. Despite tough internal competition, their positions were comfortable and secure. High wages and high incomes were taken for granted. They became accustomed to the formula of high tech and high wages in the industrialized nations, low tech and lower wages elsewhere. But times are changing.

Reasons for Change

Southeast Asia is gaining competitiveness and is already competitive in terms of quality and quality standards. Yet, the region's costs are far more favorable than those in industrialized nations. Today, high tech, high quality, and low wages go together.

Low-cost Eastern European countries are also putting pressure on the traditional industrial nations. At the moment, companies in the region are not yet competitive as far as technical standards are concerned, but their cost advantages are enormous, particularly over Western Europe. As far as costs are concerned, West Europe suddenly has another Hong Kong on its doorstep. At the same time, though West European companies enjoy a solid position in their home market, the space is limited and the pace of growth is relatively weak. In booming regional markets, however—and this applies to many of those low-cost Eastern European countries—we are not so strong.

Probable Consequences

Dynamic growth in Southeast Asia and new challenges from Eastern Europe will force countries in Western Europe to prove that they are fit enough to respond. To do this, they will have to meet the global challenge with new strategies. The task of redefining the basic assumptions of corporate leadership will therefore emerge as the highest priority for the management of every West European company. It will be a question of survival.

Proposed Actions

There are two remedies. First, improve Europe's position as a place to do business in order to revive and maintain dynamic growth. This is a task mainly for the politicians. Second, create company environments that encourage new growth. This is a job for management.

Let us look at the first of these tasks. To begin with, we must improve Europe's competitiveness. There are a number of reasons for the sluggish growth in Europe, and many of them need to be addressed by Europe's political leadership. Germany, for example, is involved in an intense debate on the country's competitiveness in the global market.

To outsiders, the European community may appear to be unified, but in reality the European market is far from homogeneous. Aggressive national interests still prevail in both human and research policies in many states, and there remains a general reluctance to formulate political objectives on a European level. However, Europe's businesses need the economies of scale provided by the single market. They also need to apply sophisticated technologies wherever possible. In the public sector, for instance, this applies particularly to such areas as telecommunications and transportation systems. It is essential that the privatization of state-owned businesses continue at full speed, with privatization of state telecommunications authorities as a top priority. This is vital for European equipment suppliers, who need strong lead customers if they are to survive in the highly competitive telecommunications market.

We also need greater flexibility in labor costs; work-time standard regulations and solutions no longer provide the answers. Part-time work and reduced or extended work-times could provide the flexibility needed for survival. Flexibility is essential—to work only four days a week could be a good solution for some companies, a bad solution for others.

In addition, we must focus on research and development. Only then can Europe utilize its full innovative potential. We must make every effort to advance the best talents, the elite in our countries, and we need to be able to do this without being plagued by envy. These talents are our future. It is not only the politicians who face challenges if Europe is to continue to prosper. Europe's managers also have important work to do. They must improve productivity, accelerate innovations, and penetrate new markets to secure growth.

The first of these tasks, improving productivity, means reducing the cost of development, production, and marketing, and cutting management costs as well. It can be done—as American companies have shown over the past few years—and it must be done.

The second task, the acceleration of innovation, means that we have to bring new products on to the market faster than ever before, products that have greater customer benefits. We must therefore speed up production processes and improve quality. Microelectronic technologies are playing a key role in this process, and Europe is catching up in this field. Major contributions are being made by the French microelectronic center in Grenoble, for example, while in Dresden, Europe's largest semiconductor project is being implemented under Siemens' leadership. Efforts like these clearly signal Europe's innovative spirit and capability.

The third challenge facing Western European companies is winning new markets. The dynamic pace of growth in Asia Pacific is a major challenge for Europe. We must respond, and not merely by increasing our exports to that region. Our primary job is to build up local content. That is where our future lies.

West Europe's global strategies must also take into account its reforming neighbors in Eastern Europe. These countries are more than just attractive production locations, and for our own sake, we have the political and economic mission to help them join the international division of labor. We want to, and have to, integrate them step by step into the global economy. In a time of fundamental change, this calls for a spirit of openness and innovation. We must be willing to accept those changes in business and society that are crucial for the future.

Perhaps we do not, after all, need to fear the wrath of the gods, but it is clear that we have much work to do. This means giving up the comfortable ways we have accumulated in the past, habits that have spread throughout Europe like a creeping paralysis. Only innovative strategies for the future will help Europe to prevail.

-7-
The Right Size for Global Companies
Percy Barnevik

Description of Change

There are important changes and trends in our environment that necessitate reconsideration of the organization of corporate leadership. Two issues in particular are important: globalization and size.

In the global marketplace, many companies are already big, and the tendency is for them to become bigger and fewer. Many medium-sized companies are losing out as globalization leads to acquisitions, mergers, and quite simply, bigger companies. A good illustration of this trend was BMW's 1994 takeover of the British car manufacturer Rover.

Reasons for Change

For a company, the advantage of being big is the power it has with suppliers and its ability to standardize. For instance, if a company has forty transformer factories around the world, and if each of those factories acts as an isolated island, then it might just as well be forty separate companies. There must be some kind of global coordination that ensures that those forty factories are not making nine different types of distribution transformers or buying from twenty different porcelain suppliers. What they need is to have fewer suppliers and to buy more from them. They must use the advantage of being big to standardize and integrate.

Probable Consequences

While large companies have many advantages—such as economy of scale and economy of scope—they also unfortunately have big inherent negatives. Some of them may even carry the seeds of their own destruction—in their bureaucracy, rigidity, slow decision making, lack of entrepreneurial spirit, and distance from their customers. Employees who feel like small pieces in a large machinery are less likely to take responsibility; they are less engaged.

Proposed Actions

This is a formidable challenge to tackle. One solution is to apply a far-reaching decentralization. ABB, for example, is made up of some 5,000 profit centers, each with an average work force of forty or fifty people. These profit centers are grouped into 1,300 legal entities, which means that there are 20,000 to 25,000 managers, each responsible in some way for a profit center.

It is also important to reduce layers. Ideally there should be no more than two or three layers between the top executive committee and the lowest level of supervisory management. Of course, this can bring its own negatives. For instance, there are many promotion possibilities at the bottom of this type of "flat pyramid" management structure, but there are few such possibilities higher up. However, the advantages of having few layers outweigh the disadvantages. One of the key advantages is ease of communication—something that is particularly important in a company that is in the process of implementing change. Another benefit is smaller headquarters—and if anything needs reengineering today it is the old overblown headquarters. All too often we have seen companies moving staff out of productive operations and into nonproductive service organizations. Corporate staffs not only cost a lot of money, they create jobs for other people and they disturb operating people. It is therefore a must in a big organization to keep them to a bare minimum.

Decentralization also helps to shift responsibility down the management ladder to the worker. What do all those women and men on the shop floor use of their total capacity when they are working compared to what they use in their private lives, when they are managing their households, organizing their children, or perhaps building their summer houses? At work, they may use only ten or even five percent of the thinking power they use when they are away from work. This presents another major challenge.

If workers are allowed to manage certain aspects of their jobs, it becomes to some extent a career rather than merely a series of mundane tasks. This leads to increased productivity and commitment and a decrease in absenteeism. This is a long and difficult process, but at the end of the day, a company's competitiveness depends on its people, how we motivate them, how we lift them to higher performance, how they can use a larger part of their total capability. Today, that is the ultimate challenge for corporate leaders.

As companies operate on an increasingly global basis, another challenge is to find a new category of manager—global managers who understand different cultures, who can work with mixed nationality teams, and who have open minds and high integrity. These global leaders are not born; we have to develop them. And the way to develop them is to move them around, to send them for one, two, or three years to different countries where they can learn another culture, pick up another language. In this way, they broaden their understanding and acquire the potential to be promoted into global management. Companies need these people in their hundreds rather than their thousands, but they are worth their weight in gold.

Mixed nationality teams have many inherent benefits, but it is not always easy to bring them about. It is only human nature to stick to the familiar: Germans prefer to work with other Germans in their teams; Italians prefer to work with Italians; as do the nationalities on the executive committee, at group headquarters, and so on. That is why one must interfere sometimes in hiring decisions and force people into multinational situations.

Managers need to realize too that they face a challenge with the young generation. These young people—the managers of tomorrow—are not attracted to companies because they are big or because they have a high market value. They are individualistic. They need to be offered some vision, some direction they can buy into. For example, ABB's commitment to supporting growth in Central and Eastern Europe or to environmentally responsible economic development offers more than just shareholder value.

The process of change itself is an important subject. In Europe, there is too often a tendency to stick to the status quo and regard the process of change as something abnormal, something that is only done when absolutely necessary. If companies are to survive, they must see change as a normal activity. It has been said that when you are through changing, you are through. That is a good summary.

The Need for
Business Focus

Robert B. Palmer

Description of Change

The most exasperating fact about big companies in crisis is that they got there by doing what once made them big. They come by their troubles honestly.[1]

In the computer industry, many companies grew strong and prosperous as vertically integrated systems businesses. The winners were the ones that learned how to provide everything from silicon, operating systems, and applications to delivering complete packages to their customers. Added value came from the way in which companies glued all these things together, compensating for being mediocre in some areas by excelling in others.

Reasons for Change

These companies created infrastructures that supported their vertically integrated systems businesses, which in turn spawned and supported organizational hierarchies that mirrored the vertical integration of the products and services they provided. Systems businesses were not alone in taking this approach; many of their customers developed in a similar way and are also facing the problems that are now arising from this. As the world market changes, more and more businesses are identifying their own horizontal slices of once vertical markets.

Probable Consequences

Vertically integrated businesses need to become more focused in order to compete with these highly competitive horizontal slices. To do that, it is

---

[1]Roger Martin, *The Harvard Business Review*, November/December, 1993. Martin is director of the Monitor Company.

essential to unlearn some of the philosophies that led to their success. This encompasses not only vertical hierarchies and the processes that go with them, but also the information technology that supports them. The large-scale problems that many companies face today have a great deal to do with the very information systems and technological infrastructures that were such a key contributor to their previous success.

At the same time that we are witnessing the emerging horizontal disaggregation of the marketplace itself, we are also hearing about horizontal corporations that are organized around customer-oriented processes instead of specific tasks or hierarchies. Some vertically integrated organizations are embracing this concept wholeheartedly, implementing company-wide programs that will transform them from vertically organized, internally focused businesses to process-driven, customer-focused enterprises.

Proposed Actions

It is important to stress the need to revamp the way we design and implement information technology in order to support this kind of effort. This is crucial if we are to ensure that the desired transformations take place. All too often, information systems based on aging mainframe computers are preventing data from crossing functional and divisional boundaries. Information systems cannot be allowed to remain stubbornly mired in the old hierarchy.

Just as we all need to manage a response to the changing marketplace by reengineering and transforming the way we do business, we also need to redefine the technological foundation that supported our business in the past. Think of an information technology infrastructure as a company's immune system. As well as being a major capital investment for most companies, it is also quite literally hardwired to keep them doing the things that made them successful over the years. The challenge is to get the immune system to understand that the body it supports is going to look and behave very differently as it redesigns and reengineers itself. If technology infrastructures are not redesigned as part of the overall reengineering effort, that reengineering effort is destined to fail. A company can implement all the work force reduction and customer-focused programs and process reengineering in the world, but hardwire systems will be relentless in not allowing the organization to achieve the desired results. Despite all the efforts to restore health and profitability, the existing corporate immune system will simply work that much harder to reject the process reengineering transplant.

What is called for is a holistic view, one that recognizes the interdependence of the customer, engineering and marketing, and the information structure that supports them all. As managers, our goal must be a dramatic improvement in operating effectiveness and customer satisfaction via the redesign of the processes and support systems that are critical to our customers. A primary objective is to ensure that customers, suppliers, and employees can all create, access, disseminate, and share knowledge and exchange information wherever and whenever needed.

Because existing enterprise-wide systems frequently do not support current business needs, nor the niche markets and horizontal slices of the market in which companies need to compete, individual point solutions have been created as a way to meet these needs. The result of this approach is simply a proliferation of solutions, which drives complexity, increases expenditure, creates redundancy, and impedes effective business management. Resources are put in place that facilitate information flow often with no value added whatsoever. Intermediaries can often distort or filter information rather than share it. Companies can find themselves spending a huge amount of money each year simply to manage this proliferation. Over many years, hundreds of databases, thousands of files, and millions of on-line pages of information are accumulated, yet the tendency is not to delete or purge data that is no longer needed. In some companies, much of this data is never accessed, much of it is out of date, and worse still, it is sometimes misleading. There is no integrated browse capability and no unified catalog of subjects. This is unmanaged, expensive, and often irrelevant data at a time when managing information flow and sharing knowledge effectively to competitive advantage is the life-blood of a company. Instead of holding on to the limited concept that information is power, it is important to understand that knowledge and the sharing of knowledge is what provides the competitive edge today. There is a significant difference between knowledge and data. We have enormous strings of data at our fingertips, but if it is not usable, we cannot call it knowledge or information. To operate efficiently, companies, employees, and customers all need a steady, reliable, and accessible information system.

There is a useful analogy to be made here with an aquifer, which is a natural underlying supply of water. Just as a water supply is vital for the body, so the flow of information—one that employees, customers, suppliers, and partners can tap into where and when they need it, with appropriate security—is vital for the success of an enterprise. This knowledge aquifer is not just a database or a collection of databases or networks; rather, it represents a major revision of the concept of how information and knowledge are created, packaged, stored, and accessed.

What made many companies, especially large companies, successful has led to a hierarchy and structure and information systems that support that hierarchy and structure. The information systems themselves resist the change that we must all go through as we reengineer our companies.

In order for change to occur, it is essential that the top management is wholeheartedly behind this effort. Change is uncomfortable and without strong leadership and determination at the top, it will not happen. Nor will this change be successful if the information systems that support the enterprise are themselves not completely reengineered to be flexible and to provide the knowledge people need when and where they need it.

Conclusion

Klaus Schwab

This book marked the state of humanity at a turning point in history. Although the outlines of any new order remain obscured, it seems clear that historians will someday judge the current decade as the dawn of a new era. At a propitious moment, then, this effort to enumerate change sketched the terms of a new world.

The Four Revolutions

Four interrelated "revolutions," or radical changes in the framework of human existence, deserve recognition as points of departure for the changing basic assumptions of political, social, and economic life. These revolutions exact the responses which characterized this volume.

A survey of these revolutions reveals that two are of a constructive nature and represent opportunities to add new dimensions to our existence: *First,* the revolution of information, which I will call the "informationization" of humanity, and *second,* the revolution of the spread of the market economy.

The other two revolutions have a more destructive character and represent outright challenges to the current order. They have a particularly erosive effect on social structures: *First,* the reduced role of values in society, and *second,* the reduced input of labor in production.

These four revolutions have different causes, but reinforce each other. Together they make the end of this century a turning point which has, until now, seemed less dramatic than past periods of revolution. But the consequence of these revolutions have become evident, and people are forced to grapple with ensuing change.

Let us examine these four revolutions, for they inspire the present challenges to humanity as we approach the next millennium.

The "informationization" of humanity underlies any analysis of the human condition as it redefines the concept of communication and analysis. This revolution offers opportunities for unparalleled cooperation between peoples, but its ultimate ramifications are not yet evident. Two aspects of this revolution have already had major impact on our state of being. The first, the computer, was originally a tool to facilitate our work, to rationalize and robotize the production of goods and (later) services. But now computers, coupled with communications technologies and packaged into multimedia "personal assistants," have become partners in the management of our lives, of our relationships with human beings, and of reality. A new conceptual dimension in the form of virtual reality will transform how we think and what we do. Fantasy transgresses into reality, and our intellectual and conceptual spheres push toward new frontiers.

The second development driving the "informationization" of humanity is the increasing availability of information everywhere. With satellites beaming signals to disc-equipped television sets in tiny villages in China, India, and other formerly "remote" areas of the world, we have transformed the globe into a comprehensive real-time information net-work. The manifest implications for societies, politics, and economics are only now unfolding and will upset many of our life patterns. Over the horizon lies the potential for a unified human consciousness, but only with prudence and self-knowledge might we avoid the dangers of mis-"informationization."

The second revolution, the spread of the market economy, has been made possible by the fact that information, capital, goods, and skills move easily around the world. Facilitated by the unprecedented "informationization" of humanity, a true world market has become a reality. Not only producers, but consumers, think in global terms, reinforcing the trend toward global optimization of all factors of production. Further, the addition of newly emerging markets like China and India brings formidable competition and creates a new "ideology of competitiveness." This new ideology, which has social and political as well as economic implications, subdues all other considerations to the need to increase national productivity. Mastering the challenges of this new ethos represents a foremost mission for humanity.

Next, two additional revolutions have had more unequivocally negative ramifications. The reduced role of values in society is a particularly sobering reality. Traditional channels of the transmission of societal values have ceased to function, and valuelessness has advanced. The old assumption that ideologies, religions, and culture serve as inspiration for values to be transmitted by schools, family, church, and civic society no longer holds. Value systems are now replaced by perceptions based on "dreams and dramas," simple and insufficient messages that communicate only marketable messages on television and through advertising. Society based on a common ethos has been replaced by a mass audience with expectations devoid of moral roots and not cognizant of complex realities. A vacuum of deeply rooted values is increasingly filled by either shallow "life-style ideologies," by political demagoguery, or by religious fundamentalism. Such is the danger to our political cultures and our social sustainability.

The fourth revolution, the reduced input of labor in production, derives from the first three and has ominous implications in particular for the most developed societies. The "informationization" of humanity has transformed our hardware societies to software societies. The size of the work force (manpower) no longer creates added value, but has been supplanted by skills, above all intellectual skills. The spread of the market economy and associated competitive pressures transforms mass-produced products into commodities and requires standardized high quality at low cost, and, finally, valuelessness most afflicts those whose training proves inapplicable in the new world.

Labor, particularly in the old industrialized countries, has become a high-cost input to be squeezed in the process of restructuring and reengineering. This revolution affects not only the production of goods, but also of such services as banking and transportation. Robots and computers do·more and more sophisticated work and invade new sectors, and contrary to past industrial revolutions, no newly emerging sectors absorb the remnants of a structurally displaced work force. This revolution ironically imperils even the most successful of societies.

Three Megatrends

In addition to the fundamental revolutions described above, three general developments similarly transcend society, politics, and economics, albeit in a more gradual and less dramatic manner. Like rising water behind a swollen dike, they deserve recognition before the opportunity to avoid catastrophe passes.

The first such trend is the decreasing social and ecological sustainability of humanity's existence. The major determinant of sustainability, population growth, bears oft-cited but inadequately understood ramifications, and the threat to the environment posed by the human species intensifies. The spread of health-care information and rising levels of education throughout the world have together worked wonders for human longevity; the population of the planet has doubled since 1950 and, in all probability, will again by 2030 at the latest. Simply put, increasing consumption levels will create a situation where less and less available natural resources (including water and air) per capita have to be squeezed more and more in order to sustain our standards of living. Societies will soon have to choose between boosting material standards of living and quality of life, and the two are in danger of becoming mutually exclusive.

The second perennial trend, the compression of time, frames all the considerations of change. The acceleration of change leads us to the perception that time is compressed. Time is no longer lived as a continuity encompassing events, but purely as a succession of unrelated and unrelenting changes. We experience discontinuous and fragmented lives. Time compression reduced the meaning of experiences, either as an example from the past or as a guide to the future. The distant past counts less and less. Experiences rapidly become irrelevant and obsolete.

Paradoxically, the future also counts less. Confronted with accelerating change, we lose perspective. Witness the emergence of the "everything now" generation that lives exclusively in the realm of immediacy: quick, short-term solutions and satisfactions define existence.

The final trend underpinning the need to revise fundamental assumptions is the increasingly complex set of issues on the international agenda. Complexity itself presents a harsh reality. From a simply old global agenda consisting, essentially, of three items, multilateral trade and monetary relations, East-West military balance, and North-South resource transfer, emerges a new and lengthy list of challenges. The aforementioned population explosion, corollary challenges of urbanization, ecology and sustainability, health care, drug use, arms trafficking, terrorism, crime, racism, ethnic issues, nuclear proliferation, migration, and a host of other issues darken the headlines daily. The information explosion has put all those challenges into the consciousness of television viewers worldwide, and the international agenda must now incorporate concerns that had previously passed unnoticed.

Consequences

Linkages between the profound revolutions and the incessant trends described above suggest their insolubility. Economic restructuring and social strife no longer seem manageable through existing impotent political institutions. Stark consequences ensue and multipolarization, marginalization, and breakdowns prompt fear for our collective future.

The reduced status of leadership and the rise of competing poles marks a reconceptualization of power itself. The dissemination of information led automatically to a dissemination of power in our society, and the multipolarization of power enters every sphere. The bipolar world has become a multipolar one, where economic, political, and military power are distributed among several distinct rising and declining poles, and the new reality of people power bespeaks a new political "citizens's society." Even our new economics embraces a significant diffusion of power, and consumers' and shareholders' power defines enterprise realities.

Power itself is increasingly accepted only if it comes from the grassroots, and the multipolarization of power spurs distrust of leaders who accumulate or demonstrate power. Especially those who benefit from corporate perks or political favors are degraded, and the ultimate consequence of the multipolarization of power is a powerless society—powerless to meet the pressing challenges of our transition into the next century through historical patterns of leadership and response. Who will respond?

A new concept of power must synthesize a consensus on the basis of a common vision, a common direction, and a common value system. In the absence of those integrating common denominators, society will have a tendency to fragment. "Micro" identities will replace "macro" identities, and simplistic fundamentalist, usually egocentric, life values will dominate. A unified new ethos could mark a new renaissance, but a specter of fragmentation impoverishes humanity.

This fragmentation of society could reduce the capacity of humanity to manage the pressing problems of global and societal interdependence and bring about a situation where large parts of our world society experience more and more marginalization. Exposure to the pressures enumerated above could produce global and societal "favelas" which, like cancer, first localized, spread slowly and finally lead to a breakdown of the total system.

Such "favelas" will include all the new "have nots," who will be better described as "don't knows," as they lack the skills to cope with the software society. They will also include those whose natural resources, particularly food, water, and air, have run out, as well as those who have found salvation in membership of a new warrior class, serving racism, nationalism, and fundamentalism, and engaging in self-destructive behavior. The consequences of change unmanaged are grim.

Leadership Requirements

It is apparent that new leadership must confront numerous risks as we approach the year 2000. The revolutions and megatrends outlined above bear consequences which forewarn of chaos and complicate positive response. A new leadership must define itself in light of a new vision of power and combat the fragmentation of our societies. But, if the revolutions and trends driving change are clear, so must be the mission of those who would lead humanity into the next century.

Power no longer derives solely from status. Leaders must differentiate themselves from would-be heroes, who craft shallow images, inspire simplistic populism, and promise rebirth. While many voices distance themselves from old structures and promise an abstract idyllic new world, they will ultimately disappoint. Foundations of cleverness in business affairs will prove weaker than those of moral integrity, and true leaders must combat simplistic solutions which present no real vision.

New leaders must acknowledge the power of information and craft that information into knowledge. The "informationization" of society has created new channels of communication: these channels could inspire a new renaissance of thought and facilitate the transmission of new value systems as easily as they erode historical social patterns.

New leaders must accept without fear the inevitable spread of the market economy. One might pay homage to the attributes of such a system, which includes reduced poverty, increased life expectancy, and improved standards of living, *and* embrace justice for those who are marginalized by its spread. Though labor might be devalued in the new economy, human beings need not be.

In light of the dilution of power in our societies, leaders must earn the trust of those who follow. Leaders will deserve our trust only if they adhere to basic universal values which forward the fundamentals of peace, freedom, and justice. Fragmentation threatens to erode any ethic shared by humanity, spark conflict, and sacrifice the gains of improved communication, so leaders have a special responsibility to search for common mores.

There is hope for the future despite the manifest revolutions occurring around us. This book showed that there is no shortage of ideas on how to deal with change, so a new, inspired leadership armed with a common value system can usher in a new age. Analysis of the revolutions shaping our times and the subtle megatrends abetting change may threaten, but a new leadership can overcome the consequences. If we maintain a collective consciousness and confront our collective challenges, solutions will be found. To forward that mission is the highest aspiration of this book.

INDEX